DEFINING WEB3

RESEARCH IN THE SOCIOLOGY OF ORGANIZATIONS

Series Editor: Michael Lounsbury

Recent Volumes:

Volume 59:	The Production of Managerial Knowledge and Organizational Theory: New Approaches to Writing, Producing and Consuming Theory
Volume 60:	Race, Organizations, and the Organizing Process
Volume 61:	Routine Dynamics in Action
Volume 62:	Thinking Infrastructures
Volume 63:	The Contested Moralities of Markets
Volume 64:	Managing Inter-organizational Collaborations: Process Views
Volume 65A:	Microfoundations of Institutions
Volume 65B:	Microfoundations of Institutions
Volume 66:	Theorizing the Sharing Economy: Variety and Trajectories of New Forms of Organizing
Volume 67:	Tensions and Paradoxes in Temporary Organizing
Volume 68:	Macrofoundations: Exploring the Institutionally Situated Nature of Activity
Volume 69:	Organizational Hybridity: Perspectives, Processes, Promises
Volume 70:	On Practice and Institution: Theorizing the Interface
Volume 71:	On Practice and Institution: New Empirical Directions
Volume 72:	Organizational Imaginaries: Tempering Capitalism and Tending to Communities Through Cooperatives and Collectivist Democracy
Volume 73A:	Interdisciplinary Dialogues on Organizational Paradox: Learning from Belief and Science
Volume 73B:	Interdisciplinary Dialogues on Organizational Paradox: Investigating Social Structures and Human Expression
Volume 74:	Worlds of Rankings
Volume 75:	Organizing Creativity in the Innovation Journey
Volume 76:	Carnegie Goes to California: Advancing and Celebrating the Work of James G. March
Volume 77:	The Generation, Recognition and Legitimation of Novelty
Volume 78:	The Corporation: Rethinking the Iconic Form of Business Organization
Volume 79:	Organizing for Societal Grand Challenges
Volume 80:	Advances in Cultural Entrepreneurship
Volume 81:	Entrepreneurialism and Society: New Theoretical Perspectives
Volume 82:	Entrepreneurialism and Society: Consequences and Meanings
Volume 83:	Digital Transformation and Institutional Theory
Volume 84:	Organizational Wrongdoing as the "Foundational" Grand Challenge: Definitions and Antecedents
Volume 85:	Organizational Wrongdoing as the "Foundational" Grand Challenge: Consequences and Impact
Volume 86:	University Collegiality and the Erosion of Faculty Authority
Volume 87:	Revitalizing Collegiality: Restoring Faculty Authority in Universities
Volume 88:	Routine Dynamics: Organizing in a World in Flux

RESEARCH IN THE SOCIOLOGY OF ORGANIZATIONS ADVISORY BOARD

Series Editor
Michael Lounsbury
Professor of Strategic Management & Organization
University of Alberta School of Business, Canada

RSO Advisory Board
Howard E. Aldrich, *University of North Carolina*, USA
Shaz Ansari, *Cambridge University, UK*
Silvia Dorado Banacloche, *University of Massachusetts Boston, USA*
Christine Beckman, *University of Southern California, USA*
Marya Besharov, *Oxford University, UK*
Eva Boxenbaum, *Copenhagen Business School, Denmark*
Ed Carberry, *University of Massachusetts Boston, USA*
Lisa Cohen, *McGill University, Canada*
Jeannette Colyvas, *Northwestern University, USA*
Erica Coslor, *University of Melbourne, Australia*
Gerald F. Davis, *University of Michigan, USA*
Rich Dejordy, *California State University, USA*
Rodolphe Durand, *HEC Paris, France*
Fabrizio Ferraro, *IESE Business School, Spain*
Peer Fiss, *University of Southern California, USA*
Mary Ann Glynn, *Boston College, USA*
Nina Granqvist, *Aalto University School of Business, Finland*
Royston Greenwood, *University of Alberta, Canada*
Stine Grodal, *Northeastern University, USA*
Markus A. Hoellerer, *University of New South Wales, Australia*
Ruthanne Huising, *emlyon business school, France*
Candace Jones, *University of Edinburgh, UK*
Sarah Kaplan, *University of Toronto, Canada*
Brayden G. King, *Northwestern University, USA*
Matthew S. Kraatz, *University of Illinois at Urbana-Champaign, USA*
Tom Lawrence, *Oxford University, UK*
Xiaowei Rose Luo, *Insead, France*
Johanna Mair, *Hertie School, Germany*
Christopher Marquis, *Cambridge University, UK*
Renate Meyer, *Vienna University, Austria*
William Ocasio, *University of Illinois at Urbana-Champaign, USA*
Nelson Phillips, *University of California at Santa Barbara, USA*
Prateek Raj, *Indian Institute of Management Bangalore, India*
Marc Schneiberg, *Reed College, USA*

Marc-David Seidel, *University of British Columbia, Canada*
Paul Spee, *University of Queensland, Australia*
Paul Tracey, *Cambridge University, UK*
Kerstin Sahlin, *Uppsala University, Sweden*
Sarah Soule, *Stanford University, USA*
Eero Vaara, *University of Oxford, UK*
Marc Ventresca, *University of Oxford, UK*
Maxim Voronov, *York University, Canada*
Filippo Carlo Wezel, *USI Lugano, Switzerland*
Melissa Wooten, *Rutgers University, USA*
April Wright, *University of Queensland, Australia*
Meng Zhao, *Nanyang Business School & Renmin University, China*
Enying Zheng, *Peking University, China*
Tammar B. Zilber, *Hebrew University of Jerusalem, Israel*

RESEARCH IN THE SOCIOLOGY OF
ORGANIZATIONS   VOLUME 89

DEFINING WEB3: A GUIDE TO THE NEW CULTURAL ECONOMY

EDITED BY

QUINN DuPONT
York University, Canada

DONNCHA KAVANAGH
University College Dublin, Ireland

and

PAUL DYLAN-ENNIS
University College Dublin, Ireland

United Kingdom – North America – Japan
India – Malaysia – China

Emerald Publishing Limited
Emerald Publishing, Floor 5, Northspring, 21-23 Wellington Street, Leeds LS1 4DL.

First edition 2024

Editorial matter and selection © 2024 Quinn DuPont, Donncha Kavanagh,
and Paul Dylan-Ennis
Individual chapters © 2024 The authors.

Published under exclusive licence by Emerald Publishing Limited.

Reprints and permissions service
Contact: www.copyright.com

No part of this book may be reproduced, stored in a retrieval system, transmitted in any form or by any means electronic, mechanical, photocopying, recording or otherwise without either the prior written permission of the publisher or a licence permitting restricted copying issued in the UK by The Copyright Licensing Agency and in the USA by The Copyright Clearance Center. Any opinions expressed in the chapters are those of the authors. Whilst Emerald makes every effort to ensure the quality and accuracy of its content, Emerald makes no representation implied or otherwise, as to the chapters' suitability and application and disclaims any warranties, express or implied, to their use.

British Library Cataloguing in Publication Data
A catalogue record for this book is available from the British Library

ISBN: 978-1-83549-601-5 (Print)
ISBN: 978-1-83549-600-8 (Online)
ISBN: 978-1-83549-602-2 (Epub)

ISSN: 0733-558X (Series)

Printed and bound by CPI Group (UK) Ltd, Croydon, CR0 4YY

INVESTOR IN PEOPLE

CONTENTS

About the Editors — ix

About the Contributors — xi

Foreword: Research in the Sociology of Organizations — xvii

Acknowledgments — xix

Introduction to Web3: The New Cultural Economy
Quinn DuPont, Donncha Kavanagh and Paul Dylan-Ennis — 1

PART 1
BIG TENT

Web3 is the Opportunity We Have Had All Along: Innovation Amnesia and Economic Democracy
Nathan Schneider — 13

Entering the Field of Web3: "Infrastructuring" and How to Do it
Kelsie Nabben — 27

Business Without Firms: A Planetary Design Language for DAOs
Bernhard Resch — 43

A Progressive Web3: From Social Coproduction to Digital Polycentric Governance
Quinn DuPont — 57

Institutional Isomorphism in Web3: Same Same but Different?
Tara Merk and Rolf Hoefer — 75

Hash, Bash, Cash: How Change Happens in Decentralized Web3 Cultures
Paul Dylan-Ennis — 87

PART 2
VAUDEVILLE

Political Economy of the Crypto-art Craze
Geert Lovink — 97

When Digital Carnival? Distributed Control of the Metaverse Asset Layer to Enable Creative Digital Expression to Flourish
Eric Alston — 105

Web3 as Decentralization Theater? A Framework for Envisioning Decentralization Strategically
J. P. Vergne — 115

The Rise of Blockchain Egregores
Primavera de Filippi, Morshed Mannan and Wessel Reijers — 129

Crypto Personalities as Carnivalesque Jesters
Alesha Serada — 137

Web3: The Gentrified Carnival?
Donncha Kavanagh — 147

PART 3
DARE DEVILS

The Gambler
Sandra Faustino — 157

Web3 and the Amazing Computable Economy
Jason Potts — 163

Trying to Sell the Crow Queen in Web3: On the Resistance of Video Gamers to Cryptocurrencies, NFTs and Their Financial Logic
Diane-Laure Arjaliès and Samuel Compain-Eglin — 177

Blockchain and Web3: Mirrors, "Jouissance" and Social and Personal Identity Formation
Victoria Lemieux — 191

Blow that Mausoleum Down
Bill Maurer — 199

Immediate Gratuitousness
Finn Brunton — 207

ABOUT THE EDITORS

Quinn DuPont is an Information Scientist with subject matter expertise in cryptocurrencies, blockchains, and cybersecurity. For over a decade, he has held research and development positions at top global universities, startups, and blue chip enterprises. He has a PhD in Information Science from the University of Toronto.

Donncha Kavanagh is Full Professor of Information and Organization at University College Dublin. His research interests include the sociology of knowledge and technology, the history and philosophy of management thought, pre-modern and post-modern modes of organizing, play and creativity, and (digital) money.

Paul Dylan-Ennis is Lecturer/Assistant Professor in the College of Business, University College Dublin. His research focuses on Bitcoin and Ethereum. He is a CoinDesk Columnist.

ABOUT THE CONTRIBUTORS

Eric Alston is a Scholar in Residence in the Finance Division at the University of Colorado Boulder. His research applies methodologies and concepts from institutional and organizational analysis and law and economics to studies of constitutions, economic rights on frontiers, and digital governance specifically. He is also currently engaged in governance design for several distributed network projects.

Diane-Laure Arjaliès is an Associate Professor at the Ivey Business School, Western University, where she leads the Sustainable Finance Lab. She explores the potential role of blockchains in building financial instruments for social and environmental good. Previously, she studied the role of utopias in the workings of cryptocurrencies, from Bitcoin to alternative time monies. She is now investigating the impact of Web 3.0 (e.g., cryptos and non-fungible tokens) on society.

Finn Brunton is a Professor at UC Davis with appointments in Science and Technology Studies and Cinema and Digital Media. He is the author of *Spam: A Shadow History of the Internet (MIT, 2013)* and *Digital Cash: The Unknown History of the Anarchists, Technologists, and Utopians Who Created Cryptocurrency* (Princeton, 2019), and the co-author of *Obfuscation: A User's Guide for Privacy and Protest* (with Helen Nissenbaum, MIT, 2015) and *Communication* (with Mercedes Bunz and Paula Bialski, Meson Press and University of Minnesota, 2019). His articles and papers have been published in venues including *Radical Philosophy*, *Artforum*, *The Guardian*, and *Representations*.

Samuel Compain-Eglin is a Video Game Artist. As a self-taught artist, he started working in video games in 2009 as a concept artist. Later, he switched to three-dimensional character art and became an art director. He has worked on a large panel of games, cinematics, and ads for companies like EA, Gearbox, Unit Image, and many others. He also teaches art in different art schools.

Primavera de Filippi is a Research Director at the National Center of Scientific Research (CNRS) in Paris, a Faculty Associate at the Berkman-Klein Center for Internet and Society at Harvard University, and a Visiting Fellow at the Robert Schuman Centre for Advanced Studies at the European University Institute. Her research focuses on legal challenges and opportunities of blockchain technology and artificial intelligence, with specific focus on trust and governance. She is the author of the book *Blockchain and the Law*, published in 2018 by Harvard University Press (co-authored with Aaron Wright), and she was recently awarded an ERC grant (€2M) to investigate the use of blockchain technology to enhance institutional governance by increasing confidence and public trust and its implications on global governance. In addition to her academic research, she acts as a legal expert for Creative Commons in France and sits on the stakeholder board of the P2P Foundation. She was a Founding Member of the Global Future Council on Blockchain Technologies at the World Economic Forum, and Co-founder of the Internet Governance Forum's dynamic coalitions on Blockchain Technology (COALA).

Sandra Faustino is a Sociologist and Researcher at the Lisbon Business School of Economics and Management, University of Lisbon. Her research focuses on the material cultures and legal architectures of fintech and the digital economy.

Rolf Hoefer holds a PhD in Organizational Theory from INSEAD, where his dissertation focused on organizations and tokens. He is a core contributor to MetaCartel Ventures DAO, invests at Cultur3 Capital, builds staking infrastructure at Cultur3 Stake, and runs an educational institute called 100X. He has experience across NFT, DeFi, and Public Goods DAOs such as Public Nouns, DAOhaus, Padawan, Rarible, Cream, and Metagov. He frequently speaks on DAOs, NFTs, and Web3, most recently at Stanford, Harvard, USC, and KAIST. He has also published a book called *NFT Revolution* that sold over 100,000 copies, as well as an academic paper on the role of rhetoric in legitimacy judgments in the journal *Academy of Management Review*.

Victoria Lemieux is an experienced and multidimensional technology leader, innovator, and academic. She currently holds a position as Professor of Archival Science at the University of British Columbia's School of Information. She is also Founder and Co-lead of Blockchain@UBC, the University of British Columbia's Multidisciplinary Blockchain Research Cluster. She has consulted for the United Nations, the Commonwealth Secretariat, and the Inter-American Development Bank and has collaborated on research projects with the US Treasury, Office of Financial Research. Her academic research focuses on risk to the confidentiality, integrity, and availability of trustworthy records and how these risks impact upon transparency, financial stability, public accountability, and human rights. She is the author and editor of award-winning articles and books, including *Financial Analysis and Risk Management: Data Governance, Analytics and Life Cycle Management* (Springer, 2012); *Building Trust in Information – Perspectives on the Frontiers of Provenance* (Springer, 2016); *Building Decentralized Trust – Multidisciplinary Perspectives on the Design of Blockchains and Distributed Ledgers* (Springer, 2020); and *Searching for Trust: Blockchain Technology in an Age of Disinformation* (Cambridge University Press, 2022).

Geert Lovink is a Dutch media theorist, internet critic, and author of *Uncanny Networks* (2002), *Dark Fiber* (2002), *My First Recession* (2003), *Zero Comments* (2007), *Networks Without a Cause* (2012), *Social Media Abyss* (2016), *Organization After Social Media* (with Ned Rossiter, 2018), *Sad By Design* (2019), and *Stuck on the Platform* (2022). He studied Political Science at the University of

About the Contributors xiii

Amsterdam (UvA) and received his PhD from the University of Melbourne. In 2004, he founded the Institute of Network Cultures (www.networkcultures.org) at the Amsterdam University of Applied Sciences (HvA). His center organizes conferences, publications, and research networks such as Video Vortex (online video), The Future of Art Criticism, and MoneyLab (internet-based revenue models in the arts). His recent projects deal with digital publishing experiments, critical meme research, participatory hybrid events, and precarity in the arts. From 2007 to 2018, he was Media Theory Professor at the European Graduate School. In December 2021, he was appointed as Professor of Art and Network Cultures at the UvA Art History Department. The Chair (one day a week) is supported by the HvA. Since early 2022, he has been involved in support campaigns for Ukrainian artists, in particular UkrainaTV, a streaming art studio, operating out of Krakow.

Morshed Mannan is a Postdoctoral Research Fellow on the BlockchainGov ERC Project at the Robert Schuman Centre for Advanced Studies, European University Institute. He completed his PhD dissertation on the Emergence of Democratic Firms in the Platform Economy at Leiden Law School, Leiden University. He has extensive experience teaching comparative corporate law and European corporate law at undergraduate and graduate levels. He is currently researching blockchain governance, platform cooperatives, and data cooperatives. He has also acted as an expert or consultant on matters regarding decentralized autonomous organizations (DAOs), cooperative law and governance for the International Cooperative Alliance and NCBA Clusa International, the UN Department of Economic and Social Affairs, the OECD, the European Commission, as well as several local and national government bodies.

Bill Maurer is a cultural anthropologist and sociolegal scholar. His work explores the technological infrastructures and social relations of exchange and payment, from cowries to credit cards and cryptocurrencies. As an anthropologist, he is interested in the broad range of technologies people have used throughout history and across cultures to figure value and conduct transactions. He has particular expertise in alternative, experimental, and cooperative forms of money and finance, payment technologies, and their legal implications. He has published on topics ranging from offshore financial services to mobile phone-enabled money transfers, Islamic finance, alternative currencies, blockchain/distributed ledger systems, and the future of money.

Tara Merk is a Political Science PhD candidate at CNRS/University of Paris II, working in the ERC BlockchainGov. She is a Research Fellow with both the Weizenbaum Institute in Berlin and the Metagovernance Project. Her current research, conducted mainly through digital ethnography and action research, focuses on blockchain governance, exit to community, DAOs, and labor in Web3. She previously held various roles in the blockchain industry after studying in Maastricht, Hong Kong, and Dublin where she completed her MSc in the field of information systems management focusing on institutional entrepreneurship in Bitcoin.

Kelsie Nabben is an Ethnographic Researcher specializing in the social impacts of emerging technologies, notably decentralized digital infrastructure and artificial intelligence. She completed her PhD at RMIT University's Centre of Excellence for Automated Decision-Making & Society on the topic of "Resilience in decentralised technologies." Her postdoctoral research as a Max Weber Fellow at European University Institute with Dr Primavera De Filippi at BlockchainGov focuses on accountability in blockchain as a context of digital self-governance.

Jason Potts is a Distinguished Professor of Economics at RMIT University and Director of the Blockchain Innovation Hub at RMIT. He is also a Chief Investigator on the ARC Centre of Excellence for Automated Decision-Making and Society. His research covers evolutionary and complexity economics, creative industries and cultural science, economics of cities, innovation commons, and crypto-economics and blockchain. He is an Editor of the Journal of Institutional Economics.

Wessel Reijers is A Postdoctoral Researcher at the Department of Media Studies, Paderborn University. Additionally, he holds visiting fellowships at the Technion and at the Robert Schuman Centre, European University Institute. He received a PhD in Technology Ethics from Dublin City University. Previously, he was a Max Weber Fellow at the European University Institute and a Research Associate in the ERC project "BlockchainGov," led by Dr Primavera de Filippi. His current research explores the impacts of emerging technologies on citizenship, most notably coming from social credit systems. Additionally, he explores the nature of distributed governance, investigating its potential as well as its pitfalls. He is the author of *Narrative and Technology Ethics* and Co-editor of the edited volume *Interpreting Technology*.

Bernhard Resch is Assistant Professor of Organization Sciences at Vrije Universiteit Amsterdam. Grounded in ethnographic sensibilities, his work revolves around the affective and aesthetic intimacies of politics and power in organizing. He explores new and old modes of production beyond firms, management, and employment, seeking to understand how regenerative ways of working and organizing can contribute to the social transformations ahead of us. Topics include collaborative spaces, new work culture, creativity and learning, polycentric governance as well as commons and commoning.

Nathan Schneider is an Assistant Professor of Media Studies at the University of Colorado Boulder, where he leads the Media Economies Design Lab. His most recent book is *Governable Spaces: Democratic Design for Online Life*.

About the Contributors

Alesha Serada is currently finishing their PhD studies at the University of Vaasa, Finland. Their dissertation, which was due in 2024, discusses construction of value in games on blockchain. Their work grew out from more general interest in theory and practice of economic exploitation. Their research interest resulted in a number of papers in the area of game studies, presented at conferences such as DiGRA, IEEE Conference on Games, and International Conference on the Foundations of Digital Games. Originally from Belarus, Alesha finds comfort in studying weird and horror media. Their personal horrors are explored in publications on the late Soviet and post-Soviet visual culture, published in *Studies in Eastern European Cinema*, *Mortality*, and other journals.

J. P. Vergne is an Associate Professor of Strategy at UCL School of Management. His research examines how socially contested innovations shape the evolution of capitalist societies. His academic journal publications unpack the notion of organizational adaptation, particularly in the arms industry and in the cryptocurrency sector. In 2014, he founded the Crypto Capitalism Center to research the role of decentralization technologies in contemporary capitalism, and in 2016, he became Director of the Scotiabank Digital Banking Lab at Ivey Business School (Canada). He published the essay "The Pirate Organization: Lessons from the Fringes of Capitalism" (2013, with R. Durand) and the graphic novel *Déjà Vu* (2017, with S. Legault), whose artworks were digitalized using blockchain technology. He advises startups and asset managers on issues involving technology and industry evolution.

FOREWORD: RESEARCH IN THE SOCIOLOGY OF ORGANIZATIONS

Research in the Sociology of Organizations (RSO) publishes cutting-edge empirical research and theoretical papers that seek to enhance our understanding of organizations and organizing as pervasive and fundamental aspects of society and economy. We seek provocative papers that push the frontiers of current conversations, that help to revive old ones, or that incubate and develop new perspectives. Given its successes in this regard, RSO has become an impactful and indispensable fount of knowledge for scholars interested in organizational phenomena and theories. RSO is indexed and ranks highly in Scopus/SCImago as well as in the *Academic Journal Guide* published by the Chartered Association of Business Schools.

As one of the most vibrant areas in the social sciences, the sociology of organizations engages a plurality of empirical and theoretical approaches to enhance our understanding of the varied imperatives and challenges that these organizations and their organizers face. Of course, there is a diversity of formal and informal organizations – from for-profit entities to non-profits, state and public agencies, social enterprises, communal forms of organizing, nongovernmental associations, trade associations, publicly traded, family-owned and managed, private firms – the list goes on! Organizations, moreover, can vary dramatically in size from small entrepreneurial ventures to large multinational conglomerates to international governing bodies such as the United Nations.

Empirical topics addressed by RSO include the formation, survival, and growth or organizations; collaboration and competition between organizations; the accumulation and management of resources and legitimacy; and how organizations or organizing efforts cope with a multitude of internal and external challenges and pressures. Particular interest is growing in the complexities of contemporary organizations as they cope with changing social expectations and as they seek to address societal problems related to corporate social responsibility, inequality, corruption and wrongdoing, and the challenge of new technologies. As a result, levels of analysis reach from the individual to the organization, industry, community and field, and even the nation-state or world society. Much research is multilevel and embraces both qualitative and quantitative forms of data.

Diverse theory is employed or constructed to enhance our understanding of these topics. While anchored in the discipline of sociology and the field of management, RSO also welcomes theoretical engagement that draws on other disciplinary conversations – such as those in political science or economics, as well as work from diverse philosophical traditions. RSO scholarship has helped push forward a plethora of theoretical conversations on institutions and institutional change, networks, practice, culture, power, inequality, social movements, categories, routines, organization design and change, configurational dynamics, and many other topics.

Each volume of RSO tends to be thematically focused on a particular empirical phenomenon (e.g., creative industries, multinational corporations, and entrepreneurship) or theoretical conversation (e.g., institutional logics, actors and agency, and microfoundations). The series publishes papers by junior as well as leading international scholars and embraces diversity on all dimensions. If you are a scholar interested in organizations or organizing, I hope you find RSO to be an invaluable resource as you develop your work.

Professor Michael Lounsbury
Series Editor, *Research in the Sociology of Organizations*
Canada Research Chair in Entrepreneurship &
Innovation University of Alberta, Canada

ACKNOWLEDGMENTS

We wish to acknowledge Gitcoin and the wider Web3 community who generously supported our Gitcoin grant. We would also like to thank University College Dublin, which provided additional funding. And finally, we would like to thank our contributors, who have been immensely patient and forgiving with our little experiment.

INTRODUCTION TO WEB3: THE NEW CULTURAL ECONOMY

Quinn DuPont[a], Donncha Kavanagh[b] and Paul Dylan-Ennis[b]

[a]York University, Canada
[b]University College Dublin, Ireland

Keywords: Web3; DeFi; NFTs; emerging research; online communities

INTRODUCTION

The story of Web3 starts with the earliest "read-only" Web where users jumped from static web page to static web page. In this Web 1.0 era (circa 1990–2000), we see the beginning of the Internet in the modern sense. At this stage, the Internet is accessible through the World Wide Web but still somewhat peripheral in society. The action of the story is found in the Web 2.0 era (circa 2000 onward). Web 2.0 is the dynamic "read-write" Web defined by the rise of the FAANGs (Facebook, Amazon, Apple, Netflix, Google). It is the era of ecommerce, social media and the entrenchment of the Internet into our everyday lives. It begins optimistically, promising an opening world of knowledge and shared ideas, but devolves in time into concerns around mental health, surveillance capitalism and fake news. Arguably, Web 2.0 never ended, but there was an attempt – distinct from the blockchain concept of Web3 – to introduce the term Web 3.0. Web 3.0 was meant to capture the rise of the semantic Web, later machine learning and artificial intelligence, but it never quite stuck (though ChatGPT suggests perhaps it was simply too early).

Today, the term Web3 (as distinct from Web 3.0) exists as a challenger to name the overall space variously known as cryptocurrency, crypto or blockchain. It has an especial appeal to the post-2021 generation swept under a wave of innovation in blockchain primitives. These primitives – decentralized autonomous organizations (DAOs), decentralized finance (DeFi) and non-fungible tokens (NFTs) – captured

---

Defining Web3: A Guide to the New Cultural Economy
Research in the Sociology of Organizations, Volume 89, 1–9
Copyright © 2024 by Quinn DuPont, Donncha Kavanagh and Paul Dylan-Ennis
Published under exclusive licence by Emerald Publishing Limited
ISSN: 0733-558X/doi:10.1108/S0733-558X20240000089001

the imaginations of a new kind of user, one not necessarily plugged into the cypherpunk or crypto-anarchist ideals of Bitcoin. The term appears to partially reflect a desire to move beyond Bitcoin's strictly monetary focus. The targets for blockchain decentralization increasingly became the tech giants of Web 2.0, whose reputation had plummeted in this era.

At a more technical level, Web3 is associated with the nexus of blockchain technologies beginning with the invention of Bitcoin in 2008. At heart, a blockchain is a decentralized record-keeping system. Bitcoin, for example, is a blockchain that tracks ownership of a currency (bitcoins) designed to offer a decentralized alternative to traditional money systems. Blockchain cultures tend to be hostile to centralization, which is thought to be associated with corruption and control, and they typically engage in experiments with decentralized alternatives. For instance, the next great experiment in decentralized blockchains after Bitcoin was Ethereum, which is not a money system like Bitcoin but instead a decentralized world computer. Ethereum's key innovation is the smart contract, the nuts and bolts that allow developers to build decentralized applications (sometimes known as dApps). Ethereum itself is intended to be a neutral infrastructure for anyone to build what they wish. For the Web3 community specifically, the attraction is the ability to build decentralized analogues to centralized forms of organization (DAOs), finance (DeFi) or art and collectibles (NFTs). To some, this means building regenerative projects with positive externalities, and to others, it means little more than accelerated financial speculation.

Web3 truly emerged in 2021, which one might see as linked to the coronavirus lockdowns. Whatever the reason, the post-2021 generation was certainly presented with novel decentralized mechanisms but also, with their consequences, a chaotic lawlessness that can be both enthralling and intimidating. Manic financial nihilism reigns in Web3 in the form of influencer scams, social engineering, convoluted Ponzi schemes, digital muggings and CEOs acting as wildmen (FTX, Celsius, Terra Luna). The domain is exciting, but exciting like a dangerous downtown; it's where the action is, but make sure you watch your wallet. The push and pull of Web3 is always between the affordances decentralization offers, whether positive or negative. Everyone is always a little bit compromised in Web3, including us.

The editors of the volume walk the line between Web3 enthusiasts and critics. We find in it much to support and encourage and much that makes us question our research choices. On the positive side, Web3's emphasis on experimental decentralization and non-hierarchical organizing is intriguing, sometimes even appealing. We decided the best course of action would be to produce an experimental volume, one that involved some of the risk-taking characteristics of Web3 cultures. To this end, we decided that the book would also explore next-generation methods of publishing. While we typically associate Web 2.0 with Big Tech behemoths like Apple and Amazon, only five companies hold an equally dominant position in the smaller world of academic publishing. The largest of these, Elsevier, holds 16% of the market and has a profit margin approaching 40%, which is higher than that of Google and Microsoft. We saw our initiative as a counter to this dominance and a prefigurative experiment in a different form of academic publishing. In particular, we wanted to emulate the commitment to

Defining Web3 3

openness found in open-source cultures, ensuring that the texts would be freely available to download online, as well as published traditionally. Regarding funding, we also wanted to explore novel funding methods using the native tools of Web3. This was achieved by securing a grant from Gitcoin, which is an open-source project where anyone can request funds for a (non-profit) project that is useful to the wider Ethereum community.

To truly embrace the Web3 world, we created a website that sought to reflect both the transgressive, fun side of Web3 and its chaotic, tumultuous nature. Inspired by early Internet art, flash games, multiplayer online role-playing games (MMORPGs) and the emerging NFT culture, we sought to produce an experience that goes beyond the traditional page or screen by leveraging smart contracts, NFTs and the metaverse, in order to appeal beyond the academy. We decided on the theme of the carnival because, as others have previously observed, Web3 exhibits aspects of the carnivalesque, such as a fascination with games and the ludic, masks and misrepresentation, scams, chancers, various forms of excess, transgression and exhibitionism and a communal ethos that pushes against central authority. We are particularly fascinated by the curious mixture of the playful and the political that we see in both carnivals and Web3.

PAPER SUMMARIES

Part 1: Big Tent

Nathan Schneider argues that Web3 can give us more and better democracy, since distributed ledger technologies enable, by design, shared ownership and control by the system's participants. Unlike the conventional corporation, where the owners of capital and labor are clearly distinguished, the expectation in Web3 is that the user is also the owner. That, at least, is the hope. However, just as corporate power colonized the early Internet, quashing the pioneers' utopian dreams, a centralization power grab is already underway in Web3 creating new forms of feudalism and plutocracy. To counter this, Schneider argues that we need to study and learn from the shared ownership models that already exist in sectors such as credit unions, agricultural cooperatives and rural electrification. And the learning can go both ways: cooperatives can embrace some of the governance and financing practices emerging in DAOs, while some DAOs are already incorporating as cooperatives. But if the potential for a democratic renaissance is to be realized, then Web3's infrastructures need to be explicitly designed to foster democratic governance.

Kelsie Nabben presents "infrastructuring" as a useful analytical lens for understanding Web3. For her, Web3 is not so much an infrastructure but rather the playful, prefigurative and political practice of infrastructuring. The playfulness builds on the field's hacker heritage, the deep embedding of game logics in the underlying technologies and the anarchic and bohemian traditions that inform the communities' practices and esthetics. But that play ethos sits on top of quite serious modular pieces of cryptography, computing hardware and software that provide the underpinnings for the myriad collection of DApps, DeFi, NFTs and

DAOs that constitute Web3. Moreover, these boring technologies are resolutely political in that they purport to offer a free market and a decentralized alternative to existing institutions. Nabben emphasizes that the practice of infrastructuring is prefigurative as the communities enact a vision of a desired society through BUIDLing things that are new and valuable. But the ethos of experimentation means that much of the learning is through trial and error, which, she argues, is necessary as the community must discover "how to infrastructure."

Bernhard Resch proposes nests, stewardship and weaving as three primary vectors to guide the design of new digital ecosystems in Web3. As a counterpoint to a modular worldview centered on firms and individuals, nests are small, interdisciplinary teams held together by collaborative community spirit, shared purpose and a nurturing of collective well-being. Nests are embedded in complex relationships that link pods (small groups of 5–7 people), nests (100–200 members) and flocks (circa 1,500 people). DAOs have the potential to be organized thus, but their structures and practices must be carefully designed and managed to avoid the toxic behaviors that self-organizing can sometimes facilitate. The logic of stewardship is centered on contributing, sharing, caring and commoning, which Resch contrasts with the externalities, exploitation and short-termism of the extractive commodity logic. Again, he believes that DAOs can, and should, embrace this logic of stewardship. Finally, he weaves into his metaphor a form of distributed leadership practice, fluid hierarchies (heterarchies) and wayfinding that DAOs should adopt as their preferred mode of organizing.

Quinn DuPont's wide-ranging paper critically evaluates the political economy and polycentric governance of Web3. Building on extant critiques of Web3 – which often fail to recognize the domain's diversity – he maps out multiple issues that a "progressive Web3" must address. For instance, DAOs can turn everything they touch into a valuable digital asset, while Web3, with its reconfiguration of work and play, can produce problematic forms of commodity fetishism. And even though "smart contracts" might appear to be fairer, they may actually exacerbate inequality. These concerns are present in Web3, which in some ways is "a petri dish for our future online lives" that produce interesting, if sporadic, cases of digital, decentralized, polycentric governance. For DuPont, Elinor Ostrom's ideas of polycentric governance need to be refashioned for Web3 where there are only artificial rather than material constraints. Likewise, trust is transformed rather than eliminated, contrary to the frothy talk about "trustless" transactions. DuPont argues that ideas centered on scarcity, work and profit maximization are ill-suited to understanding Web3, and so, instead he draws on Hardt and Negri's model of social coproduction, social movement theory and sociological models of collective identity. He concludes with a program of research into the polycentric governance of digital common pool resources (DCPRs).

While also recognizing shared ownership as a pivotal characteristic of Web3, *Tara Merk and Rolf Hoefer* strategically diverged from concentrating on prevalent issues such as equality, trust and collective identity, choosing instead to direct their academic scrutiny toward the neoinstitutional foundations that undergird Web3 organizations. Their investigation into how DAOs strive for self-governance led them to examine the effects of both competitive and institutional isomorphism. In their paper, Merk and Hoefer adopt a theoretical approach to decipher the formation of institutions, adapting previous studies to underline three varieties of institutional isomorphism: coercive, mimetic and normative. The core premise here is that institutions emulate competitors to enhance their effectiveness and efficiency. They argue that coercive institutional isomorphism induces homogeneity among institutions due to external threats and opportunities. This mirrors the concept of competitive isomorphism, which is driven by factors such as regulatory scrutiny, legal threats and market opportunities. Mimetic isomorphism, on the other hand, provides an explanation for DAO's adoption of analogous technologies and operational strategies amid significant market uncertainty, even when these practices seemingly conflict with other strategic priorities, such as using centralized services like Discord. Lastly, normative isomorphism shifts our view toward the formation of associations, trade groups and communities of practice. These entities play crucial roles in establishing industry behaviors and norms. In conclusion, Merk and Hoefer argue that institutional isomorphism can significantly contribute to organizational legitimacy, a persistent concern for online organizations with high voice and exit dynamics.

Paul Dylan-Ennis tackles the thorny issue of institutional change. Specifically, he outlines how Web3 culture is framed by social imaginaries, which define a community's goals, its behavioral norms, its shared history and, finally, its taboos. By zeroing in on the culture associated with the Ethereum platform, Dylan-Ennis offers the "Hash, Bash, Cash" model of decentralized organization, where he finds change flows through its technical (hash), social (bash) and financial (cash) spaces. To elucidate this model, Dylan-Ennis dissects the "vampire attack" on Uniswap, which gave birth to a competitor, SushiSwap. While this level of transformative change is somewhat commonplace in the Web3 realm, scholarly attention devoted to these rapid organizational disruptions is sparse; the hash, bash, cash model offers one interpretative lens.

Part 2: Vaudeville

In his paper, *Geert Lovink* explores the rise of NFTs, their esthetic and market value and their impact on the art world. NFT art emerged in the midst of (another) debate in contemporary art about the end of art. One position in that debate holds that the artistic idea is all that matters, and hence, its material production is unimportant, as is the buying and selling of such productions. Crypto, Lovink argues, misses this key point when it envisages "art" as just a digitized asset that can be bought and sold. Hence, NFTs do not truly represent a source of income for artists but instead simply contribute to the speculative nature of crypto investments, which is a world dominated by right-wing techno-libertarians. Consequently, Lovink concludes, debates about "crypto art" are distracting and moot unless they engage with wider issues around power, race and gender in Web3.

Eric Alston asks Web3 to embrace the productive polycentrism of carnivals, from Lent to Burning Man. In his paper, Alston recognizes the governance challenges that emerge with large festivals and gatherings and how scaling often has a homogenizing, detrimental effect. To counter this tendency, Alston recommends that producers seek greater personal power, especially by enhancing bargaining power. While reminiscent of Michael Porter's Five Forces model of competition, Alston instead shifts our attention to the new bargaining opportunities in the metaverse (whenever or whatever it may be). Alston probes into the unknown of this anticipated metaverse in search of the driving forces behind innovation. Ultimately, however, he identifies enhanced ownership as a key component (technologically facilitated by NFTs). Alston concludes his paper in search of a more liberated metaverse.

J. P. Vergne takes on one of the most enduring utopian visions of Web3: decentralization. He observes that decentralization is not only the raison d'être for Web3 but that it also serves as a form of theater, akin to political or security "theater." In this theatrical context, Vergne unfolds the narrative of decentralization through an eclectic ensemble of characters – Hamlet, Godot, Bucket and Figaro – as archetypes embodying efforts at decentralization in Web3. Vergne's narrative method downplays the influences of technologies, corporate strategies and neoclassical economic reasoning and instead accentuates the situatedness, or essentially contextual nature of decentralization in Web3. This distinctive approach enables him to assert that the desired model of decentralization in Web3 should be understood as a continuum, which requires setting system boundaries, and is a process that must be regarded as distinct from associated concerns like inequality or disintermediation. In his concluding argument, Vergne advances the concept of "authority dispersion" as a candidate for achieving decentralization. His insight adds a fresh perspective to the discourse on how to balance power within decentralized systems effectively.

In their paper, *Primavera de Filippi, Morshed Mannan* and *Wessel Reijers* examine Web3 through the lens of memes. For them, cryptocurrencies like Dogecoin and Shiba Inu are not only playful and absurdly self-referential but are also make-believe: they are "pretend" currencies – a deliberate and knowing charade – and they are also subversive depictions of a possible alternative world, with different forms of money and authority. These memecoins, it is suggested, are digital instantiations of the trickster, an archetype with conflicting attributes: at once clever and foolish, serious and facetious, loyal and rebellious, selfish and kind, a sneak and a hero. They can also become an "egregore," a spirit that manifests itself in the collective imagination of a group of people – Santa Claus is a good example. Web3 has its own egregores, such as the mythical figure of Satoshi Nakamoto, memes like Dogecoin and Rare Pepes and profile pictures (PFPs) like the Bored Ape Yacht Club. However, countermovements can be inverted and captured by the system they seek to subvert, and egregores can be intentionally designed and marketed through using the power of communities to make worthless objects seem valuable. As in the carnival, what you see is often not what you get. Or want.

Alesha Serada also sees the trickster as one of Web3's primary archetypes, but her analysis of Crypto YouTube celebrities from 2020 to 2022 widens the focus to jesters and adventurers too. Adopting an anthropological and narrative approach, Serada finds in the myths of many cultures that the trickster is neither a deity nor a person but an outlier in a stable order, an agent of chaos, prone to causing harm to others, obsessed with sexual desires, while sexually ambiguous, the subject of unbelievable stories and a discoverer of new things. The most-watched crypto personalities are not really tricksters, Serada concludes, instead, they are jesters or maybe adventurers. The jester (a fool) has many of the trickster's attributes but, importantly, is a symbolic foil to the king who is expected to mock royal authority and, by triggering carnivalesque laughter, can inspire the masses to imagine an alternative truth and new freedoms. But, Serada points out, the face of crypto is boredom, not laughter, and so, the jester is neither as pervasive nor as important as one might expect. More common is the adventurer, typically a person from the impoverished or lower middle class who infiltrates and dupes the upper class – someone who exhibits exotic tastes and conspicuous consumption, an agent for chaos, a seducer with dubious morals and a magnet for misfortune. In the end, Serada finds the Crypto YouTube community too tame today but points to the trickster, the jester and the adventurer as opportunities for productive disruption.

Donncha Kavanagh makes the case that Web3 is part of a broader cultural shift toward games, a "ludic turn" of recent decades. Marking out new theoretical grounds, he extends the analysis of games to the carnival and highlights the rich extent of the metaphor. In so doing, he explores anonymity, crime, myths, hierarchy, authority, regulation and control as major themes. But turning directly to Web3, Kavanagh finds scant evidence of these tensions. Rather, he finds a gentrified carnival, lacking the exciting rebelliousness of early Bitcoin culture and without any of the viscera of the carnival. Moreover, Kavanagh points out, neither Web3 nor Bitcoin have much "ilinix," a special form of play associated with vertigo and confusion, which carnivals specialize in.

Part 3: Dare Devils

Instead of the trickster or jester, *Sandra Faustino* sees the gambler as Web3's more significant archetype. She begins her narrative with the "casino capitalism" that led to the 2008 financial crisis and the general distrust of financial institutions and states. The working through of that crisis resulted in states bailing out banks and then paying for it through austerity programs that left citizens impoverished and alienated by the larger forces of macro-economics and global computational infrastructures. Just then, DAOs, NFTs, blockchains, cryptocurrencies, DeFI and Web3 arrived, offering a potential out and a belief that "if you cannot escape the casino, you might as well try to improve your odds." Moreover, the code, algorithms and gamified environments fit nicely with the experiences of post-work, digital natives. But the gambler is also something of a parasite, disrupting for its own self-interest, happy to play the game but unwilling to design new games or to critique the games the rest of us play.

Jason Potts focuses on a new type of economy emerging through the integration of digital technologies such as blockchain, smart contracts and digital identity that have enabled digitally native institutions – money (cryptocurrencies), property (tokens, NFTs), organizations (DAOs), markets (DEXs) and security (consensus protocols). Not all readers will buy his argument that capitalism and technology, through substituting machines for people and capital for labor, have brought wealth and freedom, but Potts offers an unashamedly techno-utopian view that sees the process continuing and extending in Web3. This new economy, he argues, is "computable" by which he means that it operates according to a system of rules that produces outputs that become part of the world and so can become, in turn, inputs to the same process. The computable economy, then, is an integrated, algorithmic process of computation that constructs, implements and connects all economic actions (transactions). The computable economy is not just like a computer; it is a computer. And this computer is not a tool we use but rather an environment we live in. Computable economies, he argues, will be massively cheaper to set up and run, and so he envisages a world of "pop-up," configurable economies built for particular purposes and at different scales.

Diane-Laure Arjaliès and *Samuel Compain-Eglin* situate Web3 in the universe of games by addressing the players themselves. In their paper, Web3 is the disruptor in an already established video gaming industry. Arjaliès and Compain-Eglin go on to describe how players in North America and Europe resisted Web3's financialization of their play, whereas poorer, Asian-Pacific gamers embraced the movement as an alternative source of income. More than just an output of research, Arjaliès and Compain-Eglin experiment with the narrative form by establishing a dialogue between them, part professional and part personal, to discuss the esthetics of play. Their discussion revolves around the Crow Queen, a digital artwork produced by Compain-Eglin and offered to readers as a free NFT, which reveals the esthetic tensions of Web3.

Victoria Lemieux also extends the analysis of Web3 to games, accounting for the popularity of more extreme elements of Web3. She focuses on carnivalesque practices that produce degenerate, pleasurable and borderline erotic feelings, what she calls jouissance. By moving her analysis away from technological features and functions, Lemieux is able to focus on the symbolic structures that bring people together to experience collective lifeworlds. Distinctively, Web3 reflects back these inner desires and, in the hands of Lemieux, mirrors the formation of a social epistemology. Like Dylan-Ennis (this volume), Lemieux invokes Charles Taylor's notion of imaginaries to understand how utopian communities come together despite never fully realizing the dream of Web3. Specifically, as people experience separation from the objects of their desire, the resulting feelings of jouissance creates space for the rejection of normal rules and permits the debasement of the individual. Rather than focusing on how Web3 potentially or actually is "good," in her concluding analysis of meme coins and NFTs, Lemieux demonstrates the importance of catharsis, allowing her to excavate the symbolic aspects of Web3. The result is a highly novel, critical reflection on the tensions between individuals and their communities.

Bill Maurer's paper considers the symbolic elements of Web3 but drives his analysis into the heart of capitalism in questioning the role of fungibility, newly reinvented by NFTs. Whereas Lemieux built her argument on the foundation of Lacanian symbols, Maurer looks to the sign systems of Saussure and Peirce.

Here, Maurer finds deep philosophical and historical connections between money – which can, famously, "stand for" anything – and fungibility. This leads him to consider other, perhaps non-capitalist, systems of reckoning value. In turning to Web3, Maurer considers the DeFi practice of seeking "alpha" and finds valiant efforts to use technologies to "hold down" loosely coupled objects for valuation – to transform the fungible into the non-fungible. Economic "singularities" are the result of these valuation processes. Taken to its capitalist extreme, Maurer thinks this is a foolish, illogical task. As a sign system, Web3 tries to fend off the decay and rot implicit in all processes, what the 20th century called entropy. Intriguingly, Maurer finds new pockets of extropianism in these valuation processes but concludes that it is a deficient ideology unable to address political and economic realities.

Finn Brunton anchors the edition with his playful analysis of waste. Like Vergne, Brunton introduces a cast of characters drawn from theater. This play-acting explains how self-destruction, waste and gratuitousness emerge in crypto communities, what Brunton calls You Only Live Once (YOLO) ideology. YOLO ideology is unique in that the past is meaningless and the future is opaque, so inhabitants remain stuck in a perpetual present. YOLO in finance is similar in that it has no stake in the future, a point Brunton drives home with a statement by the US Security and Exchange Commission, where rule 156 notes that "past performance does not guarantee future results." Of course, the extreme of a finance with no future is destruction, which Brunton unpacks through his description of the K Foundation. Most famous for burning a million British pounds in 1994, the K Foundation was responsible for liberating the cash made by the successful pop band KLF. They found many ingenious ways of disposing their cash, but as Brunton describes, burning that much cash takes persistence. Since it "just wants to be a fire," Brunton concludes by reflecting on the password to a wallet of worthless crypto as a pure expression of theater.

PART 1
BIG TENT

WEB3 IS THE OPPORTUNITY WE HAVE HAD ALL ALONG: INNOVATION AMNESIA AND ECONOMIC DEMOCRACY

Nathan Schneider

University of Colorado Boulder, USA

ABSTRACT

The class of technology variously referred to as Web3 or crypto has been heralded as a democratizing force for economics and governance. This chapter argues that, to the extent such hype is justified, it is only partly due to the affordances of the technology itself. Perhaps more important is the amnesia it has induced, as an innovative paradigm whose novelty inclines people to neglect once-stable norms. In both economics and governance, crypto offers opportunities for greater democracy, but following through on them is guaranteed by neither the technology nor the amnesia it invites.

Keywords: Blockchain; cooperatives; decentralized autonomous organizations; governance; economic democracy; finance

Web3 is an opportunity to do what could have been done before but wasn't done, which is already being squandered with what *is* being done. Nevertheless, I will argue, it is an opportunity we need.

The kind of opportunity I refer to is not necessarily the opportunity everybody sees in Web3 – which I will subsequently include in the broader terminology of *crypto*. Common accounts of what crypto is good for include keywords such as trustlessness (De Filippi et al., 2020; Nakamoto, 2009), openness (Caliskan,

2020), coordination (Owocki, 2022; Soleimani et al., 2019; Swartz, 2017), decentralization (Schneider, 2019; Walch, 2019), and freedom (Golumbia, 2016). But the opportunity I am most interested in would be better phrased with another floating signifier (Mehlman, 1972): *democracy* – specially, the pursuit of equitable economics and decision-making. Democracy is also widely cited among crypto's possible or actual affordances (e.g., Allen et al., 2019; Buterin et al., 2018; Linares & Cabaña, 2019; Magnuson, 2020; Reijers et al., 2016), and for some, it is the end for which the other keywords are means. Crypto comes by these democratic associations honestly; its distributed ledger technology enables novel means of circulating wealth and power among a system's participants. Unlike Internet technology that operates through a central server, shared ownership and control are the default setting. Crypto meanwhile has the wherewithal to enable new degrees of consolidation in wealth and power.

The democratic opportunities of crypto are real. But those opportunities are not unique to the technology at hand. They could have been taken before, although for the most part they were not.

The most salient opportunity that crypto presents, more than any particular technical feature or affordance, arises from the amnesia of innovation: that deer-in-the-headlights effect as a new technological paradigm shines brightly enough that people freeze and forget to apply once-stable, and still applicable, social contracts to it. Much as gig platforms made regulators forget labor laws (Cherry, 2015–2016) and cloud services did not face the same privacy rules governing older telecoms (Zuboff, 2019), the strange new tech of crypto has made space for breaking and remaking norms about how networked assets are to be owned and governed. What once seemed (but did not have to be) fixed is now (by no particular necessity) in flux.

Adapted by the Author from Public Domain Images with the GNU Image Manipulation Program.

As Langdon Winner (1980) put it, in the final paragraph of his seminal essay "Do Artifacts Have Politics?" (p. 135):

> In our times people are often willing to make drastic changes in the way they live to accord with technological innovation at the same time they would resist similar kinds of changes justified on political grounds.

That is: What was always possible for humans to do in politics, but never quite feasible, can happen all of a sudden if it can be made to seem the inevitable result of technology.

With Web3, we find ourselves in a throwback to Web1, which is to say the days when John Perry Barlow (1996) could proclaim a "Declaration of the Independence of Cyberspace." The years since have insisted that cyberspace was never its own space and was certainly not independent from its surroundings. Meatspace regimes of law, finance, wealth, and power have had their way with Internet technology, turning that open and decentralized technology into unprecedented concentrations of corporate power. So goes the story again with incipient crypto.

Once again, under the cover of decentralization talk, the centralization power grab is well underway. Venture capitalists have recognized that crypto protocols represent an even greater chance for value capture than platforms did in Web1 or Web2 (Wilson, 2016). Platforms operate within rules; protocols write the rules (Galloway, 2006). A further advantage for the power grabbers lies in the amnesia: crypto's ability to operate ambiguously with respect to territorial law and regulation, carrying out forms of ownership, governance, and financial chicanery that could not be gotten away with using more familiar technologies. In this respect, the disruption of

Adapted by the Author from Public Domain Images with the GNU Image Manipulation Program.

crypto runs the risk of enabling "disaster capitalism" (Klein, 2008): the use of a rupture in the way of things to enact an anti-democratic power grab by capital holders, enabling them to accomplish what would otherwise face too much popular resistance.

So far, actually existing practice appears to be making good on that risk. Available data on blockchain activity are plentiful and precise, but they rarely reveal much about the effects on real human lives. Viral tokens attract hopeful retail investors, who may reap astonishing gains or see large chunks of their savings wiped away in hours. Venture capitalists meanwhile hold large stakes in important decentralized autonomous organizations (DAOs) and protocols, through which they can dominate governance processes (Buterin, 2018; Ferreira et al., 2019; Jensen et al., 2021). The crypto advocates' long-standing promise of financial inclusion for the world's poor appears to remain mostly deferred. Any opportunities that crypto presents on behalf of democracy, therefore, accompany opportunities for democracy's enemies.

Capital, and crypto-capital especially, is itself a form of media (Schneider, 2020b) – malleable, transmissible, vulnerable to subversion, and a vessel for culture. Like any other media, it shapes us, and perhaps even more than we recognize, we shape it. We can bend it beyond recognition, even to the point of its abolition.

I offer this chapter as an explanation for the cautious but determined hope I have for the opportunity that crypto and its cognates present – even if we shouldn't need this opportunity, because the possibility for more democratic ownership and governance has been with us all along. As Kei Kreutler (2021) puts it, those earlier chances represent a kind of "prehistory" for crypto. I will consider crypto's contexts, prospects, and potential tactics for ownership and governance, centered too much on my particular life-world of the United States tech economy, which is at once parochial and outsized in influence. Despite my ambivalence about turning to any technology as a lever of social change – can't we humans do this on our own? – I write in order that, through the amnesia, we might better remember the stakes and defeat exploitation in all its forms.

OWNERSHIP

In capitalist economies, wealth accumulation tends to derive from business ownership (Smith et al., 2019). Particularly since the 1970s in the United States, the returns to capital ownership have continued to grow while wage income has stagnated (Alvaredo et al., 2013; Michel, 2012). There are many contributing reasons for this. Labor-union membership has declined while the financial sector grew. Public policies in much of the world have privileged accumulations of investor wealth and discouraged widespread participation in early-stage businesses. Taxes on capital gains are generally lower than on wages. Stock ownership is highly concentrated, and the bottom half of American income-earners own almost none of it (Wolff, 2017). Redlining and other exclusions have prevented people racialized as non-White from accessing ownership. Private equity funds can access financing to purchase a business, but its own employees rarely can do the same. When even the likes of Uber and Airbnb seek to distribute company stock to their contract workers, the US Securities and Exchange Commission declines to permit it (Robbins et al., 2018). Business structures based on shared ownership such as cooperatives have consistently faced barriers to growth, due to a lack of capital access and other signs of structural neglect (Molk, 2014; Spicer, 2021). Cooperatives have been particularly rare in the platform economy, where venture capital has excelled in deploying large quantities of investment that co-ops cannot access.

This is not a natural or inevitable condition. In sectors such as credit unions, agricultural cooperatives, and rural electrification, public policy has enabled shared ownership to flourish by enabling frameworks for financing it (Schneider, 2018). Economic democracy works when the system allows it to happen. Tools such as dividends from sovereign wealth funds and "baby bonds" could have spread the benefits of capital gains much more universally. Programs for expanding homeownership could have targeted, rather than excluded, marginalized populations. And policy could have ensured that workers who want to buy their factory, or neighborhoods that want to set up their own broadband networks, can access financing just like wealthy investors do (Kelso & Kelso, 1986; Schneider, 2020a).

Those things didn't happen. Now, crypto presents another chance to try.

Shared ownership is the basic value proposition of a blockchain – a database that distinct stakeholders agree on together. Achieving the hallowed goal of decentralization requires having many participants jointly managing their network. Users of a blockchain or a DAO typically hold its associated tokens, which can accrue value with the system as a whole. Use and equity, roughly, go hand in hand; to be a user is to be an owner. The classic distinction between labor and capital could thus be poised to dissolve into an alignment through a common token. Where regulators blocked Uber and Airbnb, crypto seems to find a way. When Gitcoin conducted a financing round in 2021 and created a DAO, it distributed tokens to users (Owocki, 2021). When the Ethereum Name Service released its own token, it distributed thousands of dollars' worth to anyone who had bought a domain (Thurman, 2021). In the culture of crypto early adopters, co-ownership is an expectation and a norm.

The old and new are beginning to learn from each other. Present-day cooperatives, recognizing the constraints that the mainstream economy imposes on them, are turning to tokens and DAOs to open new financing opportunities (Prado, 2021; Robey, 2022). Some DAOs are legally incorporating as cooperatives (Radebaugh & Muchnik, 2021). Even investors such as Variant Fund have adopted widespread user ownership as an investment thesis, citing the cooperative tradition as an inspiration (Walden, 2019). The narrative of "exit to community" (Mannan & Schneider, 2021) – transitioning to community ownership, in one form or another – has become a byword in some corners of crypto culture.

None of this presents a guarantee of equity, fairness, or justice. Achieving those will require intention. For instance, protocols can ensure that token allocations accrue to contributors of labor and use-value, rather than just to those who can afford to pay for them at the outset. Mechanisms akin to antitrust enforcement may be necessary to counteract consolidation and excessive inequality.

Perhaps most importantly, financial instruments should ensure that communities of less-capitalized people can participate in this new economy with relative safety. Whereas the imagined user of many decentralized finance (DeFi) apps seems to be the speculative day-trader, the lone gambler, truly decentralized finance would need to focus on enabling groups of under-capitalized people to access capital for reasonable, practical undertakings.

If more equitable ownership arrangements arise through crypto, however, it is not because they were impossible before. For instance, non-fungible token (NFT) enthusiasts celebrate that the technology enables artists to receive royalties from the resale of their works. However, few seem to recognize that resale royalties have been in use in Europe since the 1920s and more recently in the United States (van Haaften-Schick & Whitaker, 2022). No NFTs required. Still, if crypto can make fair pay for artists easier to enforce and more widespread, all the better.

Adapted by the Author from Public Domain Images with the GNU Image Manipulation Program.

GOVERNANCE

Those of us in the United States experience periodic dismay about institutions like the Electoral College and the Senate filibuster; these are reminders that the government's basic mechanisms date to an 18th-century experiment of aristocratic slaveholders. Their experiment has thus far lasted longer than any other regime of modern republicanism, and yet it joins countries around the world in a general pattern of declining efficacy and public confidence (Diamond, 2022; Papacharissi, 2021; Silva-Leander, 2021). Polarization and gridlock have become increasingly synonymous with democracy.

This is not for lack of opportunities. Recent decades have seen social movements and technologists develop numerous experiments in more textured, responsive, and participatory forms of collective decision-making. These include participatory budgeting (Cabannes, 2004), liquid democracy (Hardt & Lopes, 2015), sortition (Bouricius, 2013; Fan & Zhang, 2020; Gastil, 2000; Pek, 2019), citizens' assemblies (Chwalisz, 2017; Giraudet et al., 2022; Niemeyer, 2014), crowdsourcing (Bernal, 2019; Hsiao et al., 2018), and various alternative voting systems (Emmett, 2019; Posner & Weyl, 2014). A growing field of platforms for online citizen engagement has emerged to facilitate these processes (Stempeck, 2020). Yet in even the most advanced applications of technology-enabled governance, from Madrid to Taiwan (Hsiao et al., 2018; Smith & Martín, 2021; Tseng, 2022), the new mechanisms serve in solely advisory roles; participatory budgeting processes, while more likely to be binding, apply to only small fractions of public budgets.

Governments could be eagerly transforming themselves into the vibrant, creative, networked institutions that the networked world arguably needs them to be, but they are not.

Meanwhile, governance in everyday online life has been guided by a design pattern of "implicit feudalism" (Schneider, 2021), according to which platforms and user-moderators alike wield power with little accountability to the communities they govern. Forms of governance common in offline civic associations – such as elected boards, bylaws binding on leaders, and clearly defined rights – are almost nonexistent in Facebook Groups, "creator economy" platforms, and group chats, for instance. If political thinkers like Alexis de Tocqueville ([1840] 2006) and Robert Putnam (Putnam et al., 1994) are right that small-scale democratic experience contributes to the possibility of mass democracy, then what happens in these online spaces may be contributing to the decline of confidence in the democratic government.

Online democracy certainly could have become far more widespread before – though with crypto, it may be easier. Implicit feudalism emerged partly as a result of a particular socio-technical confluence: From early bulletin-board systems to Web2's corporate social media platforms, central servers and their associated legal entities have been inescapable facts of online social life. Democratic power-sharing, therefore, would probably be infeasible without something like cooperative ownership of a platform's servers. Whoever owns the server holds important legal responsibility for what occurs on it – and most often that means a platform's profit-seeking investors. To the extent that blockchains bypass such sites of central control through user ownership and control, Web3 represents an historic opportunity to break from platform feudalism to digital democracy.

In this specific sense, Web3 boosters' proclamations about the democratizing power of their innovations is true.

Crypto may also help short-circuit the logjam that has hobbled experimentation among democratic governments. In a promotional video for Aragon, a platform for blockchain governance, co-founder Luis Cuende boasts, "Today, we are in the first time in history that we can actually try out new governance models without the need of people getting killed" (Aragon, 2018). It is actually the case that many of the governance innovations listed above – the ones being used either as mere advisors or not at all by governments – are already at work in crypto protocols, organizing decisions and moving resources. Programmable smart contracts enable mechanisms to be tried without asking whether an external legal system will enforce them. Experimentation becomes easier to imagine when it doesn't require a political revolution, just a tweak to the source code.

Crypto's democratic opportunities, however, are not guaranteed. Software protocols can become as entrenched and inflexible as political constitutions (Alston, 2019). The dominant design logic for blockchain governance today is "cryptoeconomics," which relies on economic incentives in ways that risk making democratic deliberation on the common good inadmissible (Schneider, 2022). Too often, the actual practice of participatory governance that crypto makes possible would be better described as plutocracy (Buterin, 2018) or technocracy (Postman, 1993), as opposed to democracy.

For crypto to usher in a democratic renaissance, it needs to be designed that way. For example, even leading advocates of cryptoeconomic designs have begun calling for systems with "soulbound" features that center people, not tokens, as their basic unit (Buterin, 2022; Weyl et al., 2022). This is an important prerequisite for fostering spaces of political, rather than just economic, deliberation, and decision-making – for imagining a common good, not just an optimal return on investment. Drawing on the much longer tradition of cooperative business (Schneider, 2018), crypto systems might more intentionally allocate governance rights accordingly: perhaps only to the workers who build value in their systems or to people making the most widely appreciated contributions, rather than flattening all forms of citizenship into token-holding.

In the meantime, it is a predictable irony that the fate of crypto governance may lie with old-world governments. As policy-makers scramble to regulate crypto – or strategically not regulate it – they also decide whether to turn crypto into a subsidiary or an autonomous zone. Will widespread use of blockchains depend on their adherence to territorial governments' laws? Or will the technology enable new governance layers, as distinct from existing governments as the most libertarian partisans have hoped? In either case, the reshuffling of social contracts underway presents a chance to catch up on the democratic experimentation that has otherwise gone neglected.

CONCLUSION

There is a tendency among some crypto enthusiasts to imagine that, thanks to the marvelous new technology at hand, a green solarpunk paradise of abundant wealth and close-to-effortless coordination is at hand (e.g., Owocki, 2022; Swartz, 2017; Wenger, 2016). It is an echo, amplified with a new kind of hyper-volatile money, of the "solutionism" familiar from the heyday of Web2 (Morozov, 2014). The disappointments of Web2, combined with a steady stream of Web3 cataclysms (White, n.d.), give cause to dismiss such utopianism. Yet it remains undeniable that Web2 produced a kind of rupture with its round of innovation and amnesia – reshaping society, economics, and politics in ways we are still grasping to understand. The result is hardly utopian. To a greater degree than early enthusiasts expected, the rupture was shaped by external forces: venture capital, racism, colonial power relations, and authoritarian politics, for instance.

If Web3 ushers in a similar rupture, it runs a similar risk of amplifying outside forces that do not necessarily contribute to human and ecological flourishing. From the carbon footprint of Bitcoin mining to the surge in crypto-enabled ransomware attacks, the negative externalities are well underway. But with every change comes opportunity. In this chapter, I have sought to identify very real opportunities that crypto presents to radically advance democratic ownership and governance – in ways that both were possible before crypto and are well-suited for crypto's particular affordances.

What is missing from the crypto-optimist culture, as with Web2 solutionism, is a sober recognition of the forces arrayed against happy outcomes. The rewards

Adapted by the Author from Public Domain Images with the GNU Image Manipulation Program.

are great for a small minority to capture the wealth and power of this new paradigm and to prevent democratic possibilities from taking hold. Many contenders seeking to be that small minority are already actively at work in doing so. If people building, regulating, and using crypto are serious about advancing democracy, they will need to design for democracy with determination comparable to what they now apply, for instance, to system security. Tremendous energy – intellectual and computational – goes toward securing property rights on blockchains. What if similar energy were also devoted to ensuring these systems produced more democratic outcomes than their predecessors? What if designers' threat models were not just double-spending and distributed-denial-of-service attacks but also plutocracy and wealth inequality?

This is not the first time advancing democracy has been an option, an opportunity. Too often, other forces won out, and they are well on their way to doing so again.

REFERENCES

Allen, D. W. E., Berg, C., & Lane, A. M. (2019). *Cryptodemocracy: How blockchain can radically expand democratic choice*. Lexington Books.

Alston, E. (2019). *Constitutions and blockchains: Competitive governance of fundamental rule sets*. Center for Growth and Opportunity, Utah State University. https://www.growthopportunity.org/research/working-papers/constitutions-and-blockchains

Alvaredo, F., Atkinson, A. B., Piketty, T., & Saez, E. (2013). The top 1 percent in international and historical perspective. *Journal of Economic Perspectives*, 27(3), 3–20. https://doi.org/10.1257/jep.27.3.3

Aragon. (2018, March 29). *The fight for freedom*. https://www.youtube.com/watch?v=AqjIWmiAidw

Barlow, J. P. (1996, June 1). A declaration of the independence of cyberspace. *Wired*. https://www.wired.com/1996/06/declaration-independence-cyberspace/

Bernal, C. (2019). How constitutional crowdsourcing can enhance legitimacy in constitution making. In D. Landau & H. Lerner (Eds.), *Comparative constitution making* (pp. 235–256). Edward Elgar Publishing. https://www.elgaronline.com/view/edcoll/9781785365256/9781785365256.00017.xml

Bouricius, T. (2013). Democracy through multi-body sortition: Athenian lessons for the modern day. *Journal of Public Deliberation*, 9(1), 1–19. https://www.publicdeliberation.net/jpd/vol9/iss1/art11

Buterin, V. (2018, March 28). *Governance, part 2: Plutocracy is still bad*. https://vitalik.ca/general/2018/03/28/plutocracy.html

Buterin, V. (2022, January 26). *Soulbound*. https://vitalik.ca/general/2022/01/26/soulbound.html

Buterin, V., Hitzig, Z., & Weyl, E. G. (2018). *Liberal radicalism: A flexible design for philanthropic matching funds*. Social Science Research Network. https://papers.ssrn.com/abstract=3243656

Cabannes, Y. (2004). Participatory budgeting: A significant contribution to participatory democracy. *Environment and Urbanization*, 16(1), 27–46. https://doi.org/10.1177/095624780401600104

Caliskan, K. (2020). Data money: The socio-technical infrastructure of cryptocurrency blockchains. *Economy and Society*, 49(4), 540–61. https://doi.org/10.1080/03085147.2020.1774258

Cherry, M. A. (2015–2016). Beyond misclassification: The digital transformation of work. *Comparative Labor Law & Policy Journal*, 37, 577–602. https://heinonline.org/HOL/P?h=hein.journals/cllpj37&i=613

Chwalisz, C. (2017). *The people's verdict: Adding informed citizen voices to public decision-making*. Rowman & Littlefield International.

De Filippi, P., Mannan, M., & Reijers, W. (2020). Blockchain as a confidence machine: The problem of trust & challenges of governance. *Technology in Society*, 62, 101284. https://doi.org/10.1016/j.techsoc.2020.101284

De Tocqueville, A. ([1840] 2006). *Democracy in America* (Translated by H. Reeve). Project Gutenberg. https://www.gutenberg.org/ebooks/815 & https://www.gutenberg.org/ebooks/816

Diamond, L. (2022). Democracy's arc: From resurgent to imperiled. *Journal of Democracy, 33*(1), 163–179. https://journalofdemocracy.org/articles/democracys-arc-from-resurgent-to-imperiled/

Emmett, J. (2019, November 18). *Conviction voting: A novel continuous decision making alternative to governance.* Medium. https://medium.com/commonsstack/conviction-voting-a-novel-continuous-decision-making-alternative-to-governance-62e215ad2b3d

Fan, J., & Zhang, A. X. (2020). *Digital juries: A civics-oriented approach to platform governance.* Association for Computing Machinery. http://dx.doi.org/10.1145/3313831.3376293

Ferreira, D., Li, J., & Nikolowa, R. (2019). *Corporate capture of blockchain governance* [Finance Working Paper 593/2019, European Corporate Governance Institute]. https://www.ssrn.com/abstract=3320437

Galloway, A. R. (2006). *Protocol: How control exists after decentralization.* MIT Press.

Gastil, J. (2000). *By popular demand: Revitalizing representative democracy through deliberative elections.* University of California Press. http://books.google.com?id=SH_TSsKpQfoC

Giraudet, L.-G., Apouey, B., Arab, H., Baeckelandt, S., Begout, P., Berghmans, N., Blanc, N., Boulin, J.-Y., Buge, E., Courant, D., Dahan, A., Fabre, A., Fourniau, J.-M., Gaborit, M., Granchamp, L., Guillemot, H., Jeanpierre, L., Landemore, H., Laslier, J.-F., Macé, A., ... Tournus, S. (2022). '*Co-construction' in deliberative democracy: Lessons from the French citizens' convention for climate.* https://hal-enpc.archives-ouvertes.fr/hal-03119539

Golumbia, D. (2016). *The politics of bitcoin: Software as right-wing extremism.* University of Minnesota Press.

Hardt, S., & Lopes, L. C. R. (2015, June). *Google votes: A liquid democracy experiment on a corporate social network* (Defensive Publications Series). Technical Disclosure Commons. https://www.tdcommons.org/dpubs_series/79

Hsiao, Y.-T., Lin, S.-Y., Tang, A., Narayanan, D., & Sarahe, C. (2018, July). *vTaiwan: An empirical study of open consultation process in Taiwan.* SocArXiv. https://doi.org/10.31235/osf.io/xyhft

Jensen, J. R., von Wachter, V., & Ross, O. (2021). *How decentralized is the governance of blockchain-based finance: Empirical evidence from four governance token distributions.* arXiv. https://doi.org/10.48550/arXiv.2102.10096

Kelso, L. O., & Kelso, P. H. (1986). *Democracy and economic power: Extending the ESOP revolution through binary economics.* Ballinger Publishing. http://books.google.com?id=_R5XDQAAQBAJ

Klein, N. (2008). *The shock doctrine: The rise of disaster capitalism.* Picador.

Kreutler, K. (2021, July 21). *A prehistory of DAOs.* Gnosis Guild. https://gnosisguild.mirror.xyz/t4F5rItMw4-mlpLZf5JQhElbDfQ2JRVKAzEpanyxW1Q

Linares, J., & Cabaña, G. (2019). *Towards an ecology of care: Basic income beyond the nation-state.* https://basicincome.org/wp-content/uploads/2020/01/Julio-Linares-Gabriela-Caba%C3%B1a.pdf

Magnuson, W. (2020). *Blockchain democracy: Technology, law and the rule of the crowd.* Cambridge University Press.

Mannan, M., & Schneider, N. (2021). Exit to community: Strategies for multi-stakeholder ownership in the platform economy. *Georgetown Law Technology Review, 5*(1), 1–71. https://georgetownlawtechreview.org/exit-to-community-strategies-for-multi-stakeholder-ownership-in-the-platform-economy/GLTR-05-2021/

Mehlman, J. (1972). The "floating signifier": From Lévi-Strauss to Lacan. *Yale French Studies (48),* 10–37. https://doi.org/10.2307/2929621

Michel, L. (2012). *The wedges between productivity and median compensation growth* [Issue Brief 330, Economic Policy Institute].

Molk, P. (2014). The puzzling lack of cooperatives. *Tulane Law Review, 88*(5), 899–958.

Morozov, E. (2014). *To save everything, click here* (Reprint ed.). PublicAffairs.

Nakamoto, S. (2009, February 11). *Bitcoin open source implementation of P2P currency.* P2P Foundation on Ning. http://p2pfoundation.ning.com/forum/topics/bitcoin-open-source

Niemeyer, S. (2014). Scaling up deliberation to mass publics: Harnessing mini-publics in a deliberative system. In A. Bächtiger (Ed.), *Deliberative mini-publics: Involving citizens in the democratic process* (pp. 177–202). ECPR Press.

Owocki, K. (2021, December 15). *A brief history of Gitcoin from 2017–2022*. Gitcoin Governance. https://gov.gitcoin.co/t/a-brief-history-of-gitcoin-from-2017-2022/9431

Owocki, K. (2022). *GreenPilled: How crypto can regenerate the world*. Gitcoin.

Papacharissi, Z. (2021). *After democracy: Imagining our political future*. Yale University Press.

Pek, S. (2019, August). Drawing out democracy: The role of sortition in preventing and overcoming organizational degeneration in worker-owned firms. *Journal of Management Inquiry*, *30*(2), 193–206. https://doi.org/10.1177/1056492619868030

Posner, E. A., & Weyl, E. G. (2014). Quadratic voting as efficient corporate governance. *The University of Chicago Law Review*, *81*(1), 251–272. http://www.jstor.org/stable/23646377

Postman, N. (1993). *Technopoly: The surrender of culture to technology*. Vintage.

Prado, J. B. (2021, November 28). *DAOs are interesting, likely, and terrifying* [Substack newsletter]. https://venturecommune.substack.com/p/daos-are-interesting-likely-and-terrifying

Putnam, R. D., Leonardi, R., & Nanetti, R. Y. (1994). *Making democracy work*. Princeton University Press.

Radebaugh, J., & Muchnik, Y. (2021, December 16). *Solving the riddle of the DAO with Colorado's cooperative laws*. The Defiant. https://thedefiant.io/solving-the-riddle-of-the-dao-with-colorados-cooperative-laws/

Reijers, W., O'Brolcháin, F., & Haynes, P. (2016). Governance in blockchain technologies & social contract theories. *Ledger*, *1*(December), 134–151. https://doi.org/10.5195/ledger.2016.62

Robbins, R. B., Schlaefer, C. V., & Lutrin, J. (2018, October 25). *From home sharing and ride sharing to shareholding*. Pillsbury Law. https://www.pillsburylaw.com/en/news-and-insights/rule-701-revision-uber-airbnb.html

Robey, A. (2022). *What co-ops and DAOs can learn from each other* [Blog]. Friends with Benefits. https://www.fwb.help/wip/what-co-ops-and-daos-can-learn-from-each-other

Schneider, N. (2018). *Everything for everyone: The radical tradition that is shaping the next economy*. Nation Books.

Schneider, N. (2019). Decentralization: An incomplete ambition. *Journal of Cultural Economy*, *12*(4), 1–21. https://doi.org/10.1080/17530350.2019.1589553

Schneider, N. (2020a). Digital Kelsoism: Employee stock ownership as a pattern for the online economy. In D. Pohler (Ed.), *Reimagining the governance of work and employment* (pp. 234–246). Cornell University Press. https://osf.io/7wrab/

Schneider, N. (2020b). Mediated ownership: Capital as media. *Media, Culture & Society*, *42*(3), 449–459. https://doi.org/10.1177/0163443719899035

Schneider, N. (2021). Admins, mods, and benevolent dictators for life: The implicit feudalism of online communities. *New Media & Society*, *24*(9), 1965–1985. https://doi.org/10.1177/1461444820986553

Schneider, N. (2022, August 11). Cryptoeconomics as a limitation on governance. *Mirror*. https://ntnsndr.mirror.xyz/zO27EOn9P_62jVlautpZD5hHB7ycf3Cfc2N6byz6DOk

Silva-Leander, A. (2021). *Global state of democracy report 2021: Building resilience in a pandemic era*. International IDEA. https://www.idea.int/gsod/global-report

Smith, A., & Martín, P. P. (2021). Going beyond the smart city? Implementing technopolitical platforms for urban democracy in Madrid and Barcelona. *Journal of Urban Technology*, *28*(1–2), 311–330. https://doi.org/10.1080/10630732.2020.1786337

Smith, M., Yagan, D., Zidar, O., & Zwick, E. (2019). Capitalists in the twenty-first century. *Quarterly Journal of Economics*, *134*(4), 1675–1745.

Soleimani, A., Bhuptani, A., Young, J., Haber, L., & Sethuram, R. (2019). *The Moloch DAO: Beating the tragedy of the commons using decentralized autonomous organizations*. https://raw.githubusercontent.com/MolochVentures/Whitepaper/master/Whitepaper.pdf

Spicer, J. (2021, October). Cooperative enterprise at scale: Comparative capitalisms and the political economy of ownership. *Socio-Economic Review*, *20*(3), 1173–1209. https://doi.org/10.1093/ser/mwab010

Stempeck, M. (2020, May 12). *Next-generation engagement platforms, and how they are useful right now (part 1)*. Civicist. https://web.archive.org/web/20201101012224/https://civichall.org/civicist/next-generation-engagement-platforms-and-how-are-they-useful-right-now-part-1/

Swartz, L. (2017). Blockchain dreams: Imagining techno-economic alternatives after bitcoin. In M. Castells (Ed.), *Another economy is possible: Culture and economy in a time of crisis* (pp. 82–105). Polity.

Thurman, A. (2021, November 9). *Ethereum name service tokens soar after $500M+ airdrop.* https://www.coindesk.com/business/2021/11/09/ethereum-name-service-tokens-soar-after-500m-airdrop/

Tseng, Y.-S. (2022). Rethinking gamified democracy as frictional: A comparative examination of the decide Madrid and vTaiwan platforms. *Social & Cultural Geography*, *24*(8), 1–18. https://doi.org/10.1080/14649365.2022.2055779

Van Haaften-Schick, L., & Whitaker, A. (2022). From the artist's contract to the blockchain ledger: New forms of artists' funding using equity and resale royalties. *Journal of Cultural Economics*, *46*, 287–315. https://doi.org/10.1007/s10824-022-09445-8

Walch, A. (2019). Deconstructing 'decentralization': Exploring the core claim of crypto systems. In C. Brummer (Ed.), *Cryptoassets* (pp. 39–68). Oxford University Press. https://doi.org/10.1093/oso/9780190077310.003.0003

Walden, J. (2019, March 2). *Past, present, future: From co-ops to cryptonetworks* [Blog]. Variant Fund. https://variant.fund/past-present-future-from-co-ops-to-cryptonetworks/

Wenger, A. (2016). *World after capital.* http://archive.org/details/WorldAfterCapital

Weyl, E. G., Ohlhaver, P., & Buterin, V. (2022). Decentralized society: Finding Web3's soul. *Social Science Research Network.* https://doi.org/10.2139/ssrn.4105763

White, M. (n.d.). *Web3 is going just great.* Retrieved June 8, 2022, from https://web3isgoinggreat.com/

Wilson, F. (2016). *The golden age of open protocols.* AVC. Retrieved July 31, 2016, from https://avc.com/2016/07/the-golden-age-of-open-protocols/

Winner, L. (1980). Do artifacts have politics? *Daedalus*, *109*(1), 121–136. http://www.jstor.org/stable/20024652

Wolff, E. N. (2017). *Household wealth trends in the United States, 1962 to 2016: Has middle class wealth recovered?* [Working Paper 24085, National Bureau of Economic Research]. https://doi.org/10.3386/w24085

Zuboff, S. (2019). *The age of surveillance capitalism: The fight for a human future at the new frontier of power.* PublicAffairs.

ENTERING THE FIELD OF WEB3: "INFRASTRUCTURING" AND HOW TO DO IT

Kelsie Nabben

European University Institute, Italy

ABSTRACT

"Web3" is a practice in participatory digital infrastructures through the ability to read, write, and control own digital assets. Web3 is hailed as the alternative to the failings of big tech, offering a participatory mode of digital organization and shared ownership of digital infrastructure through algorithmic governance. This paper offers an introductory playbook to researchers entering the field of Web3 by providing an analytical lens to approach the emergent field of Web3 as "infrastructuring." It argues that Web3 can be understood as a collective, community exploration of "how to infrastructure." Drawing on qualitative examples derived from digital ethnographic methods, the study reveals that play, politics, and prefiguration are fundamental qualities underpinning Web3's vision of offering an "exit" from established institutional infrastructures. Therefore, a primary challenge Web3 faces in its governance experiments centers around the question of how to effectively build and manage infrastructure.

Keywords: Blockchain; Web3; infrastructure; ethnography; digital

INTRODUCTION

The decentralized, digital technologies that comprise Web3, such as public blockchains and digital token economies, are born out of the idea that access to encryption technology is an essential right in the age of information and computers.

Encryption technology is fundamental to the ability to control one's own digital assets. Accessing and entering the field of Web3 involves navigating the boundaries of deep online and offline community participation, including "sliding into the DMs" (direct messages) of Web3 personalities, interacting with individuals using pseudonyms, and managing numerous coins, wallets, and "seed phrase" passwords.

This paper demystifies Web3 for researchers by approaching it as infrastructure, identifying where it occurs, how to enter it, and how to understand it through cultural dynamics, politics, and master narratives. Web3 is characterized by several distinct attributes, including:

- *Permissionless access*: Web3 is accessible without the need for authorization from a third-party authority, allowing for anyone to participate freely, according to a predefined ruleset.
- *Pervasiveness*: It features participatory infrastructures and personal entanglement, indicating a deeply integrated and all-encompassing nature.
- *Prickly characters*: Web3 is known for its unique and sometimes challenging personalities and pseudonymity that shape its community and culture.
- *Playful asthetics*: The environment of Web3 is marked by playful elements, such as the widespread use of memes, adding a light-hearted and creative dimension.
- *Political origins and ambitions*: Web3 has a political aspect, rooted in its ideological origins and aspirations, reflecting a vision of societal impact and change.
- *Prefigurative bias*: It demonstrates a tendency toward prefigurative practices, suggesting an inclination to embody and experiment with the future ideals and structures it advocates for.

These themes of "permissionless," "pervasiveness," "prickly," "playful," "political," and "prefigurative" are subtly and deliberately threaded throughout this paper as "easter eggs" in theoretical explorations and qualitative examples for the reader to uncover, apply, and make meaning of. By analyzing some of Web3's key themes and politics, I argue that Web3 is about "exiting" existing institutions to build its own structures of self-governance from within the prevailing societal hierarchies and power structures. The verb "to infrastructure" denotes the activities, processes of integrated materials, tools, methods, and practices that make up and change an infrastructure. The development of "good" information infrastructures requires adaptability to changing circumstances and environments (Star & Bowker, 2010, p. 159). Applying this perspective to Web3 as infrastructure, highlights a core challenge that community members must grapple with in the pursuit of Web3's developmental ambitions, that is, *how to effectively build and manage infrastructure*.

GAINING ACCESS

The secret of change is to focus all of your energy not on fighting the old, but on building the new. (Millman, 1984)

It was worth leaving the house for the local "WEB3 HACK" meetup that Thursday evening, despite my post-COVID social anxiety about being in crowds

Entering the Field of Web3 29

and having to make small talk. In reward for our interest and attention, each attendee was "airdropped" Zcash privacy coin to our digital wallet address. To receive the equivalent of 18 cents in the privacy coin, I chose the mobile wallet brand called "Nighthawk." The transaction included a secret memo containing a "shielded love note," which was a message from the sender to the receiver that was cryptographically hidden from external surveillance or snooping.

I was late to provide my wallet address to register for the airdrop, somewhat desperately "DMing" (direct messaging) the well-known founder on Twitter in the middle of their talk to include me in their software script that would drop to all the addresses at once.

> Hi! *wave emoji*. Please add me to your bash script. Wallet address: zs1tegqkd6ll92ktc2gxr-874ljy7qjau5aa7pspp6rrktnaeyl82fgrdh6zxlr5pjznsdgpjmyqaef.[1]
>
> Ty! *thank you hands emoji*.
>
> Also, I would love to interview you for a research article on the Cypherpunk's and origins of decentralized technologies to test some assumptions.

To my surprise, they responded.

> Hi.
>
> Check your Shielded Love Notes!

Opening up my Nighthawk wallet, the transaction memo read:

> Hi, Kelsie, nice to meet you! How did you think the meetup went yesterday? What assumption are you trying to test?

With the tiny amount of coins I had received, I could still afford to send micro transactions of cryptocurrency with a memo attached each time. Each message exchanged was shielded by "zero knowledge" cryptography on the Zcash privacy coin blockchain.

I thought to myself, "I'm interviewing a well-known cryptographer and privacy coin founder, mediated by cryptographically shielded love note transactions on the blockchain they invented!" as I responded: "There are not enough characters in the memo or Zcash in my wallet …. Also, I need your approval to interview ☺," referring to the ethics form I needed them to sign to consent to an interview to comply with university processes.

WHAT IS WEB3? A BRIEF BACKGROUND

The invention of the World Wide Web, known as "Web 2.0," offered a revolutionary shift in digital media. It enables any individual to access information through browser-based search engines and share content via web pages, blogs, and eventually social media platforms. "Web 3.0" is an evolution of the internet, with greater data portability to shift power away from corporates to individuals (Stevens, 2022). In contrast, Web3 is a general term used to refer to platforms that leverage blockchain technology to enable verifiable ownership of digital assets (including data). Web3 is hailed as offering an alternative, decentralized internet (although it still depends on existing internet infrastructure). If Web 2.0 gave people the ability to read as well as "write" digital media on the World Wide Web (e.g., blogs), then Web3 is a platform infrastructure to read, write, and "own" (insofar as anything digital can really be "owned"). For ownership, the cryptographic properties of private key management in cryptocurrency (a.k.a. fancy maths for secure communication over insecure channels), combined with the shared, distributed consensus of blockchain-based ledgers (databases), provide the foundations for cryptocurrency tokens that represent property rights and ownership of decentralized digital assets and networks. As such, this paper largely focuses on blockchain technology as an enabling infrastructure for Web3, and blockchain communities as a field site by which to enter Web3.

Promises, Promises

The promise of Web3 is a decentralized infrastructural base that anyone can build on, and everyone can collectively own. Web3 provides a next-generational, peer-to-peer network for participatory self-organizing and a new infrastructural "archetype" (Stefik, 1996). The unique components of public blockchains are the combination of distributed computing, cryptography, and self-provisioning public infrastructure (such as financial networks) to coordinate without central intermediaries. This gives rise to what has been labeled as a new field of "cryptoeconomics," which is the application of cryptography and economics for new forms of institutional infrastructure (Berg et al., 2019b; Nabben, 2023a). Grounded in the purity and infallibility of mathematics, cryptoeconomic systems combine cryptography and economics to "produce new methods of communication, cooperation, and organization" (Cowen & Tabarrok, 2022). Blockchains are touted as a technical expression of the politics of "exit, choice, and loyalty" (Hirschman, 1972). This means that individual freedom is pursued through optionality, with the choice to split the technology and the community if there is strong disagreement (known as "forking") (Berg & Berg, 2017). This infrastructure provides an alternative, free market response to the decline in organizations and nation-states.

In response to these features, public blockchains have been described as creating "new institutional possibilities" and providing a "blueprint for a new economy" (Berg et al., 2019a; Swan, 2015). In blockchain systems, the rules of collective governance are designed and encoded for software to enact through ordered, distributed consensus. When applied to governance procedures, this purportedly minimizes the need for trust in institutions by relying on computational processes, especially transparent and verifiable software code and cryptography (Szabo, 2017). In theory, code reduces the need for third-party regulators, as the system can regulate itself (Wright & De Filippi, 2015). This procedural "input–processing–output" perspective of the world is referred to as "blockchain thinking" (Swan, 2017). What can be built on these infrastructural foundations include decentralized autonomous organizations (DAOs) for coordination (as represented in Fig. 3.1 in the form of a meme), decentralized finance (DeFi), non-fungible tokens for digital representation of unique items (NFTs), and "open" metaverses for immersive digital experiences (Nabben, 2021a).

Entering the Field of Web3

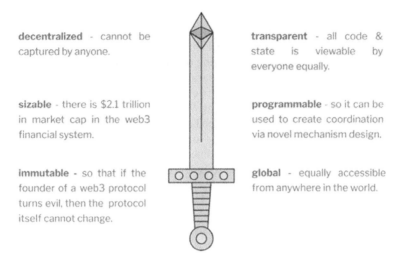

Fig. 3.1. "The Sword That Can Slay Moloch" (the God of Coordination Failure) (Owocki, 2022).

RESEARCHING WEB3

Relatively little has been written about conducting research in the field of blockchain communities as an enabling component of "Web3." Web3 is a multidisciplinary construct, combining principles and practices from cryptography, software engineering, network security, and economics. Rella (2021) describes the ethnography of blockchain communities as digital, multi-sited, and "radically networked." Rennie (2021) highlights the cooperative, participatory nature of decentralized technologies, posing the question: "what would it be like to be *part of* an autonomous robot or infrastructure that makes decisions?" Generating ethnographic connections and identifying patterns, especially in socio-technical systems, is analogous to human–machine entanglement between heterogenous, connected elements (Murray-Rust et al., 2019; Strathern, 2004). In this ethnographic engagement between constellations of people, artifacts, and algorithms, it is impossible not to get subsumed by the pervasive nature of crypto culture.

As an ethnographer, entering the field of Web3 requires entanglement. Communities are relatively open and easy to access. This aligns with the ethos of "permissionlessness," meaning "possible to participate in the use, development, and governance of that system or infrastructure without requiring permission from an authority, by adhering to publicly stated procedures" (Nabben & Zargham, 2022, n.p.). Participation consists of "lurking" in numerous online Discord application chats, community and company Slack groups, engagement in full-blown Discourse forum discussions, and voting in DAOs. Yet, everyday immersion in the field of crypto is unrelenting and consuming. In markets that never close, traders don't stop trading, and developers in time zones around the world don't stop developing. One early and long-term contributor and "cypherpunk"

Vinay Gupta (2022) states: "You've never seen burnout till you've seen blockchain burnout: 24h a day, 7 days a week ... I remember working on the web: it was never *anything* like as intense as the blockchain space is." Even crypto researchers have announced a leave of absence, citing burnout (Walch, 2022).

In entering the field, Web3 is inseparably intertwined across the digital and physical. Blockchain research has been described as both a theoretical and logistical pursuit (Rella, 2021). Researching Web3 occurs in and through information infrastructures, often those of Web3 itself. Amid the COVID-19 pandemic, and for me in the city with the world's longest lockdown, the moving circus of crypto conferences slowed but the online forums and sheer volume of conversation continued to rage. The intense cadence of discussions, proposals, votes, and market twists and turns that are maintained in these online spaces all form ethnographic research data to identify, keep track of, document, analyze, reflect on, and transform. Meanwhile, the moving feast of crypto conferences charged ahead throughout the pandemic where personal relationships are built for "high signal, low noise" communications that lubricate deals, projects, governance decisions, and development. In many cases, catching COVID-19 was "proof of attendance." When I was able to return to my first crypto conferences in three years (actually three conferences in two and a half weeks), I was physically exhausted but intellectually invigorated.

Researching decentralized technology communities uncovers both the inspiring aspirations of internet subcultures, as well as the dank corners of the Dark Web. Here, the worst of human nature can be displayed in a pseudonymous atmosphere of meritocracy based on intellectual prowess, extreme libertarianism ("anything goes as long as I don't impinge on your personal property"), and a value for hard-edged incentive alignment ("make the humans do what you want via money"). Crypto can be described as a "repugnant market," meaning one that is viewed unfavorably in the eyes of society due to the real or perceived harm to participants (Allen et al., 2021). The underbelly of crypto's "dank meme culture" occasionally bubbles up and spills over from one of the "Chans" (i.e., "4Chan" or "8Chan"), an online platform that is government censored in numerous geographies but thriving. For example, the crypto craze around saying "Good morning" or "GM" for short is thought by many participants to be a way of welcoming others to a Discord chat or the Twittersphere as a way to kick off a day's work, especially during the pandemic. With a little more digging, it seems that the morning ritual emerged from a known sex cult in America and perpetuating it in unknowing online communities was seen as funny (Prabhu, 2018; Wikipedia, n.d.). In this field, I've seen many lose their identity, quit their job to become a "sovereign individual," give up one residency to gain another in a tax haven, separate from their long-term partner and declare polyamory, and forego their human decency in the hope of "mooning" (getting rich quick). I have also met wonderfully interesting people, worked on cutting-edge projects, travelled the world, and established long-term friendships.

As time progresses, I have remained entangled in Web3. As an academic researcher, people and projects seem genuinely interested in my research outputs. In such a fast-paced setting and with little sensemaking occurring in near real time, I am invited to speak, write, participate, govern, steward, and advise (thank goodness my husband refuses to come to all the events, so I am forced to return home from the conference circuit and maintain a life on the outside). These projects too want to know "how does technology become resilient?" "What are DAOs vulnerable to?" and "what is good governance?" Why these questions are even relevant is connected to the origins of Web3.

WHERE DID WEB3 COME FROM?

In the study of infrastructures, one way to identify emerging ecosystems is by their master narratives (Star & Ruhleder, 1996). In this chapter, I reject the notion of Web3 as a Venture Capital marketing term designed to capture emerging technologies, instead (briefly) focusing on the historical origins of public blockchains. Blockchain, and by extension Web3, can be known by its political imaginaries and expressions (Husain et al., 2020). Blockchains configure our social reality by configuring social relations and constituting new social realities (Reijers & Coeckelbergh, 2016). Decentralized technologies offer an information infrastructure with unique attributes, in that it is participatory, open source, and encrypted, which suggests the possibility for social coordination that is free from unwanted third-party interference. The combination of distributed computing, cryptography, and the idea of self-provisioned digital monies led to the invention of Bitcoin, the first functioning, "peer-to-peer digital cash" (Nakamoto, 2008). This concoction of an invention is largely credited to the Cypherpunks, a 1990s subcultural group of cryptographers, computer engineers, philosophers, and political extremists (Brunton, 2019; Maurer et al., 2013; Nabben, 2023a; Swartz, 2018). The Cypherpunks have been described as key political protagonists in the engineering of Web3 political economies (Brekke, 2020).

Cryptocurrencies and Web3 emerge as an early reaction to the potential of computing to greatly enhance the surveillance state and surveillance capitalism (Nabben, 2023; Nabben, 2021b). The advent of public key cryptography enabled access to the ability for identities to communicate securely over insecure networks (Diffie & Hellman, 1976). The Cypherpunks converged over the shared belief that public key cryptography was a powerful tool in restructuring society. According to Timothy C. May, author of the Crypto Anarchist Manifesto and one of the co-founders of the Cypherpunks Mailing List, cryptography has the ability to "fundamentally alter the nature of corporations and of government interference in economic transactions" (although we know that public blockchains as an instantiation of this vision are indeed very traceable, with professional organizations offering this service to governments and other companies) (May, 1992). Such tools for communication, commerce, and self-organization were first embraced by repugnant markets, such as the "silk road" online drug marketplace.

Web3 also perpetuates computer subcultures of old by embracing the hacker ethic of participatory organizing. Hacking is about political reordering. The cultural politics of Web3 are in many ways a continuation of hacker traditions of political reordering, embracing political ambition through "playful tinkering" (Coleman, 2011). Although serious in its underlying ambition, development is conducted playfully and for the "lulz" (laughs) (Coleman, 2014), as both an intellectual challenge and a game. Yet, in Web3, hackers are not breaking, but the overarching memetic phrase known as "BUIDLing."

Web3 has emerged from encryption massive expansion in digital possibilities for coordination, and anarchy, not for tearing down but for creating value networks that restructure society in ways where people have more control. For hackers, "code is speech," meaning a sphere for free speech and protest (Coleman, 2009). The saying "code is law" in Bitcoin communities refers to the immutable, software code that acts as legal enforcement of the rules of the system (somehow perverted from its application in academic circles (Lessig, 2000)). In Web3, code is *creation*. Its playful origins that were once surmised in the meme phrase "HODL" (meaning, hold your tokens despite market bear and bull runs) are now described as large-scale infrastructure engineering projects, encapsulated in the surprisingly sticky meme "BUIDL" (meaning, build). Creation speaks of iterative "experiments" in new institutional infrastructures and societal possibilities for self-organization. Yet, the subliminal but fundamental question behind Web3 is, what is being built?

THE PREFIGURATIVE POLITICS OF WEB3

The cultural politics of digital media is a seminal lens for the analysis of software communities (Coleman, 2010), as "no tool is neutral" (Star, 1999). Decentralized, public blockchains have been described as both a "theory of the larger social order" and a challenge to it (Swartz, 2018). The political philosophy of these infrastructures includes self-provisioning of public goods via technological tools, free markets, and governance minimization (Ennis, 2021; Swartz, 2018). The Ethereum public blockchain project positions itself as the infrastructural backbone for distributed, global, coordination that will emerge from within the existing system.

> "[…] money is a fundamentally social thing in a much deeper way than, say, two-party encrypted communication," Buterin [co-founder of the Ethereum blockchain] states. "You have to start thinking about governance, social contracts … common shared expectations in this community, how do changes get made, how do we decide how changes get made, how do we discuss things …. These are all very political things." (As quoted by Morris, 2019)

While admiring the Cypherpunks' anarchist ideologies and creations, Ethereum's politics have been gently redirected to emphasize a culture of software development, immersed in cultural diversity and belonging, and epitomized in memes and motifs of rainbows and unicorns, (as demonstrated in Figure 3.2, which shows co-founder of the Ethereum blockchain, Vitalik Buterin, wearing pyjama pants and hugging a person in a "Spork" suit at a cryptocurrency software developer conference). By taking a more subtle but still political path to societal change, "Ethereum is not in the business of countering the state" directly (Ennis, 2021). This has allowed for the gradual advancement in the development of decentralized infrastructure for financial markets, governance, government, identity, and coordination between digital and physical assets into the mainstream. Relatively little reprimand from regulators to stop this burgeoning industry has occurred along the way, despite some SEC notices being served and US Treasury Sanctions against virtual currency mixer "Tornado Cash."

Entering the Field of Web3

Fig. 3.2. "This is the man that has all your money!". Image courtesy of Amasihy Photography (ETHDenver, 2022).

These themes underpinning the political propensities of public blockchains are encapsulated in the concept of prefigurative politics.

Prefiguration is a politics of creation in response and opposition to existing institutions to embody personal and anti-hierarchical values through participatory action to enact a vision of a desired society in place of what is (Boggs, 1977; Swain, 2019). Blockchain communities embrace a politics of prefiguration by embodying the politics and power structures that they want to enable in society (noting that they are heterogeneous and fraught with political infighting and alliances). In parallel with existing forms of government, blockchain introduces a novel form of self-governance with its own power dynamics (Miscione & Kavanagh, 2015). This disintermediation of centralized actors emerges from within existing structures in society, including that of communications, money, digital media, and recreation. What is not completely clear is what society is being prefigured toward.

If blockchain is about infrastructural experiments in reordering society, then Web3 is the configuration of these new social worlds. Of course, the risk with any strategy of prefiguration is that rather than offering an escape from government, technological infrastructures just offer another, competing governance system with its own politics (Reijers & Coeckelbergh, 2016). The reimagining of Web3 is ambitious, broad-scale, self-made societal improvement, where local actions, such as a shielded love note, lead to global change. Thus, the question begging Web3 is not just "what is good governance?" but "what is good infrastructure?" In trying to design coordination infrastructures for societal scale, the subliminal, unaddressed, question staring Web3 in the face is, "how to infrastructure?" in line with the cultural values of Web3's developmental ambitions, which has been referred to as "self-infrastructuring" (Nabben, 2023b).

WEB3 AS INFRASTRUCTURE

One way to examine Web3 that integrates its prefigurative ambitions and the technical details of its everyday functioning is by viewing it as infrastructure. Information infrastructures are the array of social and technical elements, characterized by people and processes of human organization that support the creation, use, transmission, storage, and destruction of information (Akrich, 1992; Star & Ruhleder, 1996). The attributes of infrastructure include "embedded, transparent, learned as part of membership, linked, embodied, built, modular" (Star, 1999). They are "shared, evolving, open, standardized, heterogenous" to provide an installed base on which to build (Hanseth & Lyytinen, 2016, p. 109). Bowker et al. (2009) argue that when dealing with information infrastructures, we need to look at the whole array of organizational forms, practices, and institutions that accompany, make possible, and inflect the development of new technology, their related practices, and their distributions. Institutional infrastructures are the sets of political, legal, and cultural institutions that form the backdrop for economic activity and governance, which enable or constrain operations to organize and configure societal relations (Hinings et al., 2017). In this context, Web3 is both technical infrastructure and institutional infrastructure. The challenge, in this novel context of decentralized social infrastructure, is learning *how* to infrastructure. This necessitates not only creative ambition, but a deep understanding of infrastructural lifecycles, in terms of design, development, operation, and maintenance.

HOW TO INFRASTRUCTURE

Web3 is innovating in reaction to the much-anticipated failures of Web 2.0 and the "myth of digital democracy" (Hindman, 2009). The purpose of infrastructure is to support a particular activity (Zurkowski, 1984). This is an inherently political undertaking. "The politics of technology are about ways of building order in our world" states infrastructure scholar Langdon Winner (1985). Proponents of Web3 want to create and build better information infrastructures. They just don't know how yet.

"To infrastructure" denotes the ongoing activities, processes, tools, methods, and practices that make up and change an infrastructure (Star & Bowker, 2010). Good information infrastructures are those that are adaptive to changing circumstances and environments, yet, designing for flexibility in relation to a clear purpose is not an easy task (Star & Bowker, 2010). Innovation that is predicated on past examples can lead to a lack of imagination (Star & Bowker, 2010) or, worse, degradation of "the layer of institutions that keeps individuals from eating each other" (Turner, 2019).

Public blockchains enable social, political, and economic modes of self-organization through the ability for members of a network to enter and exit infrastructures, according to their values and preferences, and the rules of the infrastructure in which they shape and participate. This flexibility cannot always be planned in advance as changes in social, technical, and economic settings are often unpredictable. Already, public blockchains are composed of the "infrastructural legos" of cryptography, computing hardware, software, and ledger, and are being composed still of decentralized applications (DApps), DeFi, NFTs, and decentralized organizations (DAOs). How these can and should be combined, and to which emergent models of data governance they will ascribe (whether based on cooperative data governance models, more legalistic data trust structures, or by emphasizing personal data sovereignty) will greatly influence the social outcomes of Web3 infrastructure.

Furthermore, the work of creating and building infrastructure is secondary to the work of ongoing maintenance. In building coordination infrastructure, it's all a coordination game. Public infrastructures traditionally emerge out of significant bureaucracy. In other networks, such as the Web, standard bodies and social arrangements make the development and ongoing maintenance of large-scale technological infrastructure possible. Although standards are essential in the development of large-scale infrastructures, they are a messy entanglement of social processes, across numerous layers of a technology stack, require practice, and evolve over time (Star & Bowker, 2010). This highlights a potential contradiction to be planned and solved if Web3 is to fulfill its vision (although as Buterin (2022) himself points out, there are many contradictions). Decentralized infrastructure cannot be governed by centralized bureaucracies in the long term, yet infrastructures require long-term maintenance strategies.

Ultimately, infrastructure requires people, and it is the social consequences of infrastructures that matter (Edwards et al., 2009). The challenge of broad-scale infrastructures is the "gateway moments" when technical, political, legal, and social innovations link previously separate systems to form far more powerful, far-reaching networks. Here, infrastructures must "adapt to, reshape, or even internalize elements of their environment in the process of growth and entrenchment" (Edwards et al., 2009). As Web3 scales in development, general interest, adoption, and the rise of challengers to it (such as nation-state-based "Central Bank Digital Currencies"), it must have a clear purpose to unite and guide its infrastructuring if it is to deliver on the hopes of its roots and its promises as a genuine alternative to Web 2.0 failings. Perhaps Web3 needs a new meme, from "BUIDL" to "COORDINAET" (meaning, coordinate – also, this is why my Web3 job title is not "Dank Meme Lord").

WEB3 AND THE EVERYDAY

Depending on the cryptocurrency market cycle, Web3 is the most hype-beasted field of what are essentially the mundane but fundamental aspects of human coordination. Societal coordination is what humans have spent generations trying to figure out. Web3 is the same goals but with new tools, situating coordination as distributed among participants across physical and digital domains, rather than hierarchical and administered via traditional institutions.

I am convinced that many people don't understand why they are here. A cause to believe in, a community, a "GM" to wake up for in the morning and, of course, an exit (either from existing social hierarchies or financially to quit the "rat race"). Yet, when there is little understanding of the history of where Web3 has come from, developers often unknowingly adopt cypherpunk sentimentalities and hacker asthetics to forward the subversive tide of Web3. Others are masters of their craft, the subtle art of coordination games of "political goals, via technological means" (Nabben, 2023b), and prefigurative "acting through building" (Coleman, 2011). The privacy coin airdrop and love note interaction elaborated in this chapter are about hiding cryptographic communications in a modern-day smartphone to incentivize migration to an alternative infrastructure. This alternative infrastructure, "Web3," is one undergirded by cryptography, powered by blockchain technology, and political in its affordances of creation toward "exit" from traditional infrastructures of communication, banking, and governance.

These quite serious matters of governance, politics, autonomy, and society are oftentimes a far cry from what I observe in the day-to-day Discord channels and memes of the crypto Twittersphere. Almost in contrast with the vast structural and political visions of Web3 projects is the way its materiality as a technological infrastructure is embedded in everyday encounters that shape our world. The everyday experiences of Web3 occur subtly, through regular columns in the local newspaper on "Web3 and me" or "GameFi" decentralized applications where furry animals "breed" with one another and players are rewarded in tokens (Axie Infinity, n.d.; Ihde, 2009). Keen attention must be paid to the underlying processes, politics, material infrastructures, and social protocols that enable and direct Web3.

This is not necessarily because Web3 is so special in the history of technological development, new media, and cultural adaptation but because wherever individuals and groups deploy and communicate with digital media, "there will be circulations, reimaginings, magnifications, deletions, translations, revisionings, and remakings of a range of cultural representations, experiences, and identities," (Coleman, 2010), and the precise ways that these dynamics unfold can never be fully anticipated in advance. Thinking about how to organize infrastructures that we can and want to live with might help.

CONCLUSIONS

Web3 offers an "exit" from existing institutions by building infrastructures for self-governance from within prevailing societal hierarchies and power structures. This paper has provided a practical outline of the core tenants of Web3 for those seeking to "enter the field" as researchers, as well as a theoretical framework for further research into Web3 as infrastructure. The historical origins, cultural asthetics, and prefigurative politics of Web3 demonstrate how Web3 is a process of community discovery in learning how to infrastructure in digital realms. The challenge for proponents of Web3 is to create good information infrastructure – meaning infrastructure that provides a genuine alternative to the governance and ownership downfalls of Web2.0 to allow people to adapt and change to their environment, in line with their values and goals and in relation to existing institutions (including the law).

Engaging with Web3 reflects profound shifts in modes of social interaction, economic, and cultural life. By encountering Web3's pursuit of collectively building better institutional infrastructure, I have presented a mirror of Web3 and a mirror to Web3 of "how to infrastructure." This infrastructural lens helps frame "success" as neither getting in early on a Ponzi scheme or orchestrating a social movement but as conscious design and maintenance for the everyday human experience.

Despite offering an analytical lens, there is no reason to presuppose that researchers *should* engage with Web3. Indeed, academic bureaucracies epitomize the antithesis of Web3, built on sluggish hierarchies, with little incentive toward practical action, in favor of climbing "publish or perish" rankings (not my team but so I'm told occurs elsewhere). According to the logic of prefiguration that organizes Web3, open, permissionless, peer-to-peer systems playfully seek to reorder, mend, and re-create seemingly broken structures from within, to enable choice. Thus, this entire exercise in institutional reimagining and building is not really about entering the field, but true to the nature of cryptoeconomic systems, it is about *exiting* it. This is in many ways the goal of this publication.

NOTE

1. Alas, I have edited the figures so this is not my actual wallet address.

ACKNOWLEDGMENTS

Thank you to RMIT University Blockchain Innovation Hub and BlockScience for ongoing research collaborations, and the editors of this special collection for the invitation to contribute.

REFERENCES

Akrich, M. (1992). The de-scription of technical objects. In W. E. Bikjer & J. Law (Eds.), *Shaping technology/building society. Studies in sociotechnical change* (p. 205). MIT Press.
Allen, D., Berg, C., & Davidson, S. (2021). *Repugnant innovation*. Retrieved May 2022 from https://ssrn.com/abstract=3932730
Axie Infinity. (n.d.). Axie Infinity. Retrieved May 2022 from https://axieinfinity.com/
Berg, A., & Berg, C. (2017). Exit, voice, and forking. *Cosmos + Taxis*, 8(8 + 9), 76–89. https://ssrn.com/abstract=3081291
Berg, C., Davidson, S., & Potts, J. (2019a). Blockchain technology as economic infrastructure: Revisiting the electronic markets hypothesis. *Frontiers in Blockchain*, 2(22), 1–6. https://doi.org/10.3389/fbloc.2019.00022
Berg, C., Davidson, S., & Potts, J. (2019b). *Understanding the blockchain economy*. Edward Elgar.
Boggs, C. (1977). Marxism, prefigurative communism, and the problem of workers' control. *Radical America*, 11(6), 99–122.

Bowker, G. C., Baker, K., Millerand, F., & Ribes, D. (2009). Toward information infrastructure studies: Ways of knowing in a networked environment. In J. Hunsinger, L. Klastrup, & M. Allen (Eds.), *International handbook of internet research*. Springer. https://doi.org/10.1007/978-1-4020-9789-8_5

Brekke, J. (2020). Hacker-engineers and their economies: The political economy of decentralised networks and 'cryptoeconomics.' *New Political Economy*, *26*(4), 646–659. https://doi.org/10.1080/13563467.2020.1806223

Brunton, F. (2019). *Digital cash: The unknown history of the anarchists, utopians, and technologists who created cryptocurrency*. Princeton University Press.

Buterin, V. [vitalik.eth, @VitalikButerin]. (2022). *Thread: Some still open contradictions in my thoughts and my values, that I have been thinking about but still don't feel like I've fully resolved* [Tweet]. Twitter. Retrieved May 2022 from https://twitter.com/VitalikButerin/status/1526378787855736832

Coleman, G. (2009). Code is speech: Legal tinkering, expertise, and protest among free and open source software developers. *Cultural Anthropology*, *24*(3), 420–454. https://doi.org/10.1111/j.1548-1360.2009.01036.x

Coleman, G. (2010). Ethnographic approaches to digital media. *Annual Review of Anthropology*, *39*, 487–505. https://doi-org.ezproxy.lib.rmit.edu.au/10.1146/annurev.anthro.012809.104945

Coleman, G. (2011). Hacker politics and publics. *Public Culture*, *23*(3(65)), 511–516. https://doi.org/10.1215/08992363-1336390

Coleman, G. (2014). *Hacker, hoaxer, whistleblower, spy: The many faces of anonymous*. Verso Books.

Cowen, T., & Tabarrok, A. (2022). *Cryptoeconomics*. Retrieved May 2022 from https://marginalrevolution.com/marginalrevolution/2022/05/cryptoeconomics.html.

Diffie, W., & Hellman, M. (1976). New directions in cryptography. *IEEE Transactions on Information Theory*, *22*(6), 644–654. https://doi.org/10.1109/TIT.1976.1055638

Edwards, P., Bowker, G. Jackson, S., & Williams, R. (2009). Introduction: An agenda for infrastructure studies. *Journal of the Association for Information Systems*, *10*(5), 369. https://doi.org/10.17705/1jais.00200

Ennis. P. J. (2021). *Ethereum's political philosophy explained*. CoinDesk. Retrieved January 2022 from https://www.coindesk.com/markets/2021/07/09/ethereums-political-philosophy-explained/

ETHDenver. (2022). *Official album. Amasihy photography*. February 18. *Flickr*. Retrieved April 1, 2024 from https://www.flickr.com/photos/162230196@N03/51923335532/in/album-72177720297192832/.

Gupta, V. [@leashless]. (2022). You've never seen burnout 'till you've seen blockchain burnout.... Twitter. Retrieved May 2022 from https://twitter.com/leashless/status/1504575667320537101

Hanseth, O., & Lyytinen, K. (2016). Design theory for dynamic complexity in information infrastructures: The case of building internet. In L. P. Willcocks, C. Sauer, M. C. Lacity (Eds.), *Enacting research methods in information systems* (pp. 104–142). Palgrave Macmillan.

Hindman, M. (2009). *The myth of digital democracy*. Princeton University Press.

Hinings, C. R., Logue, D. M., & Zietsma, C. (2017). Fields, institutional infrastructure and governance. In R. Greenwod, C. Oliver, T. B. Lawrene, & R. E. Meyer (Eds.), *The Sage handbook of organizational institutionalism* (Chapter 6, pp. 163–189.). Sage.

Hirschman, A. O. (1972). *Exit, voice, and loyalty*. Harvard University Press.

Husain, S. O., Franklin, A., & Roep, D. (2020). The political imaginaries of blockchain projects: Discerning the expressions of an emerging ecosystem. *Sustainability Science*, *15*, 379–394. https://doi.org/10.1007/s11625-020-00786-x

Ihde, D. (2009). *Postphenomenology and technoscience*. Sunny Press.

Lessig, L. (2000). Code is law: On liberty in cyberspace. *Harvard Magazine*. Retrieved May 2022 from https://www.harvardmagazine.com/2000/01/code-is-law-html

Maurer, B., Nelms, T. C., & Swartz, L. (2013). 'When perhaps the real problem is money itself?': The practical materiality of Bitcoin. *Social Semiotics*, *23*, 2–17. https://doi.org/10.1080/10350330.2013.777594

May, T. (1992). *The crypto anarchist manifesto*. Retrieved August 15, 2020, from https://www.activism.net/cypherpunk/crypto-anarchy.html

Millman, D. (1984). *Way of the peaceful warrior: A book that changes lives* (pp. 113). H J Kramer, Inc.

Miscione, G., & Kavanagh, D. (2015). *Bitcoin and the blockchain: A coup d'état through digital heterotopia?* Humanistic Management Network, Research Paper Series 23/15. https://papers.ssrn.com/sol3/papers.cfm?abstract_id=2624922

Morris, D. (2019). Vitalik Buterin is embracing a new role: Political theorist. *Breaker Magazine*. Retrieved February 2022 from https://web.archive.org/web/20210905043323/https://breaker-mag.breaker.io/vitalik-buterin-is-embracing-a-new-role-political-theorist/

Murray-Rust, D., Gorkovenko, K., Burnett, D., & Richards, D. (2019). Entangled ethnography: Towards a collective future understanding. In *Proceedings of the halfway to the future symposium 2019 (HTTF 2019)* (Article 21, pp. 1–10). Association for Computing Machinery. https://doi-org.ezproxy.lib.rmit.edu.au/10.1145/3363384.3363405

Nabben, K. (2021a). *Building the metaverse: 'Crypto States' and corporates compete, down to the hardware*. Retrieved May 2022 from http://dx.doi.org/10.2139/ssrn.3981345

Nabben, K. (2021b). Is a "decentralized autonomous organization" a panopticon? Algorithmic governance as creating and mitigating vulnerabilities in DAOs. In *Proceedings of the interdisciplinary workshop on (de) centralization in the internet (IWCI'21)* (pp. 18–25). Association for Computing Machinery. https://doi-org.ezproxy.lib.rmit.edu.au/10.1145/3488663.3493791

Nabben, K. (2023a). Cryptoeconomics as governance: An intellectual history from 'crypto anarchy' to 'cryptoeconomics.' *Internet Histories*, 7(3), 1–23. https://doi.org/10.1080/24701475.2023.2183643

Nabben, K. (2023b). Web3 as 'self-infrastructuring': The challenge is how. *Big Data & Society*, 10(1). https://doi.org/10.1177/20539517231159002

Nabben, K., & Zargham, M. (2022). Permissionlessness. *Internet Policy Review*, 11(2). https://doi.org/10.14763/2022.2.1656

Nakamoto, S. (2008). *Bitcoin: A peer-to-peer electronic cash system*. Retrieved February 20, 2022, from https://bitcoin.org/bitcoin.pdf

Owocki, K. [@owocki]. (2022). *The sword that can slay Moloch* [Tweet]. Twitter. Retrieved May 2022 from https://twitter.com/owocki/status/1486112437241745408

Prabhu, V. (2018, August 25). *Nxivm: How a sex cult worthy of influencing power was formed in America* [blog]. VoxSpace. Retrieved May 2022 from https://www.voxspace.in/2018/08/25/nxivm-sex-cult/

Reijers, W., & Coeckelbergh, M. (2016). The blockchain as a narrative technology: Investigating the social ontology and normative configurations of cryptocurrencies. *Philosophy & Technology*, 31, 103–130. https://doi.org/10.1007/s13347-016-0239-x

Rella, L. (2021). Assembling the fieldless field site. In M. O. Ajebon, Y. M. C. Kwong, & D. A. de Ita (Eds.), *Navigating the field: Postgraduate experiences in social research* (pp. 37–48). Springer International Publishing. https://doi.org/10.1007/978-3-030-68113-5_4

Rennie, E. (2021). *The governance of degenerates part I: Emerging dynamics* [blog]. Medium. Retrieved May 2022 from https://ellierennie.medium.com/the-governance-of-degenerates-part-i-emerging-dynamics-527e697aee36

Star, S. L. (1999). The ethnography of infrastructure. *American Behavioral Scientist*, 43(3), 377–391. https://doi.org/10.1177/00027649921955326

Star, S. L., & Bowker, G. C. (2010). How to infrastructure. In *Handbook of new media: Social shaping and social consequences of ICTs* (Updated Student Edition, pp. 151–162). SAGE Publications Ltd. https://dx.doi.org/10.4135/9781446211304.n13

Star, S. L., & Ruhleder, K. (1996). Steps toward an ecology of infrastructure: Design and access for large information spaces. *Information Systems Research*, 7, 111–134.

Stefik, M. J. (Ed.). (1996). *Internet dreams: Archetypes, myths, and metaphors*. MIT Press.

Stevens, R. (2022). *What is Web 3 and why is everyone talking about it?* Coin Desk. Retrieved May 2022 from https://www.coindesk.com/learn/what-is-web-3-and-why-is-everyone-talking-about-it/

Strathern, M. (2004). *Partial connections* (Updated ed., p. 38). Rowman & Littlefield.

Swain, D. (2019). Not but not yet: Present and future in prefigurative politics. *Political Studies*, 67(1), 47–62. https://doi.org/10.1177/0032321717741233

Swan, M. (2015). *Blockchain: Blueprint for a new economy*. O'Reilly Media, Inc.

Swan, M. (2017). *Blockchain thinking: The brain as a decentralized autonomous corporation*. IEEE Technology and Society. Retrieved May 30, 2022, from http://technologyandsociety.org/blockchain-thinking-the-brain-as-a-decentralized-autonomous-corporation/

Swartz, L. (2018). What was Bitcoin, what will it be? The techno-economic imaginaries of a new money technology. *Cultural Studies*, 32(4), 623–650. https://doi.org/10.1080/09502386.2017.1416420

Szabo, N. (2017). *Money, blockchains, and social scbility*. Unenumerated Blogspot. Retrieved July 2021 from https://unenumerated.blogspot.com/search?updated-max=2017-02-23T23:48:00-08:00&max-results=11&start=1&by-date=false

Turner, F. (2019). Machine politics. *Harper's Bazaar Magazine*. Retrieved May 30, 2022, from https://harpers.org/archive/2019/01/machine-politics-facebook-political-polarization/
Walch, A. [@angela_walch]. (2022). *Some personal news from me. I will be taking a leave of absence from St. Mary's for the 2022–2023 school year* [Tweet]. Twitter. Retrieved May 2022 from https://twitter.com/angela_walch/status/1523794404665823232
Wikipedia. (n.d.). *NXIVM*. Wikipedia. Retrieved May 2022 from https://en.wikipedia.org/wiki/NXIVM
Winner, L. (1985). Do artifacts have politics?. *Daedalus, 109*, 26–38. https://doi.org/10.4324/9781315259697-21
Wright, A., & De Filippi, P. (2015). *Decentralized blockchain technology and the rise of Lex cryptographia*. SSRN. http://dx.doi.org/10.2139/ssrn.2580664
Zurkowski, P. G. (1984). Integrating America's infostructure. *Journal of the American Society for Information Science, 35*(3), 170–178. https://doi.org/10.1002/asi.4630350310

BUSINESS WITHOUT FIRMS: A PLANETARY DESIGN LANGUAGE FOR DAOs

Bernhard Resch

Vrije Universiteit Amsterdam, The Netherlands

ABSTRACT

Decentralized autonomous organizations (DAOs) promise to be an incubator for a regenerative, mutualist, and democratic economy. But if business is no longer done in firms and workers are neither employed nor managed – what else? This paper argues that a new production architecture inevitably involves an uncomfortable look at the idea of "business" itself, requiring us to reconsider deeply ingrained ideas of scale, ownership, and control. Here, you will find three provocations to institutionally reimagine DAOs for a planetary-conscious future. Bear with me.

Keywords: Decentralized autonomous organizations; new organizational forms; nest; stewardship; weaving

Doing business is synonymous with the organizational architecture of firms, employment, and management. Designed in the industrial era, these forms of collective action and production are premised on the imperialist idea of ever-expanding growth, consumption, and profit (Banerjee & Arjaliès, 2021). Even though we know too well that this setup nudges us to treat humans and nature as exploitable resources while avoiding the systemic consequences of shareholder maximization as mere "externalities," it proves hard to imagine alternatives (Mulgan, 2022).

In this paper, I look at DAOs as in-between creatures. Emancipatory spaces of collective imagination for a new regenerative production architecture oriented towards planetary thriving (Butler & Loacker, 2022), but also communities animated and burdened by Web3's coin hype. The instability, fraud, and enrichment inherent to the blockchain ecology could thwart their aspirations within a day. Often attributed as "Discords with a bank account" (Kreutler, 2021), DAOs equip peer-to-peer forms of organizing with a decisive new feature: Multi-signature accounts like Gnosis Safe Multisig that enable like-minded people scattered around the globe to hold funds together. By issuing a token, groups can make collective ownership, participatory budgeting, and collaborative decision-making significantly easier.

The vision goes like this: The power to build may soon rest in Web3 communities and their interconnected microeconomies. Here, people organize localized, sustainable production processes based on commonly held global knowledge resources. In such cosmolocal production networks (Papadimitropoulos, 2023; Ramos et al., 2021), workers turn into contributors and curators, unlocking the freedom of freelancing without the precariousness of the gig economy. As various DAOs integrate into a modularized production process, former stakeholders, like employees, customers, investors, communities, and natural habitats, become co-owners and thus equitable "relationholders" (Woermann & Engelbrecht, 2019). Based on the democratic limits of self-organized teams, DAOs present a technologically induced opportunity to free cooperatives from their prison of the "firm" structure (Hassan & de Filippi, 2020).

AFTER THE FIRM?

Nathan Schneider (this volume) reminds us that this seemingly unique opportunity for economic democracy is one we have had all along. I underscore his call to learn from the wins and misses of coops, communes, social movements, P2P communities, gaming guilds, or coworking spaces. However, there is a more profound reckoning waiting. If the Web3 crowd wants to use cryptocurrencies to solve the problems of funding and scale plaguing their predecessors, they must also unearth the mythopoetical foundations that invisibly govern our understanding of business and work. This means questioning the modern image of success and happiness based on our ability to control and possess – but also the modularization of work and life in mass institutions (Suzman, 2020) and, ultimately, our place at the center of the cosmos separated from nature, from each other, and ourselves (Arendt, 1958).

Beyond our culturally contingent horizon of "business," "work," and "the economy," DAOs are a window of opportunity to expand on what Yochai Benkler (2017) sees as the limits of commons-based peer production: Combining self-governance, shared meaning, and intrinsic motivation characteristic of flash teams and ad hoc networks with persistent social relationships. Enjoying the freedom of freelancing while participating in equitable ownership structures and mutualistic venture communities. And most importantly, cultivating shared resources or commons as the soil on which markets, property, and more-than-capitalocentric (Gibson-Graham, 2006) values can grow. Maybe the historical moment of DAOs is to squander their giddy crypto resources for a carnival of collective imagination, a burst of denormalization to tinker with a new digital production architecture.

Building on the lessons of alternative organizing and social anthropology, I propose three main impulses to consider on this journey. First, instead of distributed firms, DAOs could be thought of as *nests*: interlaced, polycentric group constellations, not individuals as basic organizational design units, embracing ecological and multi-generational thriving as their measure of success. Second, in the digital era, the idea of owning resources, land, and other species turns into *stewardship* – a custodial stance operating, for instance, in stark contrast to the non-fungible token (NFT) philosophy. It is oriented toward regenerative impact, embracing more economic values than just transactions and profits. Third, the management of subordinates gives way to distributed leadership that invites participation: *weaving* connections, rhythms, and tools developed and maintained by a community of users without recreating "tyrannies of structurelessness" (Freeman, 1972) as playgrounds for informal elites.

The contours of digital production architectures have been discernable before the advent of Web3, but DAOs may push networked localization to an unprecedented scale. However, technophile utopias promising effortless governance, trustless coordination, and federated NFT copyrights are undermining the realization of this very potential. DAOs will inevitably fail. Hangover, crypto crisis, or the legacy of big money will kick in. In this paper, I argue that their true strength is to enable a carnivalesque celebration of renewal (Ehrenreich, 2007): Boundary-spanning experiments with different forms of collaborating, voting, enterprising, sharing, co-owning, and kin-making. An unregulated, exuberant space for collective imagination, yet another step along a journey that has neither begun with DAOs nor will it end with them.

In what follows, I propose nests, stewardship, and weaving as the outset of a design language for regenerative production architectures and caution against likely pitfalls to keep this party going.

FIRST, A CONFESSION

My coding skills never went beyond HTML tags and Squarespace design. I am a social researcher, geeking out on new forms of work and cultural theory. I do love gadgets and gaming, though, and am fascinated by the impact of tech on society. My first encounter with Web3 was in 2016 when people in my vicinity started to invest or engage in crypto projects. Curiously, I observed how they bought houses or took time off to start passion projects. Since I was doing my PhD and moving my family across the continents, money was scarce, and investments were a faint wish.

But so came the opportunity to put 500 dollars into a Web3 project: An ethically inspiring DAO, an initial coin offering, a recent ditch in crypto stocks. The time was ripe! I consider myself a savvy user who never got ripped off, never caught serious malware. Soon, my Metamask and Coinbase accounts were set. I learned on their Discord and bought my tokens at an attractive price, silently wondering about the economics behind those insane gas costs. Nevermind. Instead, my mind started rattling: What if those 500 bucks multiplied 10×, 100×? Maybe 1,000×? Then, a minor technical issue popped up. A helpful Discord support person guided me to a website. It looked cheap. I typed in my recovery phrase. Ouch!

It is still embarrassing to face how I got so caught up in my desires for fast money that I naïvely let down my guard. This is the Wild West, not a village in the Swiss Alps! At least my foolishness serves to make a point: The vibes that keep Web3 humming are caught between capitalist and communitarian desires. On the one hand, hyper-exaggerated expectations for growth, security, and success – a shortcut to modern longings for a house, car, pool, and holidays. On the other hand, the quest for fulfillment through belonging to a community that has your back and is guided by a shared purpose.

Research holds that only the latter can lead to sustained well-being and fulfillment. Prosocial behavior is the source of our species' success (Raihani, 2021). We are multiple times more collaborative than primates. Living in connected and stable social worlds adds 10 years to our lifespan (Dunbar, 2022). Humans inherently want to belong to something bigger, to take over the baton, to perform good and valued work in a caring place, where it gets easier to walk the rocky path of life because we do it together.

MODULAR LIVES

Unfortunately, mass institutions have largely replaced communities as species-appropriate spheres of (re-)productive socioeconomic activity. Social anthropologist Ernest Gellner (1994) recognized that Modernity split historically integrated lifeworlds into differentiated areas with limited role expectations: work, family, church, and club. The resulting "modular personality fragments" (Kallinikos, 2003) could then be integrated into hierarchical mass organizations as "human resources," "consumers," or "clients." From daycare, through school, to the workplace, hospital, and retirement home – we spend most of our time in institutions, showing up as functional pieces of ourselves. Pandemic work-from-home settings have made it palpable how onerous this separation of lifeworlds, genders, and generations actually is.

Robin Dunbar's (2022) primate research, relating neocortex size to cohesive groups, tells us that our cognitive limit for stable interpersonal relationships caps around 150 people. Here, at the community level, we know who each person is and how they relate to each other. At the margins of our socio-cognitive capacities, humans can maintain five intimate friendships but remember the names of 1,500 people. Historically, societies developed within these bounds as multi-level systems comprised overlapping group constellations: families within bands, bands within communities, communities within tribes (Graeber & Wengrow, 2021).

Giving up layered group structures as the basic principle of organizational architecture in favor of mass-organized modular individualism was useful in controlling large aggregations of people, assets, and value chains. However, we have dangerously surpassed the lifespan of this design. It is ill-equipped to deal with the levels of environmental destruction, technological risk, and organized immaturity that it has spawned as "externalities." Moreover, in recent decades, the "role module" work has dominated and marginalized the other modules, resulting in high levels of burnout (Petersen, 2019), excessive self-expression (Ekman, 2013), and loneliness (Dunbar, 2022).

My point is that underneath the challenge to tackle centralization, hierarchy, and bureaucracy is a deeper layer of organizational form and collective desire that needs to be transformed. Modularized individualism and socialized longings for wealth and consumption are the real obstacles to a regenerative, fair, and alive production architecture.

NESTS: SCALING ACROSS

In the knowledge economy, success results from relational quality, not efficiently assembling stuff. As creative and service-based components of products become the real deal, effective production relies on a collaborative spirit between us (Lee & Edmondson, 2017). It facilitates trust, serendipitous encounters, openness to fresh ideas, or the vulnerability to utter raw thoughts and silly questions. Togetherness, care, and creativity between people, as well as reciprocal connections between organizations and their ecosystems, are the pillars of digital enterprise. Just as the industrial imperative of "efficiency" bore the "corporate firm," the primacy of "co-creative intimacy" (Rouse, 2020) demands a new organizational form (Buterin, 2022a).

Heeding Dunbar's multi-level design of social architecture, "nest" is an intriguing metaphor to describe such an emerging digital form (Fig. 4.1). *First*, nests are not based on individuals but on small, interdisciplinary, autonomous delivery teams held together by collaborative community spirit and shared purpose.

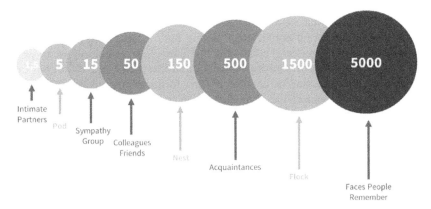

Fig. 4.1. The Pod–Nest–Flock Structure, Based on Dunbar's (2022) Anthropologically Grounded Group Sizes and Fractal Organizational Composition.

Second, depending on the task, teams assemble an evolving fabric of interlaced group constellations on nested scales. The center of nests comprises a strong core providing governance and support. *Third*, collective well-being, healthy systemic relations, and people's personal development are the most important guideposts. Such a nurturing stance is also expressed in fledgling groups and projects moving out to build their own nests. Nests are growing by "scaling across" complex relationships instead of "scaling up" individual report lines. They assemble into multi-generational flocks held together by a scaffolding conducive to connection, care, and co-creation on a human scale.

The web knows a wild mess of names for these nested formations, but the main scales are crystallizing. Small collaborative groups, no larger than 5–7 people, are at the core, called *pods*, *squads*, or *crews*. Akin to an agile team, they are functionally integrated, deliver products closely interacting with the market, and embrace role portfolios instead of job titles. The main difference is that you would never apply for a job in a pod but engage in a community of co-owning peers. The next scale, themed *hubs*, *guilds*, *neotribes*, *metalables,* or henceforth nests, encompasses 100–200 members. Projects are typically developed in a modularized way – people within their pods take on work packages, or in DAO speak: *missions, milestones,* and *raids* (Kreutler, 2021). To keep up the requisite variety, every person is engaged in multiple, partially overlapping pods intended to build products and earn livelihoods but also to facilitate communities of interest, peer support, or learning.

The ownership, budgeting, and participation infrastructure provided by DAOs is ideally suited to develop the following scale of around 1,500 people or several nests coming together in a flexible DAO ecosystem (Kreutler, 2021). As "demodularized" spheres of work, life, and play, these associations might be called *flocks*. Here, the carnivalesque and experimental character of Web3 communities is most needed. Projects like *Metagov* or *Metropolis*, which want to advance emergent organizing capabilities in DAOs, are breaking new ground. The trickiest challenge they face is blending the paradoxical cultural properties of collaborative communities – marked by vulnerability, trust, and reciprocity – with the instrumental, anonymous, and potentially isolating logic of networks (de Vaujany et al., 2020).

Research shows that self-organization historically faced the danger of "falling out" due to internal conflicts or "selling out" to traditional management structures. Jo Freeman (1972) coined the "tyranny of structurelessness" to warn against tacit hierarchies, friendship networks, and toxic behaviors of the cool kids as the inevitable outcome of community-first forms of organizing. DAOs can build on the experience of their predecessors in cooperatives (Rothschild, 2016), who realized that they need more, not less, structure compared to traditional corporate governance. Lessons can be learned in such different corners as agile corporations (*Spotify, Atlassian*), the creative industries (*Pixar, Valve*), bossless and self-organized firms (see *W.L. Gore, Haier,* or *Buurtzorg*), networked cooperatives (*Mondragon* in Spain or the Bologna region in Italy), freelancer coops, like *Enspiral, Dark Horse,* or *The Ready,* and open-source communities (*Drupal*).

Scaling across requires a "prepared environment" to speak with pioneering educator Maria Montessori. Distributed leadership starts by agreeing upon and evolving a context of interaction. Clear participation architectures (Massa &

O'Mahony, 2021) are inevitable: pod–nest–flock scales; dedicated spaces for newcomers and core contributors; a distinction between service, governance, and strategic pods in the center and delivery-oriented ones at the periphery; but also circular career paths, where veterans become coaches. Sharing practices, like check-ins to expand the emotional repertoire of the organization and regular retrospectives to reflect how people work together, are essential (Resch & Steyaert, 2020). Similarly, explicit decision-making structures, like sociocracy (Pohler, 2022), synchronous and asynchronous workspaces (chats & forums), the embrace of dissent (Brekke et al., 2021), and open documentation of processes help avert the "iron threat of oligarchy" (Diefenbach, 2019).

STEWARDSHIP: CUSTODIAL DEEDS

The move from firms to nests is undergirded by a mythopoetic leap from separation to entanglement, acknowledging the shape-shifting multiplicity of our existence, enmeshed and emerging with all that surrounds us, human or not, "real" and not (Akomolafe & Ladha, 2017). Modernity's foundational myths of individualism, modularization, and massification have not only disconnected us from ourselves, each other, and nature but also brought up the idea that there is such a thing as the "economy" removed from society.

Next to "valuable" transactional activities, other economic practices such as contributing, sharing, caring, or commoning appeared relatively "worthless." The indigenous scholar Tyson Yunkaporta (2020) reminds us that this extractive commodification mentality, with its well-known downsides (externalities, exploitation, and short-termism), is not without historical alternatives. Aboriginal Australians, for example, perceive themselves as a custodial species, focusing on multi-generational life cycles, composting, and commons. Similar to the knowledge economy, increasing relational quality to unfold potential in a human–non-human-ideational nexus becomes the economic *raison d'être*.

To legally embed such a nurturing custodial deed, stewardship has become a widely discussed concept. DAOs could build on the experience of traditional firms, like *Patagonia*, *Bosch*, *Carlsberg*, and *Zeiss*, which are owned by stakeholder foundations safeguarding that all profits are reinvested in the company, used to cover capital costs, or donated. In line with the nest metaphor, profits become a means for purpose and regenerative impact. For DAOs, stewardship is an invitation to think "exit to community" (Schneider, 2020) a step further: Developers, users, investors, regulators, communities, and non-human relationholders, like natural habitats, stewarding a nest or parts of its value chain as a commons. Here, the majority of voting rights are always held by people closely connected to the organization, its operation, and its values.

The open-source software scene has long grasped the revolutionary character of informational goods as non-rivalrous. They do not degrade when used. "You" can get a copy without "me" losing it (Papadimitropoulos, 2018). Paradoxically, the more people use them, the more valuable they get. Think of social networks, for example. Massively successful projects, like *Linux*, *Apache*, or *Wikipedia*, were built as a commons by communities of peers. On the soil of this stewarded produce, commercial offers could grow. DAOs as stewarded nests can provide the organizational backbone for the next wave of communities that grow their livelihood on design, engineering, and coding commons or simply steward empty shops on their high street and renewable energy production on their roofs. In that sense, crypto and Web3 have to be careful to use their superpower of non-fungible code, not in a way that erects artificial rivalrous containers around non-rivalrous goods.

Of course, one could ask: What would prevent people from selling out to a Web2 giant? Indeed, the spirit of commoning tends to crackle spectacularly fast (Waters-Lynch & Duff, 2021). Much like a social movement, such communities are highly active for some years, then the collaborative spirit fades. A major contributing factor to this phenomenon, especially in online self-organization, is the 1:9:90 rule. One percent of participants are usually highly engaged, 9% are somewhat active, and 90% are lurking. The inevitable consequences are frustration and burnout, leading to increasing inertia. The mission for Web3 collectives is to experiment with tools and practices that encourage rotating active participation by the many.

Research on successful commoning (Ostrom, 2015; Rozas et al., 2021) gives some clues. In contrast to Web3's dictum of trustless collaboration and openness, DAOs are advised to draw boundaries around their communities, for example, through carefully curated membership tiers (Pohler, 2022). Instead of one-size-fits-all algorithms, rules should be based on local conditions and be amenable to participatory governance. Moreover, mechanisms for rule monitoring, conflict resolution, and sanctions must be in place. Face-to-face events, from small, emergent drinks to carefully planned retreats, are another tool to foster togetherness, mutuality, and dissensus – the capacity to trust in recurring reciprocal exchanges, address problematic issues, and have a good fight (Resch & Rozas, 2024).

The legal genie is out of the bottle: If we can attribute rights to abstract entities like corporations, why can't we give them to rivers, too, as New Zealand did? Or why can't houses maintain themselves, with us as residents and custodial stewards (prototyped by *Dezentrum* in Switzerland)? In the end, we might even reckon that if we rediscover the singular value of shared things and places, their sacredness, they will hold ample opportunities for thriving livelihoods.

WEAVING: INVITING PARTICIPATION

Conventional management techniques are poor instruments for coordination in collaborative communities (Gregg & Lodato, 2018). Professional "community managers" typically feel overburdened, cannot sufficiently motivate voluntary contribution, and are in a precarious position regarding income and gender dynamics. Looking at collaborative leadership as a relational practice and not as a behavioral trait of individual leaders, we have suggested (see Resch & Steyaert, 2020) *weaving* as an alternative lens. Weaving is a form of distributed leadership that invites participation instead of managing outputs and delegating tasks.

It works through instigating connections, rituals and rhythms, and seasonal learning. While some individuals might temporarily hold a professional role in creating scaffolding and weave by example, it is crucial to encourage broad and alternating participation from the community.

Weaving encompasses introducing and referring people to each other, internal journalism or blogging to keep the flow between hybrid work settings, and event organizing to create connections, strategic discussions, and trust (Ehrlichman, 2021). At the same time, it means fostering awareness of problems and momentum for solutions by establishing working groups, missions, and bounties or facilitating decision-making between consent and direct action (Chen, 2016; Leach, 2016). Weaving also includes running retrospectives on how people work together, uncovering festering power dynamics and detrimental behavior. Harmony requires dissonance, and people in nests must learn to have courageous conversations. In that sense, weaving works as a distributed practice that sets up processes, rituals, and rules for relating, planning, working, and learning.

We should not think overly romantically about distributed leadership and fluid hierarchies in DAOs (Resch et al., 2021). Our research found that collaborative communities are held together by powerful collective longings for growth, purpose, and belonging – desires that motivate passionate voluntary contribution, intimate, co-creative relationships, and inquiry into personal growth issues. The dark side of all this dedication and self-discovery is frustration and overwork. In our case, unacknowledged care work clustered on the shoulders of leading female contributors, who consequently burnt out or left the organization. There is much to learn about inviting sustainable, distributed contributions, especially regarding typically undervalued economic practices like sharing or caring.

Weaving is embedded in a mindset shift from navigation to wayfinding: "knowing as you go" rather than "knowing before you go" (Nayak & Chia, 2011). Instead of planning, forecasting, and fixing the future, wayfinding is a preference for feeling out questions in a participatory and collaborative manner. In this image, the goal is to learn from polycentric experimentation and to be able to take a greater variety of stances. Weaving challenges people to become more comfortable with the unknown, open to being transformed, grasping how the many shades of gray between right and wrong allow us to see how connections between things form patterns, how parts may embody the whole.

JUST HERE FOR THE COTTON CANDY

I have argued that DAOs are successors in a long line of alternative organizing (Parker et al., 2014) that sought to replace the industrial production architecture comprising shareholder firms, employment relations, and hierarchical management. At the same time, Web3 is deeply interwoven with the industrial model, requiring computer chips, data centers, broadband cables, transport systems, and electric grids. It has also aroused the desires of established actors: from banks and insurance firms to mafia organizations rogue governments and Web2 giants. Amid these clashing trajectories, it is crucial to realize that at the heart of the challenge for economic democracy are not decentralization, governance, and smart contracts but the squishy, emotional, and mutualist task of reinserting communities and commons into the enterprising process.

DAOs should not press themselves into the mold of the firm. They adapt corporate elements that work, like limited liability, but build on the social physics of layered group structures – pods-nests-flocks – laid out in social anthropology. Neither fully hierarchically corporate nor democratically statist (Buterin, 2022a), they move between various polycentric modes of governance depending on the task requirements or environmental constraints. Here, weaving as distributed collaborative leadership rests on a paradigmatic shift to emergence, experimentation, and care. Most importantly, and curiously, in an environment that thrives on the prospect of exponential growth and non-fungibility, the DAO carnival could be living proof that belonging, meaningful work, and multi-generational responsibility are key to much higher levels of happiness and thriving (Adler & Heckscher, 2018). Its legacy could be the prefiguration of stewardship, bringing systemic relations into view and making space for both transactional and reciprocal economic practices by breaking up Modernity"s "modular" boundaries between the economy, society, and nature. Fig. 4.2 summarizes the DAO design principles emerging from this paper's argument.

Within this framework, is it not conceivable that gig workers, trade unions, foundations, municipalities, and transnational bodies band together to fund a ridehailing open-source software co-developed, stewarded, and used by ridehailing DAOs in cities worldwide? Can we dare to imagine a food economy drawing on open designs for three-dimensional (3D)-printed agricultural equipment, accessible vertical farming blueprints, and gene-editing peer learning platforms? Imagine if, instead of Monsanto, global open-source communities steward the synthetic biology revolution with multiple generations in mind. Our forbears

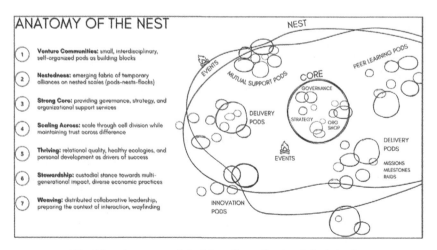

Fig. 4.2. Anatomy of the Nest: Seven Design Principles for Planetary-conscious DAOs.

upended the feudal social fabric of nobles, clerics, and farmers not by fighting against it but by collectively imagining and prototyping much more livable futures.

Like medieval cities providing respite for second sons, serfs, and tradespeople to develop their businesses, guilds, and councils, DAOs can be a home for today's misfits. If they heed the lessons of the past, they can be an incubator without repeating the bullying and abuse of their predecessors in coops, communes, and other movements. It is time for a carnival: mocking moribund systems, quitting bullshit jobs (Graeber, 2018), and slipping into new skins. The Web3 community might invite as many non-techies as possible into their celebration, focusing on accessible plug-and-play solutions to pool funds, steward value-creating ecosystems, and experiment with voting mechanisms. Many might just come for the cotton candy of fast wealth but end up infected by new ways of being.

A CAUTIONARY TALE

At last, a warning: Every feast ends, every frenzy turns into a hangover. Deep down, these Web3 experiments force us to face that the Western civilizational model, its cosmology, and production architecture, on a planetary level, have brought environmental devastation, structural violence, and organized immaturity to all but a happy few. Even those at its center are traumatized and wounded by its separation, massification, and exploitation logic. Engaging with the mythopoetic paradigm shifts from separation to entanglement, from ownership to stewardship, and from control to emergence is a necessarily painful process. It entails breaking away from the stories we grew up with, from cherished self-conceptions, and, worst, many possible cul-de-sacs.

Douglas Rushkoff (2022) reminds us that the medieval city economies with their guild-based community structures, their technological, institutional, and cultural innovations (Arvidsson, 2020), like market monies, which were issued in the morning and expired at the end of the day, were ultimately captured by the elites. The aristocracy wanted its monopoly over value creation back, so they "taxed the bazaar, broke up the guilds, outlawed local currencies, and bestowed monopoly charters on their favorite merchants" (Rushkoff, 2022). The history of Webs1 and 2 taught us that such land-grabbing attempts are in store for Web3 as well.

Nevertheless, I am hopeful that the carnival can further prototype examples of a "soulbound" (Buterin, 2022b) production architecture, creating so much thriving, connection, and contemplation that a decisive number of people obviously want to engage with it. After all, there is always an alternative. Collective imagination is the gift of our species. Current money systems did not arise spontaneously and teleologically out of free trading. They are a creation of emperors to maintain their governments (Doctorow, 2022). Research is only now uncovering how our species' evolution from hunting and gathering to agriculture and cities is not a one-way street toward centralization and domination (Graeber & Wengrow, 2021). Human history knows many examples of democratically governed ancient cities and vast bureaucratically managed nomad lands. We craft our collective efforts through the stories we tell, the aesthetics we create (Freinacht, 2022), and the shared purpose we crave (Arvidsson, 2018). These are our shores to play.

REFERENCES

Adler, P. S., & Heckscher, C. (2018). Collaboration as an organization design for shared purpose. In L. Ringel, P. Hiller, & C. Zietsma (Eds.), *Research in the sociology of organizations* (Vol. 57, pp. 81–111). Emerald Publishing Limited. https://doi.org/10.1108/S0733-558X20180000057004

Akomolafe, B., & Ladha, A. (2017). Perverse particles, entangled monsters and psychedelic pilgrimages: Emergence as an onto-epistemology of not-knowing. *Ephemera: Theory and Politics in Organization*, *17*(4), 819–839.

Arendt, H. (1958). *The human condition*. University of Chicago Press.

Arvidsson, A. (2018). Value and virtue in the sharing economy. *The Sociological Review*, *66*(2), 289–301. https://doi.org/10.1177/0038026118758531

Arvidsson, A. (2020). Capitalism and the commons. *Theory, Culture & Society*, *37*(2), 3–30. https://doi.org/10.1177/0263276419868838

Banerjee, S. B., & Arjaliès, D.-L. (2021). Celebrating the end of enlightenment: Organization theory in the age of the Anthropocene and Gaia (and why neither is the solution to our ecological crisis). *Organization Theory*, *2*(4). https://doi.org/10.1177/26317877211036714

Benkler, Y. (2017). Peer production, the commons, and the future of the firm. *Strategic Organization*, *15*(2), 264–274.

Brekke, J. K., Beecroft, K., & Pick, F. (2021). The dissensus protocol: Governing differences in online peer communities. *Frontiers in Human Dynamics*, *3*, 1–15. https://doi.org/10.3389/fhumd.2021.641731

Buterin, V. (2022a). *DAOs are not corporations: Where decentralization in autonomous organizations matters*. Vitalik Buterin's Website. https://vitalik.eth.limo/general/2022/09/20/daos.html

Buterin, V. (2022b). *Soulbound*. Vitalik Buterin's website. https://vitalik.ca/general/2022/01/26/soulbound.html

Butler, N., & Loacker, B. (2022). Capitalist unrealism: Countering the crisis of critique and imagination. *Ephemera: Theory & Politics in Organization*, *22*(2), 1–17.

Chen, K. K. (2016). "Plan your burn, burn your plan": How decentralization, storytelling, and communification can support participatory practices. *The Sociological Quarterly*, *57*(1), 71–97. https://doi.org/10.1111/tsq.12115

De Vaujany, F.-X., Leclercq-Vandelannoitte, A., & Holt, R. (2020). Communities versus platforms: The paradox in the body of the collaborative economy. *Journal of Management Inquiry*, *29*(4), 450–467. https://doi.org/10.1177/1056492619832119

Diefenbach, T. (2019). Why Michels' 'iron law of oligarchy' is not an iron law – And how democratic organisations can stay 'oligarchy-free.' *Organization Studies*, *40*(4), 545–562. https://doi.org/10.1177/0170840617751007

Doctorow, C. (2022). *Moneylike*. Medium. https://doctorow.medium.com/moneylike-78ebe88e44d

Dunbar, R. (2022). *Friends: Understanding the power of our most important relationships*. Little, Brown UK.

Ehrenreich, B. (2007). *Dancing in the streets: A history of collective joy*. Holt Paperbacks.

Ehrlichman, D. (2021). *Impact networks: Create connection, spark collaboration, and catalyze systemic change*. Berrett-Koehler Publishers.

Ekman, S. (2013). Fantasies about work as limitless potential – How managers and employees seduce each other through dynamics of mutual recognition. *Human Relations*, *66*(9), 1159–1181. https://doi.org/10.1177/0018726712461812

Freeman, J. (1972). The tyranny of structurelessness. *Berkeley Journal of Sociology*, *17*, 151–164.

Freinacht, H. (2022). *We must reclaim solarpunk from authoritarian regimes*. Medium. https://medium.com/@hanzifreinacht/we-must-reclaim-solarpunk-from-authoritarian-regimes-73d4d4f6833d

Gellner, E. (1994). *Conditions of liberty: Civil society and its rivals*. Viking Adult.

Gibson-Graham, J. K. (2006). *A postcapitalist politics*. University of Minnesota Press.

Graeber, D. (2018). *Bullshit jobs: A theory*. Allen Lane.

Graeber, D., & Wengrow, D. (2021). *The dawn of everything: A new history of humanity*. Farrar, Straus and Giroux.

Gregg, M., & Lodato, T. (2018). Managing community: Coworking, hospitality and the future of work. In B. Röttger-Rössler & J. Slaby (Eds.), *Affect in relation: Families, places, technologies* (pp. 175–196). Taylor & Francis Group. https://doi.org/10.4324/9781315163864-9

Hassan, S., & De Filippi, P. (2021). Decentralized Autonomous Organization. *Internet Policy Review*, *10*(2). https://doi.org/10.14763/2021.2.1556

Kallinikos, J. (2003). Work, human agency and organizational forms: An anatomy of fragmentation. *Organization Studies*, *24*(4), 595–618. https://doi.org/10.1177/0170840603024004005

Kreutler, K. (2021). *A prehistory of DAOs: Cooperatives, gaming guilds, and the networks to come*. Gnosis Guild. https://gnosisguild.mirror.xyz/t4F5rItMw4-mlpLZf5JQhElbDfQ2JRVKAzEpanyxW1Q?utm_source=pocket_mylist

Leach, D. K. (2016). When freedom is not an endless meeting: A new look at efficiency in consensus-based decision making. *The Sociological Quarterly*, *57*(1), 36–70. https://doi.org/10.1111/tsq.12137

Lee, M. Y., & Edmondson, A. C. (2017). Self-managing organizations: Exploring the limits of less-hierarchical organizing. *Research in Organizational Behavior*, *37*(Supplement C), 35–58. https://doi.org/10.1016/j.riob.2017.10.002

Massa, F. G., & O'Mahony, S. (2021). Order from chaos: How networked activists self-organize by creating a participation architecture. *Administrative Science Quarterly*, *66*(4), 1037–1083. https://doi.org/10.1177/00018392211008880

Mulgan, G. (2022). *Another world is possible: How to reignite social and political imagination*. Hurst.

Nayak, A., & Chia, R. (2011). Thinking becoming and emergence: Process philosophy and organization studies. In H. Tsoukas & R. Chia (Eds.), *Philosophy and organization theory* (Vol. 32, pp. 281–309). Emerald Group Publishing Limited.

Ostrom, E. (2015). *Governing the commons: The evolution of institutions for collective action* (Reissue ed.). Cambridge University Press.

Papadimitropoulos, V. (2018). Commons-based peer production in the work of Yochai Benkler. *TripleC: Communication, Capitalism & Critique. Open Access Journal for a Global Sustainable Information Society*, *16*(2), 835–856. https://doi.org/10.31269/triplec.v16i2.1009

Papadimitropoulos, V. (2023). The digital commons, cosmolocalism, and open cooperativism: The cases of P2P Lab and Tzoumakers. *Organization*, 1–23. https://doi.org/10.1177/13505084231156268

Parker, M., Cheney, G., Fournier, V., & Land, C. (Eds.). (2014). *The Routledge companion to alternative organization*. Routledge.

Petersen, A. H. (2019, January 5). *How millennials became the burnout generation*. BuzzFeed News. https://www.buzzfeednews.com/article/annehelenpetersen/millennials-burnout-generation-debt-work

Pohler, N. (2022). Composite relations: Democratic firms balancing the general and the particular. *Organization*, 1–18. https://doi.org/10.1177/13505084221131637

Raihani, N. (2021). *The social instinct: How cooperation shaped the world*. St. Martin's Press.

Ramos, J. M., Bauwens, M., Ede, S., & Gien Wong, J. (Eds.). (2021). *Cosmo-local reader*. Futures Lab.

Resch, B., Hoyer, P., & Steyaert, C. (2021). Affective control in new collaborative work: Communal fantasies of purpose, growth and belonging. *Organization Studies*, *42*(5), 787–809. https://doi.org/10.1177/0170840620941616

Resch, B., & Rozas, D. (2024). Addressing durability in collaborative organising: Event atmospheres and polyrhythmic affectivity. *Human Relations*, 1–32. https://doi.org/10.1177/00187267241229344

Resch, B., & Steyaert, C. (2020). Peer collaboration as a relational practice: Theorizing affective oscillation in radical democratic organizing. *Journal of Business Ethics*, *164*(4), 715–730. https://doi.org/10.1007/s10551-019-04395-2

Rothschild, J. (2016). The logic of a co-operative economy and democracy 2.0: Recovering the possibilities for autonomy, creativity, solidarity, and common purpose. *The Sociological Quarterly*, *57*(1), 7–35. https://doi.org/10.1111/tsq.12138

Rouse, E. D. (2020). Where you end and I begin: Understanding intimate co-creation. *Academy of Management Review*, *45*(1), 181–204.

Rozas, D., Tenorio-Fornés, A., Díaz-Molina, S., & Hassan, S. (2021). When Ostrom meets blockchain: Exploring the potentials of blockchain for commons governance. *SAGE Open*, *11*(1). https://doi.org/10.1177/21582440211002526

Rushkoff, D. (2022). *Digital distributism.* Medium. https://rushkoff.medium.com/digital-distributism-28a14bc8c4c8
Schneider, N. (2020). Exit to community. *Noema Magazine.* https://www.noemamag.com/exit-to-community
Suzman, J. (2020). *Work: A history of how we spend our time.* Bloomsbury Circus.
Toraldo, M.-L., & Islam, G. (2019). Festival and organization studies. *Organization Studies, 40*(3), 309–322. https://doi.org/10.1177/0170840617727785
Waters-Lynch, J., & Duff, C. (2021). The affective commons of coworking. *Human Relations, 74*(3), 383–404. https://doi.org/10.1177/0018726719894633
Woermann, M., & Engelbrecht, S. (2019). The Ubuntu challenge to business: From stakeholders to relationholders. *Journal of Business Ethics, 157*(1), 27–44. https://doi.org/10.1007/s10551-017-3680-6
Yunkaporta, T. (2020). *Sand talk: How indigenous thinking can save the world.* HarperOne.

A PROGRESSIVE WEB3: FROM SOCIAL COPRODUCTION TO DIGITAL POLYCENTRIC GOVERNANCE

Quinn DuPont

York University, Canada

ABSTRACT

This paper critically evaluates the political economy of Web3 and offers a neo-institutional model to explain qualitative observations of contemporary digital social movements. By starting to develop a sociological model of Web3 rooted in micro-organizational practices, including trust mediation and social coproduction, this paper re-evaluates assumptions of scarcity, economic value, and social belonging. It concludes by introducing a novel research program to study digital polycentric governance that focuses on community self-governance of digital common pool resources (DCPRs) and looks forward to empirical research using on-chain datasets from decentralized autonomous organizations (DAOs).

Keywords: Decentralized autonomous organizations; digital commons; neo-institutional theory; polycentric governance; progressive Web3

> Now, should we trust these people, no matter how well-intentioned they might be, to guide society into the future ... I'd say "no." (Evgeny Morozov, "Web3: A Map in Search of a Territory")

In a recent paper, Evgeny Morozov (2022) offers a critical biography of Web3 by tracing its popular rhetoric through Tim O'Reilly and Marc Andreessen. Inhabiting the spirit of arche-critic David Golumbia, he discovers vast "linguistic and analytical pollution" in Web3, underpinned by opportunistic hustlers. He accuses Web3 advocates of self-referentiality and performativity, questioning whether Web3 is even a meaningful analytical concept. The issue, Morozov emphasizes, is not that "Web3" or "metaverse" are poorly defined words (though they might be), nor that some "academic, intellectuals, and policy experts ... [will] accept cash for lending their names and reputations" (they have; see DuPont, 2020), rather, the value of even "well-intentioned" Web3 projects is pretty much nothing ("it's spin all the way down," Morozov chides). Worse still, these well-intentioned rubes act like capitalism's yeomen and are basically responsible for "left-washing" the Web3 brand.

Intuitively supported by a decade's worth of careful observation and scientific research on cryptocurrencies and blockchains, I agree with many of Morozov's criticisms. I consider critics like Morozov, Golumbia, Gerard, and, more recently, White astute in their analyses and much-needed voices in a conversation that tends toward credulity. But I've also found that critics sometimes paint with too broad of a brush, lumping their Bitcoiners and frens into the same lazy category. And over the years, I've also witnessed dramatic social evolution in "the scene," of which Web3 is but one frenetic little corner. Specificity matters.

So, I committed to explore Web3 and to live as close to the code as my lifestyle permits (no degen for me, thanks). I have been out on the decentralized finance (DeFi) farms in search of yield, I joined a chorus of Discord servers incessantly pinging with new notifications, I cruised the metaverse, bought some virtual art and property, and turned my digital wallet into a multitool for any situation. During my travels, I maintained a virtual open-door policy that led to dozens of conversations with dreamers, enthusiasts, hustlers, builders, and money-makers (I rounded out the haphazard selection by strategically interviewing Web3 developers and community members). Continuing my search for the holy grail of DAOs (DuPont, 2018), I also dug into the latest cryptoeconomics, blockchain-based organizational designs, and novel forms of distributed governance. I return from my Web3 sojourn with measured optimism, for I found a progressive Web3 rich with innovative ideas, designs, and technologies.

PROGRESSIVE DESIGN BEYOND THE NATION-STATE

In this paper, I'm ultimately describing progressive *design goals*, but Morozov (2022) says we need to address the lack of "engagement with the political economy of global capitalism." So let's do that.

We can start by problematizing the role of the nation-state.

Now a decade since the invention of Bitcoin, I'm surprised daily at how a faddish 1990s-era cypherpunk ideology has managed to reify into technologies that offer nascent social infrastructures – platforms – for life "without" a nation-state. Cypherpunk, Solarpunk, or not, it is possible, perhaps likely, for Web3 to exist *independently* of the state – to make a land with no government. This does not mean Web3 will be independent of the nation-state, even Bitcoin isn't, but the technological trajectory is pretty clear. However, this life isn't for everyone: for some people, living in a land where "code is law" sounds both unrealistic and risky, borderline scary. One Web3 champion, Tracheopteryx, describes this new progressive vista as "confronting" to those still steeped in traditional culture and neoclassical economics (Layer Zero, 2022). Indeed, this is the ultimate gambit of a progressive Web3: that through novel technology, culture, and economic innovation, we have powerful new tools to design the future of progressive social movements.

Of course, the critics know the history of crypto as well as I do. We all know that crypto shook awake national governments because it threatened taxation and economic sovereignty.[i] The neoliberal state responded as best it could by opening vast regulatory mechanisms (while subjugating democracy), which in turn accelerated private and public investment in – well, not exactly the radical technology promised by Bitcoin, but a sanitized, rentier version with well-monitored on and off ramps (an intelligence agent once joked to me that crypto is just "prosecution futures"). And so, in the subsequent years, the radical spirit of crypto has been all but smothered by the warm embrace of the state. In its place, a booming Silicon Valley brogrammer culture emerged and infected everything good and holy in the critic's imagination of an open Internet – incidentally, not the Internet that was *actually* developed by the US state and military for intelligence, surveillance, and the global spread of American values.[ii]

From the perspective of the "closed" Internet of 2022, largely comprised of rent-seeking platforms with supranational influence, Graeber and Wengrow's (2021) recent book is a helpful reminder to think beyond the inevitability of Hobbesian and Rousseauian political theory and its claim to Westphalian sovereignty. They invite progressives to dream of new organizational forms capable of supporting flourishing across human scales so that people meaningfully self-organize, in ways where good governance becomes essential.

Thus, one history of Web3 starts with the opportunistic labeling of a technological evolution of computer networking toward a regulated (state monitored) infrastructure for the exchange of value. This technological evolution implies that the political economy of Web3 is defined by money that is exchanged on a programmable network at a supranational scale (Swartz, 2020). But importantly, Web3 is a *programmable* money (Caliskan, 2020), having the characteristics of an "immutable mobile" because it enables "both mobilization and immutability ... at the same time" (Latour, 1986, p. 10). Like the Internet and dozens of other (notational) technologies before it, blockchain technology is *mobile* because it supports the circulation of value (an economy)[iii] and is *immutable* because transaction records are accepted as authoritative.

Immutable mobiles are not just academic curiosities – they are important because they serve to *convince*, exhibiting the same influence as maps and books did for earlier media. An important consequence of blockchain technology is that it makes things visible (DuPont & Maurer, 2015) – so that, as Latour (1986) offers, "no matter how inaccurate these traces might be at first, they will all become accurate just as a consequence of more mobilization and more immutability" (p. 12). Moreover, Latour's (1986) insight shows why any reasonable account of the political economy of Web3 must accept that materialist explanations cannot "kneel before one specific science, that of economics" (p. 3).

PREFIGURATION: A MAP FOR A PROGRESSIVE WEB3

In this paper, I offer a map – my map – to a progressive Web3, an evolution of social form from social coproduction to digital polycentric governance. Over the last year, I've been humbled by a groundswell of progressive Web3 efforts that have emerged – for example, Gitcoin's quadratic cryptoeconomics, Common Stack's bonding curves, Gnosis' explorations of polycentric governance, Tribute Lab's open legal framework, and Colony's DAO tooling, to name a few. While inspired by these wild experiments, I depart from other theorizations of Web3 insofar as I situate it in the discourse of non-state governance and apply lessons from social movements with the design goal of evolving social coproduction.[iv]

A progressive Web3 must exist beyond the nation-state to address the power vacuum in global governance that emerged with neoliberalism in the late 20th century. Due to the inefficiencies and epistemological limitations of centralized planning and failures of regulatory and representative democratic politics, neoliberal nation-states have been unable to address "local" and collective action contexts. As a decentralized social infrastructure, Web3 offers the possibility of cultivating social belonging and community self-governance by aggregating intelligence from the edges of the network (through consensus, voting, and markets).

THE TROUBLE WITH CRYPTO

Some critics still think crypto is a scam. Aside from being woefully uninformed about the preceding decade's history of crypto successes, challenges, and disasters, this view fails to register the meaningful and real issues and instead focuses on outdated criticisms of technology, regulation, and culture.

The history of crypto's first decade demonstrates that technological, regulatory, and cultural challenges are surmountable but require effective social embedding. For example, the heartbreaking environmental impact of Bitcoin could be fixed if it was more thoroughly embedded in a dynamic organizational structure capable of leadership and effective change management. Indeed, many modern blockchains have moved on from energy-intensive proof of work consensus mechanisms, adopting proof of stake or truly next-gen probabilistic byzantine fault tolerant (PBFT) protocols that use robust sub-sampling and sortition techniques for leaderless consensus in permissionless networks (e.g., Algorand, Avalanche, Cardano, EOSIO, Stellar, and Tron). Likewise, while the regulatory and legal landscape continues to evolve, crypto is no longer the state's bogeyman. Between novel uses by traditional financial institutions, e-government, and blue chip sectors, crypto has become an inextricable part of dominant capital and therefore inherits regulatory "protection" (indeed, crypto's recent move from periphery to core seems to be fueling another set of reappraisals by the Left, like Morozov's). And finally, for better or worse, crypto is no longer characterized by a monolithic culture of white, libertarian men – now everyone is in crypto (Perrin, 2021), although obviously not equally.

Similarly, many of the "old" arguments against Bitcoin no longer meaningfully apply to Web3. David Golumbia's trenchant analysis of Bitcoin comes up short today because his critique focuses on Bitcoin's anti-inflation economics, early enthusiast's weird banking conspiracy theories, and the difficulty of fitting Bitcoin into the standard tripartite model of money (Golumbia, 2016). Web3 inherits none of these issues: novel and sophisticated token engineering in DeFi is the norm, depressingly few of the people adopting crypto today are even aware of Bitcoin's unsavory political past, and I think it is obvious that crypto doesn't fit in the standard definition of money because it is an evolution of the very idea of money. David Gerard is another vocal critic and expands Golumbia's critique by focusing on technical and usability issues. Some of these issues remain (e.g., usability is still wanting), but next-generation blockchain platforms have largely resolved the issues that Gerard focused on or have engineering roadmaps for their solution. With software, technological criticisms are usually addressed in version upgrades.

While some of these challenges remain, they are also, I believe, an opportunity for a progressive Web3. But a progressive Web3 must also address three, much more difficult criticisms: (1) financialization, assetization, and quantification, (2) commodity fetishism, and (3) digital inequality. Financialization, assetization, and quantification: This assemblage of critique is intimately related to modern economics and the impact of computing – which is obviously not unique to Web3 – but is often callously celebrated within its culture. Zook and Grote (2020) describe crypto financialization as an endogenous change to financial institutions that results in the increasing prevalence of monetary and financial considerations by way of the "cultural process through which individuals are reimagined as investors." More generically, Birch and Muniesa (2020) describe assetization as the dominant form of technoscientific capitalism, marking a movement away from commodities formerly grounded in a material reality. In both descriptions, the technosocial processes of financialization and assetization result from the circulation of value which requires a prefigured quantification of things (i.e., blocks of meaning indexed to code) (DuPont, 2017). These are, of course, not new issues. They are foundational to computer history more generally, and arguably, some of these processes arose out of organizational rationalization that complemented bureaucratization (Beniger, 1986).

In an already fair and just society, financialization, assetization, and quantification don't pose any really troubling ethical issues, but when these institutional "logics" are embedded into real systems, they have the power to dramatically shape social relations. For instance, failed efforts to depoliticize money with crypto illustrate the ways that algorithmic control (still) cannot autonomously control macroeconomic forces.[v] Moreover, these issues are not exclusively "economic" and may also apply beyond cryptocurrencies to social relations in Web3. In an astute analysis, the artist Geraldine Juárez echoes Morozov's worries that even well-intentioned "[Decentralized Autonomous Organizations] DAOs are text-book [examples of] assetization as they manifest the imperative of investment as a social relation" (Juárez, 2022). The blurring of work by technologies like DAOs extends the issues of financialization, assetization, and quantification to all social realities. Ultimately, the worry is that, like King Midas, everything a DAO touches turns into a digital asset.

Commodity fetishism is an old Marxist concern emerging out of a labor theory of value. The concern with commodity fetishism is that when people come to believe an economic abstraction (value) is to be found in an object they often but mistakenly come to think the object has intrinsic value. Marxists are troubled by commodity fetishism in crypto because it contradicts their belief that value originates in labor, as part of use-value in exchange. According to John Holloway's (2010) reading of commodity fetishism – "the core of Marx's discussion of power" – social relations of labor are presented as fungible commodities measured by price (Holloway, 2010). Extending this argument, these commodities are hostile and antagonistic, "devourers of living labour" according to Marx, and simultaneously illusory and efficacious. When commodities devour labour, they alienate workers, but they also obfuscate the social character of the origin of objects and in turn separate the subject from the object, such that those who have ownership of objects have power over subjects. Web3 cannot escape the obfuscated power of commodities, but it does complicate the relationship between subjects and objects. As I describe below, work in Web3 is intimately tied to leisure (a social origin of value) and can be represented by tokens.

Nick Szabo's (1997) pioneering work on smart contracts offered an idea of "vending machine" fairness with low transaction costs, high "observability," and automatic execution. A smart contract, Szabo imagined, is like a vending machine – all interactions are secure, automatic, and fair. He then went on to imagine how contractual clauses "can be embedded in the hardware and software" to make breach of contract nearly impossible. When Szabo's dreams were later realized in Bitcoin, it became immediately obvious that "fair" does not automatically produce equality or justice. Today, the economic inequalities in crypto networks are profound and a poor basis for social cohesion.

Nonetheless, vending machine fairness has proven useful for a small – but important – set of human relations; for example, DeFi is built on this promise and has successfully mitigated online counterparty risk. But Web3 is much bigger than DeFi; it promises hypergovernance, virtual social relations, and new kinds of work and play. For these richer experiences, often embedded in DAOs today, critics rightly argue that social relations built on market-like "vending machines" may actually exacerbate inequality and stymie the development of a just Web3 society.

A SOCIOLOGICAL MODEL FOR WEB3

Web3 is a petri dish for our future online lives. In it, DAOs have emerged as challengers to traditional forms of organizational design. Due to their unusual architecture and strategic goals, DAOs have been at the forefront of digital governance, and a small research community has emerged to support them. Yet, while most DAOs claim sophisticated governance, in reality, they tend to use simple forms of coin voting (Buterin, 2021), organize and discuss on chaotic Discord and Telegram channels, and use quasi-statist apparatuses for issue resolution (e.g., Aragon's "court" or Kleros' "justice protocol"). Despite these shortcomings, collectively and imperfectly DAOs offer examples of digital, decentralized, polycentric governance in the wild.

Good Governance

Elinor Ostrom's groundbreaking work on polycentric governance showed how tough collective action problems with resource constraints can be solved without state or market solutions. In *Governing the Commons*, Ostrom (1990) discussed how a potential tragedy of the commons can often be avoided "by voluntary organizations rather than by a coercive state." Ostrom was keen to find alternatives to rational egoism that, it was presumed, necessarily devolved into over-utilization of scarce resources (the so-called tragedy of the commons). She challenged those who, failing to see past the examples outlined by Hobbes and Rousseau, thought that only a government "using what- ever force may be required" could save the commons. Others felt that, if state violence was to be avoided, it would require privatizing the commons by erecting surveillance and security features to partition resources. Ostrom pointed out that both approaches assumed institutional change must come from the outside and be imposed on the individuals affected. Ostrom's approach to polycentric governance rejects this assumption and trades state and market solutions for "difficult, time- consuming, conflict-invoking" processes (p. 14). Later, Dietz et al. (2003) proposed a list of criteria for polycentric governance that includes dialogue between resource users (analytic deliberation); complex, redundant, layered institutions (nesting); mixed institutional types (e.g., market- and state-based); and institutional designs that facilitate experimentation, learning, and change (see also Chaffin et al., 2014). Moreover, these processes rely on negotiated, self-enforcing contracts, which ultimately require communication and trust. Remarkably, Ostrom demonstrated that when all these pieces are in place, at least according to a natural resource management model (Frey et al., 2019), self-organized collective action is often more effective than state and market alternatives, potentially making way for a still unrealized "new institutionalism."

While Ostrom et al.'s model of polycentric governance demonstrates the possibility of efficient, self-organized collective action, the contexts and empirical situations they analyze are quite remote to virtual Web3 goods (see also Dylan-Ennis, this volume). This is because the tragedy of the commons is limited to material constraints – situations where over-extraction of fish, water, or grazing have deleterious effects (Chaffin et al., 2014). But Web3 has only artificial constraints, as represented by secure token ownership. So, we need to absorb the lessons of polycentric governance – negotiated governance is possible – but look beyond a political economy of material constraints to the community management of de novo DCPRs. In Web3, resource constraints are reconfigured by the environment that is *already and automatically secure* and *value laden* with token economics. Indeed, many newer environments of virtual life, such as metaverses, are rich expressions of this digital "security environment." Unavoidably, we must also acknowledge that Web3 is also a platform for producing narrow forms of private property with non-fungible tokens, the exchange of cryptoassets, and participation in game-like social interactions (Kreutler, 2021).

By using these artificial security constraints to create unique configurations of private property, DAOs offer sophisticated opportunities for robust social infrastructure. In recent years, theories of dynamic games have been developed to model bounded and artificially constrained environments, which, I suggest below, may prove helpful to understand the continuum of property rights in these digital environments. This approach builds on a long history of game theory and microeconomic modeling but, as complex systems with emergent properties, new models must also consider a variable security parameter (k). These fields of research collide to produce cryptoeconomics, the importance of which I return to later.

On the other hand, nascent theories of blockchain governance have focused on how technological consensus protocols support voting and economic staking to represent the views of relevant stakeholders (De Filippi et al., 2020; Rozas et al., 2020). Theorists of blockchain governance often argue that legitimate representation occurs by giving "voice" to individual interests with an opportunity for "exit" (Frey & Schneider, 2020; Hirschman, 1970; Mannan & Schneider, 2021). In the same vein, some authors have focused on the quasi-legal nature of blockchain smart contracts, even suggesting that they represent a new social contract (Schneider, 2021). In any case, these theories of governance and responsibility must ultimately portray a new set of values: negotiation and commitment, incentives, democratic discourse, and consensus are ultimately reconstituted by the very real "algorithmic authority" of automated systems (Pasquale, 2011). But when algorithmic authority is reified in organizational technologies, an obvious worry is that techno-social infrastructures may nurture problematic forms of power, as Kavanagh and Dylan-Ennis (2019) describe in their Weberian account of "blockocracy."

Trust and Technology

As we move from DeFi to DAOs – from financial mechanisms to organizational technology (Tan, 2021) – we also need to reconsider the role and impact of trust. Most literature on the role of trust in blockchain technology presupposes that its function is to lower transaction costs within organizations (Coase, 1937; Werbach, 2018), but empirical evidence from traditional organizations to contemporary DAOs does not show strong support for this conclusion.[vi] Rather, together with markets and hierarchy, trust is a key mechanism for managing significant vertical relationships under varying conditions. Evidence from traditional organizations also shows that trust is mostly used in the transaction process rather than during contract constitution or execution (Macaulay, 1963), although trust surely also emerges in new and unexpected ways in DAOs.

One description of the multiple conditions under which trust operates in blockchain environments is offered by Lemieux (2022), who adopts Russell Hardin's tripartite model of trust as "encapsulated interest." According to Hardin (2002), trust is "grounded in the truster's assessment of the intentions of the trusted with respect to some action," which is, typically, based on self-interest, moral commitment, or other idiosyncratic factors. In contrast, Werbach (2018) offers a structuralist account of "trustless trust" – a technology impact model of trust. Adapted from the venture capitalist Reid Hoffman, this notion of "trustless trust" attempts to bootstrap trust from executing code, in effect paraphrasing "code is law" as "code is trust" (see also "lex cryptographia" by Wright & De Filippi, 2015). A commonality among these distinct accounts is that all agree that trust does not disappear in the midst of blockchain technologies, but rather is transformed. Looking forward, exactly how trust is transformed ought to be a primary research question for DAOs in particular because, as Ostrom et al. argue, trust supports consensus, and consensus is necessary for good governance.

Not only is trust foundational for effective polycentric governance, but in Web3, it can be systematically manipulated using cryptoeconomic mechanisms. Cryptoeconomics is nascent field of research and development that combines algorithms, techniques, and design patterns from cryptography and information security engineering with (usually token-based) microeconomics to achieve the goal of network-scale behavioral control. As a complex system (Voshmgir & Zargham, 2019), cryptoeconomic mechanisms help structure but do not determine organizational evolution; rather, they enable individual actions to scale across decentralized networks to produce consensus and other emergent, relational social behaviors (like trust and cooperation but also crime; see Baumol, 1996). Cryptoeconomics also supports digital, decentralized polycentric governance because it offers organizational designers a growing menu of technologies to support broader strategic goals, such as circular or regenerative economics (Borreani, 2021; Fritsch et al., 2021; Owocki, 2022) or, as I outline below, forms of social coproduction. For the progressive Web3 designer, cryptoeconomics opens the door to virtual environments that inhibit the formation of poles of power and therein help prevent the violence and injustice that necessarily follow.

Social Coproduction

DAOs are organizational technology that, on account of being digital and decentralized, specialize in limited contact with state functions, especially state-controlled monetary functions. They are *post-operaismo* in the parlance of critical theory but emerged out of a complex socio-technical bundle of practices and people (Schatzki, 2009), not from "the workers," as with progressive movements from the last millennium.

In the utopian version, DAOs are the culmination of 200 years of post-Marxist technological automation, an evolution of the institutional form toward autonomist social goals, and an organizational technology where people directly make decisions affecting their everyday lives and seek to break free from political structures imposed from the outside, a form of agorism (Dylan-Ennis & Barlowe, 2022). Implicitly, DAOs would return autonomy to the individual with the goal of directly overcoming power relations – not as a revolutionary or vanguard movement wresting control from the state but (perhaps) as an anti-power (Holloway, 2010).

However, in my experience of nascent Web3, sophisticated organizational designs and behavioral technologies are still rare and remain highly experimental. The technologies supposedly underpinning autonomist social goals may be vital infrastructure (see Nabben, this volume) but still play a limited role in social interactions. Unfortunately, the bulk of extant scholarly work, including my own, has focused too narrowly on the imagined disruption brought about by the integration of immutable records and automatic software execution, at the expense of developing sociologically rich models of human behavior capable of explaining how Web3 designs, builds, uses, and maintains real socio-technical infrastructure. As a gesture toward thinking beyond the ways code simply replaces complex social behaviors like legal order, social trust, and cooperation, I adopt Hardt and Negri's (2017) model of social coproduction and extend it to Web3. This model reintroduces agency (Jasper, 2006), collective identity (Polletta & Jasper, 2001), and social dynamics associated with collective decision making (Ostrom, 1990) by making contributions to neo-institutional theory (Schneiberg & Lounsbury, 2017).

According to Hardt and Negri (2017), the political economy of social coproduction faces two challenges: how to create organizations without hierarchy and how to create institutions without centralization. Specifically, they call on social movement leaders to "invert the roles," by giving strategic decision-making powers to the movement (the "assembly") and tactics to the leadership. This inverted governance relationship destroys the sovereign. Of course, the sovereign must be destroyed so that the people can represent themselves, but as Rousseau (1762/2003) argues, representing oneself is an oxymoron:

> sovereignty cannot be represented for the same reason that it cannot be alienated; it consists essentially in the general will, and the will does not admit of being represented: either it is the same or it is different; there is no middle ground.

But, when Rousseau celebrates the general will in contrast to the will of all he "underwrites sovereign power," Hardt and Negri (2017, p. 27) admonish. They go on to point out that in these sovereign arrangements, "what belongs to everyone and to no one really belongs to the state" (p. 29).

As a sociological model, social coproduction draws attention to the expansive nature of biopolitics. Hardt and Negri emphasize that "all life is subject to threat and exploitation," not just those domains traditionally labeled as work. Indeed, global neoliberal capitalism has made the idea of an autonomous political realm implausible. Most obviously, sovereign nation-states have been unable or unwilling to fulfill important environmental and social goals, leaving corporations with corporate social responsibility (CSR) mandates to assume responsibility (Scherer & Palazzo, 2011), a form of neoliberalism. The social coproduction model, rather, suggests an expanded role for economics, wherein cooperation and composition naturally arise in place of political representation. Finally, in-the-streets social movements and new kinds of cooperative work organizations (Mannan, 2018) provide further evidence of the many ways that labor is ultimately cooperative (Hardt & Negri argue that "the *one* never produces"). They conclude that private property fetters social productivity and undermines social relations and that neoliberalism did not restore the freedom of the market but rather reinvented the state.

Social Movements

Hardt and Negri defend the highly practical nature of social coproduction through many rich examples and case studies of social movements, which they describe as durable social configurations reminiscent of terrorist cells and netwars (Arquilla & Ronfeldt, 2001). While the long-term durability of DAOs remains an open question (stalwarts like MakerDAO only emerged in 2017), the dynamism of their formation and transformation is well captured by social movement theory.

Social movement theory spans sociology and political science to explain contestation and collective mobilization processes (Schneiberg & Lounsbury, 2017). In particular, the sociology of collective identity has been useful to explain the emergence, trajectories, and impacts of social movements. Polletta and Jasper (2001) point out that collective identity serves as an alternative to structuralist accounts by accounting for the ways that people mobilize, why they participate, and the choices they make.

In their review of social movement theory, they ask:

> To what extent are collective identities constructed in and through protest rather than preceding it? Is the identity a group projects publicly the same one that its members experience? Are collective identities imposed on groups or invented by them? Do individuals choose collective identities to maximize their self-interest or do interests flow from identities? How is collective identity different from ideology? From interest? From solidarity? (Polletta & Jasper, 2001, p. 285)

Recent examples of popular DAOs, like Friends With Benefits, emphasize the ways that collective identities can emerge in social movements (Kitts, 2006). Friends With Benefits is a kind of VIP lounge or social club with an access token and a treasury worth millions of dollars. In their frothy Discord server, over a million messages have been posted by thousands of members who self-organize and self-promote in a riotous fashion, collectively selling merchandise, artwork, and making group investments (including purchasing brick and mortar assets). Friends With Benefits members organize parties and meetups around the globe, listen to music together in virtual rooms, and socialize with a distinct Web3 argot. In my ethnography, I found feminisms, diversity, and hustle culture abound. Notably, there is little evidence of a scarce resource debate among Friends With Benefits.

Collective identity is especially important for in-group strategic planning and communication, weathering organizational uncertainty, supporting prosocial behaviors, cultivating psychological affect, and setting social norms and limits. Most visibly, collective identities in DAOs are produced and shared through postmodern storytelling, by way of memes (Yogarajah, 2022).

Surplus and Social Money

In Web3, work is inextricably connected to leisure because the political economy of the Web3 social movement is defined by surplus – not scarcity, as in traditional capitalist models. Why surplus? Because "magic Internet money," of course (if you are unsatisfied with economic relations, just create your own!), but also because in Web3 there are no *natural* constraints. This re-imagination of value is particularly visible in the collective identity associated with Gitcoin, which valorizes reciprocity in opposition to scarcity, to claim that "in a virtual world, the scarcity of goods is just a shared fiction." Gitcoin is hardly alone in cultivating these new norms and values; at ETHDenver 2022 (one of the largest Web3 industry conferences), the organizer John Paller remarked on stage, "It's not about money. We don't care about that," and a recent *Wired* article by Gilad Edelman (2022) came to the same conclusion, finding that "Web3 is a realm where coders can feel good about working in tech." But perhaps the most persuasive evidence can be found in the many governance fora of DAOs, where an earlier Free and Open-Source model of software production has transformed into small-scale digital villages with diverse economic relations, each founded on a private money where "everyone gets paid." However, unlike the traditional Free and Open-Source model of software production – that drew in participants looking for fun, technical challenges, and work – participation in DAOs is far more diverse, social, and voluntaristic.

Of course, some people will find this naïve – as if Web3 isn't *really* about getting rich and being an egoist – but as I discussed above, these same people also struggle to understand any sense of value in digital currencies. Most critics simply assume Web3 must be a scam and move on, because *they cannot imagine a world of surplus*. Moreover, modern, neoclassical economics is built on the foundational belief that scarcity is necessary. However, their underlying assumptions about money and economic relations fail to see how crypto tokens can be used for purposes outside of exchange, a unit of account, or a store of value.

What does it mean to have a political economy of surplus? Does this imply that everyone is (equally) rich? This is an unhelpful and unlikely image – a political economy of surplus does not naturally imply equality or freedom. Rather, surplus may even lock its benefactors into a resource curse or trap, as evidenced by resource-abundant national governments like my own Canada or many African nations that founder despite great natural wealth. Unlike rationalized models of narrow "economic" relations of the sort familiar to traditional "scarcity-generating institutions" (Hoeschele, 2010), in Web3 surplus seems to be unevenly distributed through complex practices of 1) earmarking and the social use of money, and 2) the schismogenetic emergence of a subculture that defines itself through refusal and rejection of crypto's dominant culture of greed and hoarding.

Earmarking and Money's Social Context
Viviana Zelizer's (1989) observation that money is often earmarked and used in decidedly social ways suggests that it is not simply a store of value or a means of exchange, but that money is also a way to signal value. According to Zelizer, people engage in different sorts of economic transactions – gifts, taxes, or discretionary funds – to earmark money for specific purposes. This allows them to set aside funds for future use or to allocate resources according to their own priorities; they may choose to save or invest this money, earmark some of these funds for specific purposes, or use it to interact socially.

Modern monetary controls tend to flatten economic exchange, reducing the value of things to a purely numerical, exchangeable form (Nelms & Maurer, 2014). However, when we look at how money tends to be *actually* used in many different cultures – for example, as a ritual offering or as a token of access to exclusive virtual spaces – we see that value is not so straightforwardly reducible to rational economic exchange. According to Zelizer, money often retains some indexical link to its sources and owners, even as it circulates within different spheres of influence.

The Web3 software service Coordinape offers an example of the social embeddedness of money in Web3. With Coordinape, DAOs can "autonomously allocate and reward contributors with funds, ... via sybil resistant social graphs." Unlike traditional forms of human resource management that carefully structure work and compensation practices from the top down in a vertical bureaucracy, Coordinape relies on social properties to establish and validate patterns of work. As well, members of DAOs can use Coordinape's tokens to give gifts, reward prosocial behaviors, and incentivize good work. While Coordinape is an admittedly niche example, closer analysis affords an intriguing view of the ongoing and increasingly intense blurring of work. In this case, work seems to exist somewhere on a continuum of leisure – part gift economy and part social coproduction.

Looking beyond money and toward forms of plural property, Weyl et al. (2022) propose a design for socially embedded tokens that index context-specific human relations. They offer ideas for how a "decentralized society" with indelible trust and identity assets might work, wherein they claim "economic value ... is generated by humans and their relationships" by establishing social provenance across communities or clubs. Weyl et al. claim that goods exist on a continuum between public and private which invites opportunities to think about plural property regimes in place of scarcity-generating private property regimes (see also Posner and Weyl's, 2018, *Radical Markets*).

Schizmogenesis and Web3's Subculture
One of the most consistent findings of my digital ethnography of Web3 is opposition to the collective identity of Bitcoin specifically and crypto more generally. In many cases, I spoke with people who rejected Bitcoin's culture of greed, HODLing, and its programmed designs for generating scarcity; others rejected its bro culture and combative discourse. Importantly, these rejections define Web3's collective identity, and since identity fundamentally determines the status and meaning of revolt, the Web3 collective identity emerges from processes of schizmogenesis.

As first described by the anthropologist Gregory Bateson, schizmogenesis is a theory to explain how inverted or anti-social patterns can compound and grow to form an organic solidarity (Durkheim, 1893/2014). Eventually, anti-social patterns begin to challenge dominant ideology. According to Dick Hebdige (1991), evidence of these anti-social patterns can be found "reflected in the surfaces" of subculture as "expressive forms and rituals" where "objects take on a symbolic dimension" (p. 2). These subcultural symbols, he continues, warn the "straight" world of a "sinister presence – the presence of difference" (p. 3).

Using Hebdige's (1991) analysis of subculture as a guide, one approach is to read the dominant ideology by looking for connotative codes (Barthes, 1975) and then find signs of refusal in Web3. We already know many of the connotative codes associated with crypto – "whales," "lambos," and "going to the moon," for example – each marking the subconscious "maps of meaning" that are "traced and re-traced along the lines laid down by the dominant discourses about reality, the dominant ideologies" (Hebdige, 1991, p. 15). Importantly, dominant ideologies serve hegemony to create consent (p. 16). Building on Gramsci's definition of hegemony as the play of relations of force comprising a "moving equilibrium," Hebdige notes that hegemony is only ever a provisional alliance between dominant groups to exert "total social authority" over other subordinate groups. Specifically, hegemony does not result from coercion or the direct imposition of ruling ideas but by "winning and shaping consent so that the power of the dominant classes appears both legitimate and natural" (Hall, 1977, quoted in Hebdige, 1991). What we find is that mass movements emerge in refusal, to disrupt what appears legitimate and natural not by a dialectical overthrowing of the dominant classes but through collective refusal. As Eric Hoffer (2010) remarked, "mass movements can rise and spread without belief in a god, but never without belief in a devil."

Perhaps Web3 only signals a refusal of crypto's greed and need for scarcity. But even if the practices of refusal are "just the darker side ... of regulations, just so much graffiti on a prison wall," they are worth careful study. After all, Hebdige (1991) continues, "graffiti can make fascinating reading ... they are an expression both of impotence and a kind of power – the power to disfigure" (p. 3).

CONCLUSION: FROM SOCIAL COPRODUCTION TO DIGITAL POLYCENTRIC GOVERNANCE

This paper critically evaluated the political economy of Web3 and offered a neo-institutional model to better explain observations of contemporary digital social movements.

Looking forward to future research, this neo-institutional model also suggests pathways to understanding new organizational forms emerging with Web3. With this lens, rather than assume scarcity, work, and profit maximization, I pointed to some lessons we can learn by studying DAOs in terms of the social coproduction of DPCRs. Armed with rich datasets of on-chain governance proposals, voting, and token economics, in the future we can turn to data science and deep learning techniques to discover "successful" strategies of digital polycentric governance.

By drawing connections to systems modeling and data analysis in the "online communities" literature in the Information Systems field, we find complementary methodologies to search DAOs for further signs of digital polycentric governance. For instance, if governance can be meaningfully represented in an analytical model (perhaps as a time-dependent partial differential equation), safety engineering and verification become tractable goals for autonomous systems like DAOs. One approach, drawn from control system theory, recommends methods for computing backward reachable sets. Mitchell et al. (2005) introduced a differential game formulation that utilizes a viscosity solution to reach safe states, which could be explored in governance contexts. Future research might explore how control engineering could use analytical solutions like this to solve dynamic governance games, opening up new vistas for digital polycentric governance.

Still, many questions emerge out the micro-organizational structure of social movements. In addition to safety engineering, does a differential game model offer the possibility of a Nash equilibrium in governance? Furthermore, what role does revenue management play in governance, given what we now know about scarcity in DCPRs? That is, without relying on foundational theories of economic utility maximization, what are appropriate preference functions for choosing governance rules? What other constraints and limitations must a model consider to gain predictive power?

NOTES

i. Skylar Brooks' Bank of Canada (2021) report "Revisiting the Monetary Sovereignty Rationale for CBDCs" offers a rich description of the real economic threats crypto poses to nation-states. Alternatively, Manski and Manski (2018) theorize the impact of blockchain technology on various (popular, economic, and state) sovereignties in terms of seven structural elements.

ii. See Yasha Levine's (2018) *Surveillance Valley: The Secret Military History of the Internet* and DuPont and Fidler's (2016) "Edge Cryptography and the Codevelopment of Computer Networks and Cybersecurity."

iii. Foucault links circulation of value (grain, specie, gold, etc.) to the emergence of the "apparatus of security." Whereas "discipline regulates everything," the apparatus of security "lets things happen" by discriminating between "details that are not valued as good or evil in themselves, that are taken to be necessary, inevitable processes." See Michel Foucault's 1977–1978 lectures at the Collége de France, published as *Security, Territory, Population* (Foucault, 2007).

iv. Social coproduction is a term used by Hardt and Negri, who are autonomist Marxists. Wikipedia provides a useful summary of autonomist values from Katsiaficas, "In contrast to the centralized decisions and hierarchical authority structures of modern institutions, autonomous social movements involve people directly in decisions affecting their everyday lives, seeking to expand democracy and help individuals break free of political structures and behavior patterns imposed from the outside."

v. But not all cryptocurrencies aim at depoliticization. For example, according to Varoufakis (2021), CBDCs are an attempt to repoliticize money.

vi. Transaction cost economics, which predicts the emergence of firms to minimize transaction costs on an open market, is a popular model for understanding DAOs. However, DAOs rarely seek to reduce costs. For example, like most DAOs, MakerDAO contracts (no-bid) work streams externally and pays client-requested, community-approved prices.

REFERENCES

Arquilla, J., & Ronfeldt, D. (2001, November). *Networks and netwars: The future of terror, crime, and militancy*. Rand Corporation.

Barthes, R. (1975, January). *S/Z: An essay* (Trans. R. Howard). Hill and Wang.

Baumol, W. J. (1996, January). Entrepreneurship: Productive, unproductive, and destructive. *Journal of Business Venturing, 11*(1), 3–22.

Beniger, J. R. (1986). *The control revolution: Technological and economic origins of the information society*. Harvard University Press.

Birch, K., & Muniesa, F. (Eds.). (2020). *Assetization: Turning things into assets in technoscientific capitalism*. The MIT Press.

Borreani, L. (2021, October). *Applied regenerative economics*. https://blog.curvelabs.eu/applied-regenerative-economics-2219d2e1087b

Brooks, S. (2021, December). *Revisiting the monetary sovereignty rationale for CBDCs* [Technical report, Bank of Canada].

Buterin, V. (2021, August). *Moving beyond coin voting governance*. https://vitalik.ca/general/2021/10/31/cities.html

Caliskan, K. (2020). Data money: The socio-technical infrastructure of cryptocurrency blockchains. *Economy and Society*, *49*(4), 22.
Chaffin, B., Gosnell, H., & Cosens, B. (2014, September). A decade of adaptive governance scholarship: Synthesis and future directions. *Ecology and Society*, *19*(3), 56.
Coase, R. H. (1937). The nature of the firm. *Economica*, *4*(16), 386–405.
De Filippi, P., Mannan, M., & Reijers, W. (2020, June). Blockchain as a confidence machine: The problem of trust & challenges of governance. *Technology in Society*, *62*, 101284.
Dietz, T., Ostrom, E., & Stern, P. C. (2003, December). The struggle to govern the commons. *Science*, *302*, 1907–1912.
DuPont, Q. (2017, October). Blockchain identities: Notational technologies for control and management of abstracted entities. *Metaphilosophy*, *48*(5), 634–653.
DuPont, Q. (2018). Experiments in algorithmic governance: An ethnography of "The DAO," a failed decentralized autonomous organization. In M. Campbell-Verduyn (Ed.), *Bitcoin and beyond: The challenges and opportunities of blockchains for global governance* (pp. 157–177). Routledge.
DuPont, Q. (2020). Guiding principles for ethical cryptocurrency, blockchain, and DLT research. *Cryptoeconomic Systems*, *1*(1). htpps://doi.org/10.21428/58320208.a8364373
DuPont, Q., & Fidler, B. (2016). Edge cryptography and the co-development of computer networks and cybersecurity. *IEEE Annals of the History of Computing*, *38*(2), 55–73.
DuPont, Q., & Maurer, B. (2015, June). Ledgers and law in the blockchain. *King's Review*, 23.
Durkheim, E. (1893/2014). *The division of labor in society*. Free Press.
Dylan-Ennis, P., & Barlowe, W. (2022). An introduction to agorism in both theory and practice. *Agorism in the 21st Century: A Philosophical Journal*, *1*(1), 23–29.
Edelman, G. (2022, May). The Web3 movement's quest to build a 'can't be evil' internet. Wired.
Foucault, M. (2007). *Security, territory, population, lectures at the Collége De France, 1977–78*. Picador.
Frey, S., Krafft, P. M., & Keegan, B. C. (2019, December). "This place does what it was built for": Designing digital institutions for participatory change. *Proceedings of ACM Human Computing Interaction*, *3*, 31.
Frey, S., & Schneider, N. (2020). *Effective voice: Beyond exit and affect in online communities*. arXiv. Preprint arXiv:2009.12470
Fritsch, F., Emmett, J., Friedman, E., Kranjc, R., Manski, S., Zargham, M., & Bauwens, M. (2021). Challenges and approaches to scaling the global commons. *Frontiers in Blockchain*, *4*. https://doi.org/10.3389/fbloc.2021.578721
Golumbia, D. (2016). *The politics of Bitcoin: Software as right-wing extremism*. University of Minnesota Press.
Graeber, D., & Wengrow, D. (2021). *The dawn of everything: A new history of humanity*. Farrar, Straus and Giroux.
Hardin, R. (2002). *Trust and trustworthiness*. Russell Sage Foundation.
Hardt, M., & Negri, A. (2017). *Assembly*. Oxford University Press.
Hebdige, D. (1991). *Subculture: The meaning of style*. New accents. Routledge.
Hirschman, A. O. (1970). *Exit, voice, and loyalty: Responses to decline in firms, organizations, and states*. Harvard University Press.
Hoeschele, W. (2010). *The economics of abundance: A political economy of freedom, equity, and sustainability*. Gower green economics and sustainable growth series. Gower.
Hoffer, E. (2010). *The true believer: Thoughts on the nature of mass movements* (Reissue ed.). Harper Perennial Modern Classics.
Holloway, J. (2010). *Change the world without taking power*. Pluto Press.
Jasper, J. (2006, February). A strategic approach to collective action: Looking for agency in social-movement choices. *Mobilization: An International Quarterly*, *9*(1), 1–16.
Juárez, G. (2022). The ghostchain (or taking things for what they are). *Paletten*, 325.
Kavanagh, D., & Dylan-Ennis, P. (2019, July). Bureaucracy, blockocracy and power [Conference Publication]. In 35th European Group of Organization Studies (EGOS) colloquium (p. 23, Sub-theme 10: Doing process research). Edinburgh, UK.
Kitts, J. (2006, February). Mobilizing in black boxes: Social networks and participation in social movement organizations. *Mobilization: An International Quarterly*, *5*(2), 241–257.
Kreutler, K. (2021, July). *A prehistory of DAOs*. https://gnosisguild.mirror.xyz/t4F5rItMw4-mlpLZf5JQhElbDfQ2JRVKAzEpanyxW1Q

Latour, B. (1986). Visualisation and cognition: Drawing things together. In E. Long & H. Kuklick (Eds.), *Knowledge and society* (pp. 1–40). JAI Press.

Layer Zero. (2022, April). *The divine DAO with tracheopteryx*. Layer Zero.

Lemieux, V. (2022). *Searching for trust: Blockchain technology in an age of disinformation*. Cambridge University Press.

Levine, Y. (2018). *Surveillance Valley: The rise of the military-digital complex*. PublicAffairs.

Macaulay, S. (1963). Non-contractual relations in business: A preliminary study. *American Sociological Review, 28*(1), 55–67.

Mannan, M. (2018, December). Fostering worker cooperatives with blockchain technology: Lessons from the colony project. *Erasmus Law Review, 11*(3), 190–203.

Mannan, M., & Schneider, N. (2021). Exit to community: Strategies for multi-stakeholder ownership in the platform economy. *Georgetown Law Technology Review, 5*(1), 1–71.

Manski, S., & Manski, B. (2018, July). No gods, no masters, no coders? The future of sovereignty in a blockchain world. *Law and Critique, 29*(2), 151–162.

Mitchell, I., Bayen, A., & Tomlin, C. (2005, July). A time-dependent Hamilton-Jacobi formulation of reachable sets for continuous dynamic games. *IEEE Transactions on Automatic Control, 50*(7), 947–957.

Morozov, E. (2022, January). *Web3: A map in search of territory*. https://the-crypto-syllabus.com/web3-a-map-in-search-of-territory/

Nelms, T. C., & Maurer, B. (2014). Materiality, symbol, and complexity in the anthropology of money. In E. Bijleveld & H. Aarts (Eds.), *The psychological science of money* (pp. 37–70). Springer.

Ostrom, E. (1990). *Governing the commons*. Cambridge University Press.

Owocki, K. (2022). *Greenpilled: How crypto can regenerate the world*. Blurb.

Pasquale, F. (2011). Restoring transparency to automated authority. *Journal on Telecommunications & High Technology Law, 9*(235), 235–256.

Perrin, A. (2021, November). *16% of Americans say they have ever invested in, traded or used cryptocurrency*. PEW Research Centre. https://www.pewresearch.org/short-reads/2021/11/11/16-of-americans-say-they-have-ever-invested-in-traded-or-used-cryptocurrency/

Polletta, F., & Jasper, J. M. (2001). Collective identity and social movements. *Annual Review of Sociology, 27*(1), 283–305.

Posner, E. A., & Weyl, E. G. (2018). *Radical markets: Uprooting capitalism and democracy for a just society*. Princeton University Press.

Rousseau, J.-J. (1762/2003). *On the social contract* (Trans. G. D. H. Cole). Dover Publications.

Rozas, D., Tenorio-Fornés, A., & Hassan, S. (2020). Analysis of the potentials of blockchain for the governance of global commons. *Frontiers in Blockchain, 24*. https://doi.org/10.3389/fbloc.2021.577680

Schatzki, T. R. (2009). *Social practices*. Cambridge University Press.

Scherer, A. G., & Palazzo, G. (2011). The new political role of business in a globalized world: A review of a new perspective on CSR and its implications for the firm, governance, and democracy. *Journal of Management Studies, 48*(4), 899–931.

Schneiberg, M., & Lounsbury, M. (2017). Social movements and the dynamics of institutions and organizations. In R. Greenwood, C. Oliver, R. Suddaby & K. Sahlin (Eds.), *The SAGE handbook of organizational institutionalism* (pp. 281–310). SAGE Publications Ltd.

Schneider, N. (2021, August). *Cryptoeconomics as a limitation on governance*. https://ntnsndr.mirror.xyz/zO27EOn9P_62jVlautpZD5hHB7ycf3Cfc2N6byz6DOk

Swartz, L. (2020). *New money: How payment became social media*. Yale University Press.

Szabo, N. (1997, September). Formalizing and securing relationships on public networks. *First Monday, 2*(9). https://doi.org/10.5210/fm.v2i9.548

Tan, J. (2021, March). *Exploring DAOs as a new kind of institution*. https://medium.com/commonsstack/exploring-daos-as-a-new-kind-of-institution-8103e6b156d4

Varoufakis, Y. (2021, August). *A central bank cryptocurrency to democratise money*. Project Syndicate. https://www.project-syndicate.org/commentary/central-bank-cryptocurrency-democratize-money-by-yanis-varoufakis-2021-07

Voshmgir, S., & Zargham, M. (2019, November). *Foundations of cryptoeconomic systems* [Technical Report 1, WU Vienna University of Economics and Business].

Werbach, K. (2018, November). *The blockchain and the new architecture of trust*. The MIT Press.
Weyl, E. G., Ohlhaver, P., & Buterin, V. (2022, May). *Decentralized society: Finding Web3's soul*. https://papers.ssrn.com/abstract=4105763
Wright, A., & De Filippi, P. (2015). *Decentralized blockchain technology and the rise of Lex cryptographia*. http://ssrn.com/abstract=2580664
Yogarajah, Y. (2022, July). 'Hodling' on: Memetic storytelling and digital folklore within a cryptocurrency world. *Economy and Society*, *51*(3), 1–22.
Zelizer, V. A. (1989). The social meaning of money: "Special monies." *American Journal of Sociology*, *95*(2), 342–377.
Zook, M., & Grote, M. H. (2020, November). Initial coin offerings: Linking technology and financialization. *Environment and Planning A: Economy and Space*, *52*(8), 1560–1582.

INSTITUTIONAL ISOMORPHISM IN WEB3: SAME SAME BUT DIFFERENT?

Tara Merk[a] and Rolf Hoefer[b]

[a]Panthéon-Assas University Paris ii, France
[b]Cultur3, France

ABSTRACT

Like an online carnival, Web3 aims to turn the internet's social order upside down. Unlike a carnival, Web3 wants to be more than a weeklong party and morph into a legitimate substitute for the internet's status quo. Web3's secret sauce for upheaval is decentralized, permissionless technologies, in particular blockchain technologies. In this exploratory paper, we draw on the concept of institutional isomorphism to muse about Web3's future and to highlight the inherent tension between striving to be different from Web2 yet wanting to become more legitimate. We argue that technical merits are hardly enough to realize Web3's high aspirations. Regulatory pressures, rampant uncertainty, and the professional norms of Web3 participants drive the space to adopt many of the organizational structures and practices that it aims to displace. To maintain divergence from Web2, despite isomorphic pressures, we suggest that it is important to increase the overall diversity of people in Web3, to double down on the value of decentralization, and to reaffirm Web3's commitment to creatively re-imagine various institutional arrangements.

Keywords: Institutional theory; isomorphism; Web3; blockchain technology; DAOs; legitimacy

WEB3: A FOREVER CARNIVAL?

In their book *The Dawn of Everything*, the late David Graeber and David Wengrow wrote that carnivals turn social orders upside down, kings get dethroned, and taboos become acceptable. Today, Web3 evokes images of a carnival on the internet: big tech corporations are dethroned and replaced by open protocols; artwork is traded through galleries located on virtual lands; anyone can gain power in decentralized decision-making rituals; and "anons" – anonymous internet users – mint their own digital currency as internet lordlings of mini central banks. Redefined by Gavin Wood (see Vergne, this volume), the term "Web3" has gained significant traction in recent years. A popular approach to defining Web3 among the blockchain community is to place the concept in its historical context. The story is that Web3 extends the underlying capabilities offered by Web1 and Web2 by enabling digital ownership (https://ethereum.org/web3; Still, 2021).

Through digital ownership, proponents argue that Web3 facilitates a departure from large centralized platforms and their extractive business models, the possibility of owning personal data and digital assets, as well as the disintermediation of core digital infrastructure as the main differentiators (Dixon, 2021; Roose, 2022; What Is Web3 and Why Is It Important?, n.d.). Yet, Web3 is not without skeptics. Prominent figures such as Twitter founder Jack Dorsey see Web3 as merely another centralized effort hiding behind a trendy label (Kastrenakes, 2021). Signal founder Moxie Marlinspike points out Web3's technical shortcomings (Marlinspike, 2022), while articles in the *Harvard Business Review* surmise that Web3 "faces significant technical, environmental, ethical, and regulatory hurdles between here and hegemony" (Stackpole, 2022).

Whatever Web3 is, both skeptics and proponents seem to agree on what it wants: Web3 wants to be big, and Web3 most definitely, desperately wants to be different. Big means to be viewed as a legitimate alternative to the internet's status quo today. Different means different from Web2; an internet controlled by few investors and select big tech companies whose data, algorithms, and protocol changes are accountable to no government or user. In this sense, Web3 aspires to be more than just an iteration of the efficiency, scale, or user experience (UX) of Web2. Web3 aspires to be a radical change in how the internet is structured, owned, and governed. Another point of agreement within the Web3 debate is that the underlying driver for this reorganization of the internet will be decentralized, permissionless, and censorship-resistant technologies, particularly blockchain technologies.

But will the use of blockchain technologies allow Web3 to maintain its critical difference and morph into a real alternative over time? Yes, carnivals turn our social order upside down, but usually, after a while, they end and things go back to normal. Will Web3 be the same? In this paper, we draw on the concept of institutional isomorphism to argue that the blockchain may not be enough to make Web3 truly different and to turn today's carnivalesque ecosystem into tomorrow's status quo. Our intention is not to be bleak killjoys. Rather, we want to highlight the tension that exists between Web3's ambition to be fundamentally different and the need to be sufficiently legitimate to effect the changes it aspires to. Fundamentally optimistic, we close by discussing where and how Web3 may be able to navigate this tension.

THE ROLE OF INSTITUTIONAL ISOMORPHISM IN WEB3

Institutional theory is a wide field of study, broadly concerned with understanding the role of overarching, continuous and relatively stable structures, practices, norms, and values in social organization (David et al., 2019; see also DuPont, this volume). One strand of institutional theorists has asked: Why are so many organizations similar? Why do we observe imitation and similarity in organizational forms and practices? Why do organizations in industries that start as something seemingly unique soon resemble old and familiar organizations? Isomorphism is a concept that describes the environmental conditions and processes leading organizations to become more similar (DiMaggio & Powell, 1983). Understanding isomorphism is critical to understand and predict the evolution of a specific field and critically examine the source and effectiveness of established practices. However, with the exception of Laul's (2022) essay on isomorphism in decentralized autonomous organization (DAO) governance, the concept has not been widely discussed in the Web3 context. Work in neo-institutional theory has differentiated between two types of isomorphism in particular, institutional isomorphism and competitive isomorphism. Competitive isomorphism argues that organizations become similar because competition acts as a selection force, weeding out unadaptive organizations over a long-time horizon (Hannan & Freeman, 1977). In contrast, institutional isomorphism emphasizes how an organization becomes similar to other organizations because of social pressures, focusing on how organizations adapt to their environments.

In this paper, we focus on the effects of institutional isomorphism in Web3. Web3 is an empirically young, emerging, and rapidly evolving organizational field. Insufficient time has passed to establish the type of organizational structures and practices that are economically more efficient and effective than others in practice, making competitive isomorphism less applicable. DiMaggio and Powell's (1983) seminal article highlighted three distinct types of social pressures driving institutional isomorphism. Coercive isomorphism derives from political influence as well as legal and regulatory forces. Mimetic isomorphism suggests that ambiguity causes organizations to make social comparisons and copy others in response to uncertainty. In turn, normative isomorphism is associated with professionalization, which can come about via the adoption of HR practices including similar criteria for hiring, similar compensation and promotion policies, and on-the-job socialization processes. We draw on examples from the Web3 context to help illustrate each of these types of social pressures driving Web3 organizations toward isomorphism.

Coercive Isomorphism

Coercive isomorphism emerges when organizations adapt their internal structures and practices in response to outside pressures from organizations they depend on. In many cases, these are regulatory pressures. Take DAOs, defined as organizations whose operation depends significantly on blockchains (Hoefer & Ha, 2022a). In order to limit the liability claims for individual members of a DAO, many DAOs have begun to use legal wrappers by incorporating an organization in a traditional form within a traditional legal jurisdiction. Yet, DAOs do not easily fit into traditional regulatory structures. DAOs face a number of unique challenges when trying to appropriately incorporate as one or the other legal entity type: the structure of contributors may be more fluid than in traditional organizations, contributors often reside in many different jurisdictions, there might be a resistance to the centralizing forces inherent in certain models of incorporation, and the scope of the DAO's real-world operations and tax requirements might be expansive. Given these unique challenges, a very small number of legal structures have become the default mode of incorporation for DAOs. This in turn has led to the homogenization of DAOs, at least on the level of their legal structures and the operational practices required to fulfil these structures. Note that the determining factor of this emerging practice is mostly influenced from the wider social structures within which DAOs exist and therefore somewhat decoupled from the technical use of blockchain technology. For example, the rationalized myth (Meyer & Rowan, 1977) that has driven many DAOs to adopt similar formal organizational structures is the idea that projects must incorporate DAOs to "progressively decentralize" (Walden, 2020). While progressive decentralization is really a sociocultural mechanism for community involvement, it has been rationalized as a technical solution and legal strategy in an attempt to avoid powerful regulatory bodies (Hoefer & Ha, 2022b; cf. Ooki DAO, 2022). High regulatory uncertainty, limited options in terms of legal structures and jurisdictions, and widespread rational myths to avoid powerful regulatory bodies suggests coercive isomorphism is at work in Web3, consistent with DiMaggio and Powell's (1983) hypotheses that isomorphic changes increase the more dependent one organization is on another (the regulator), the higher the centralization of resources that organizations rely on and the higher the degree of engagement of the organizational field (i.e., the group of all organizations in Web3) is with the state.

Mimetic Isomorphism

Uncertainty in how to achieve an organization's goals encourages imitation in organizational structures and practices. The homogenization of organizational structures and practices driven by uncertainty is described by the idea of mimetic isomorphism. Given the high degree of uncertainty both externally (what is Web3?) and internally (what are our specific Web3 goals and strategies?), mimetic isomorphism pervades Web3. For example, mimetic isomorphism can be observed in the DAO space both on a technical level and an operational level. A DAO's resources and decision-making are typically managed on-chain via smart contracts. On-chain or blockchain-enabled smart contracts are a young technology where innovative implementations remain prone to bugs and hacks. As such, the governance and resource management contracts used by DAOs often fall into a more risky category of smart contracts. However, as DAO smart contracts are usually developed as open-source technologies that can be freely forked, imitation is virtually costless. A striking example of homogenization through imitation in the DAO space has been the adoption of MolochDAO smart contracts. MolochDAO is an early implementation of DAO smart contracts on the Ethereum blockchain. MolochDAO was launched in 2019 as an organization to fund the development of technical infrastructure. MolochDAO's smart contracts framework is designed as a minimal viable DAO in order to reduce technical risk, maximize usability, and can be extended for customizability (Graham, 2022). According to data from DAOHaus, a no-code platform used by projects to create and manage DAOs created on the MolochDAO framework, there are over 800 implementations of MolochDAO smart contracts at the time of writing (DAOhaus, n.d.). Implementing the MolochDAO framework establishes similar organizational practices (e.g., how proposals, votes, voice, and exit works), which in turn lead organizations to become more similar.

Operationally, it is also curious to observe the widespread use of the communication platform Discord among different Web3 organizations. Discord allows users to set up chat servers for free, organized in different topical discussion channels which users can easily join. While Discord offers several features that appeal to the Web3 community, such as allowing for pseudonymous identities and enabling token-gating, it is far from clear whether using Discord as the main communication platform in DAOs is the optimal choice. Many participants in the DAO ecosystem have pointed out Discord's shortcomings and weaknesses that sometimes lead to chaos and, well, discord (Quittner, 2021; rationalaussie, 2022). That most DAOs rely on Discord is not mandated from the outside or recommended by experts but rather is perpetuated as a legitimate organizational practice in the broader Web3 environment. DiMaggio and Powell (1983) predict that mimetic isomorphism will be higher when organizations face ambiguity regarding their internal goals and lack well-defined technologies. Similarly, mimetic isomorphic change within an organizational field increases if the technologies and goals of the entire field are not well understood and remain ambiguous. Given the ongoing debate on Web3's definition and purpose, as well as the fact that many core Web3 technologies such as decentralised finance (DeFi), non-fungible tokens (NFTs) and DAO smart contracts are still in their infancy, mimetic isomorphism appears to prevail widely in Web3.

Normative Isomorphism

Normative isomorphism describes the spread of organizational practices through professional groups. Previous research has highlighted the role of formal education and industry associations to encourage standardized practices among professionals in a specific field of work (Teodoro, 2014). While there are little data available on the overall educational background of people shaping Web3 organizations, the team pages of a number of large companies operating in central positions within the ecosystem are telling. For example, OpenSea, which self-identifies as "the world's first and largest Web3 marketplace for NFTs and crypto collectibles," describes its team's background as:

> Our team has varied backgrounds from Stanford, UC Berkeley, Georgia Tech, Waterloo, San Jose State University [...] The team hails from larger, more established companies like Google and Facebook, as well as smaller startups like Artsy, Lime, and a hand-crafted jewelry business. (OpenSea, 2022)

This website excerpt demonstrates OpenSea's pride in hiring professionals from top-tier universities and leading Web2 tech companies, especially those anchored and situated in the wider San Francisco Bay Area. While this hiring practice is not normatively wrong, it does encourage onboarding individuals deeply rooted in and shaped by the more traditional tech industry and inevitably transports some aspects of Web2's organizational and employee practices into OpenSea, the Web3 organization. A similar pattern can be observed in FTX, a recently disgraced cryptocurrency exchange and trading platform which described its team by emphasizing the heritage and experience from traditional finance centers: "We come from leading Wall Street quant firms and tech companies – Jane Street, Optiver, Susquehanna, Facebook, and Google" (FTX.com, 2022). Industry associations further accelerate the spread of normative isomorphism. The point here is that using blockchain technology and positioning an organization in the Web3 space does not seem to have changed the social norm of what constitutes a valuable and able team member. Instead, many of the conceptions advanced in these examples by Web3 organizations seem to be directly derived from the normative ideals developed within the Web2 industry.

DiMaggio and Powell (1983) argue that normative isomorphic change increases when organizations highly rely on academic credentials for hiring managerial staff and if such staff is heavily involved in trade and professional associations. Normative isomorphism in the organizational field is dependent on the degree of professionalization and structuration (i.e., how established and mature it is) of the field as a whole. While Web3 academic diplomas are a thing of the future, our examples above suggest that many organizations operating in the Web3 space today still rely heavily on sourcing talent from similar backgrounds as the Web2 space.

Note that the isomorphism lens privileges understanding the social rather than technical dynamics that lead to organizations becoming similar. In other words, with this lens, the use of blockchain technology is not necessarily a key determinant of organizational practice and structures. Instead, the uncertainty blockchain creates as a relatively new and malleable technology for individual organizations as well as in the Web3 space as a whole may encourage mimetic isomorphism. While institutional isomorphism is not associated with competitive advantages per se, DiMaggio and Powell (1983) argue that institutional isomorphic change can be associated with legitimacy, which is important for organizations to survive and be successful. We now turn to discuss the role of isomorphism and legitimacy in light of Web3's aspirations.

TO BE BIG, WEB3 NEEDS TO BE LEGITIMATE. ISOMORPHISM TO THE RESCUE

An increase in questions of legitimacy is frequently associated with the adoption of new technologies and practices (Strang & Meyer, 1994; Tolbert & Zucker, 1983). Legitimacy can relate both to the perceptions of stakeholders within a particular system (e.g., citizens within a democracy, users, and validators within a blockchain system) and to the perceptions of stakeholders outside the system (e.g., international community perception of a particular nation-state, legacy financial institutions perception of Web3) (De Filippi et al., 2022). In our context, we take legitimacy to broadly denote the way in which actors outside the Web3 industry, such as regulators and the public media take for granted the phenomenon as desirable, proper, and appropriate (Suchman, 1995). Previous research on the connection between legitimacy and isomorphism has shown that legitimacy can be a particularly strong driving force toward mimetic isomorphism (Deephouse, 1996; Frumkin & Galaskiewicz, 2004; Meyer & Jepperson, 2000). In Web3, mimicking other organizations' practices in the face of uncertainty is driven mostly by organizations' need for legitimation rather than economic efficiency or other performance-related reasons. As such, isomorphism in Web3 may be positively related to navigating uncertainty in the field and organizational goals of reaching widespread adoption as well as long-term viability. The core idea here is that isomorphism increases an organization's legitimacy by reducing questions about whether an organization's structures or practices appear legitimate, meaning desirable, proper, or appropriate.

In recent years, the topic of legitimacy of organizations and technologies in Web3 has been picked up by various media outlets, practitioners, and researchers alike (cf. Buterin, 2021). Articles in both Forbes and TechCrunch (https://techcrunch.com/2021/08/16/regulating-crypto-is-essential-to-ensuring-its-global-legitimacy/) highlight that establishing more regulation in Web3 and clarifying how its new technologies fit into existing regulatory frameworks is key toward strengthening Web3's legitimacy and adoption (Colbert, 2022; Siebert, 2021). In research, Rosati et al. (2021) have analyzed different discursive strategies employed by organizations in Web3, specifically the blockchain industry and their relation to legitimizing the industry's organizations and technologies. They find that organizations strive to build legitimacy in Web3 by highlighting the involvement of influential field-level actors such as institutional investors and non-Web3 mega-corporations and by emphasizing how blockchain's capabilities align with best practices in the more traditional and legitimate Web2 tech industries. From these perspectives, Web3 actors aligning with regulators and Web2 practices through strategic action and similar organizational structures and practices brings Web3 closer to its goal of achieving mainstream adoption as the next iteration of the web.

But then, where's the carnival? Legitimacy derived from isomorphic change is unlikely to result in an iteration of the web that is truly novel in how it is structured, owned, and governed. In short, it detracts from our second goal: to be different. In the next section, we explore what the institutional theory literature tells us about how this tension can be navigated.

WEB3'S EDGE: WHEN ISOMORPHISM MAINTAINS DIVERGENCE

While most research on institutional isomorphism has studied the process by which organizations become more similar to others and their external environment,

Beckert (2010) argues that depending on the underlying conditions in which isomorphism unfolds, it can create bidirectional dynamics, that is, it can lead to both convergence and divergence from the outside environment.

Specifically, Beckert (2010) shows how the direction of coercive isomorphism is dependent on the interests of powerful actors in institutional structures. For example, on the level of states, during colonialism, colonizers created specific alternative legal frameworks to ensure that the institutional structures developed in the colonized areas remained distinct from those in the "motherland." Similarly, the direction of normative isomorphism varies depending on the extent to which professional communities share cognitive and mental frames and where these frames come from. Consider a group of Web3 entrepreneurs who all have long-standing experience as cryptography researchers at different universities and now consider another group which consists of business graduates who spent their prior career consulting traditional industries. Given these distinctly different backgrounds, professional training and socialization, the two groups may be attracted to different institutional solutions when faced with the same problem. Finally, Beckert (2010) argues that the direction of mimetic isomorphism also depends on what actors within the field are attracted to. However, unlike with normative isomorphic change, the attraction here depends less on previous socialization and professionalism and more on internally established notions of legitimacy, that is, which type of institutional solutions does the Web3 community consider to be legitimate. As such, institutional divergence may prevail if external institutional solutions are not perceived as being sufficiently legitimate. These different notions of legitimacy are informed by the specific cultural context in which they operate. Overall, the direction of institutional isomorphism is shaped by the interests of strong exogenous powers, the shared understanding of what qualifies as desirable, appropriate, and proper structures shared by the professional community, as well as the cultural underpinnings of the new institutional context which influences legitimacy perceptions toward outside institutional arrangements.

We believe that the last two sets of conditions are particularly interesting when trying to understand how Web3 may be able to navigate the tension between its goals of being both different and big. The direction of normative isomorphism is influenced by the aggregate educational and professional background of the people founding and shaping Web3 organizations. Increasing the diversity –on all fronts, be it geographic, gender, age, education, and professional background – of the Web3 community should be a key goal for the field as a whole. This may be encouraged economically by supporting less represented groups (an age-old problem but hey, we have new money and means of distribution!), through various education and onboarding initiatives that bring people into the space that we would not expect (read: not the usual finance and tech professionals) and strengthen their voice and influence in media and other public discussion forums such as conferences. Drastically increasing the number of different mental frames and professional norms that people bring into the Web3 space may help to safeguard it from defaulting to the organizational processes and structures established within Web2 and adjacent industries today.

Mimetic isomorphism may maintain divergence when external institutional solutions are perceived as illegitimate. Legitimacy perceptions are deeply dependent on cultural context. This insight leads us to ask: what is Web3's culture? And which type of external institutional arrangements does it view as legitimate solutions to adopt for itself? Which are viewed as illegitimate? While there's no definite answer to these questions, previous research has drawn on the concept of imaginaries (mental frames and metaphors that individuals use to make sense of blockchain technologies, legitimize their functions, and inscribe aspirations for the projects going forward) to understand what drives various cryptocurrency communities (Brody & Couture, 2021; Dylan-Ennis et al., 2022; Maurer et al., 2013; Swartz, 2018). Particularly, Dylan-Ennis et al.'s (2022) and Brody and Couture's (2021) findings on the Ethereum community are interesting here, as the decentralized project remains central to our current understanding of Web3. Brody and Couture (2021) observe how the Ethereum community maintains various, at the same time, conflicting and complementary imaginaries of Ethereum as a world computer and Ethereum as currency and financial technology, where the former is more aligned with open-source hacker culture and an ethos of cooperation, while the latter emphasizes many of the cyberlibertarian tendencies associated with Bitcoin. Dylan-Ennis et al. (2022) expand on the economic imaginary (Ethereum as money) and technical imaginary (Ethereum as a world computer), by including public goods as a political imaginary. They further illustrate how different groups within the Ethereum ecosystem (developers, entrepreneurs, speculators, creatives, grifters, and others) draw on various imaginaries to define and redefine the purpose of Ethereum in their given contexts. Drawing on this analysis and extending it to the context of Web3 (a subset or superset of Ethereum, depending on whom you ask), we believe that particularly the communities who identify with the world computer and public goods imaginaries may be interesting to investigate further to understand their internal beliefs regarding the particular legitimacy or illegitimacy of various institutional solutions. Communities identifying with the idea of a world computer place an extraordinarily high value on decentralization. The question is whether the value of decentralization is primarily defended in the technical sense or extends toward operational decentralization as well? If this is the case, these communities are likely to perceive many Web2 institutional arrangements as illegitimate due to their operational centralization in the form of large corporations. Communities identifying with the public goods imaginary are primarily concerned with devising ways to incentivize the production of goods beyond markets and (public) institutions as we know them. As such, the entire goal here is to devise new institutional arrangements. Consequently, communities that default back to the organizational models dominant in Web2 in times of uncertainty contradict their reason for existence. Instead, these communities are likely to develop their own institutional solutions to mimic in times of uncertainty, thus perpetuating divergence, not convergence, from Web2. Our example of the diffusion of the MolochDAO framework illustrates this point.

CONCLUSION

In this paper, we drew on the concept of institutional isomorphism to argue that Web3 faces a significant tension between its aspiration to be both different and big, to be carnivalesque and live forever. Using various examples to illustrate how the concepts put forward by institutional isomorphism can explain the mechanisms by which Web3 organizations begin to resemble each other and their external environment. The advantage of institutional isomorphic change for Web3 is likely to come in the form of increased legitimacy which is an important driver on the road to mainstream adoption. The disadvantage is the decline of difference and the slow, creeping regress back to the type of structures, organizations, and governance dynamics Web3 aspires to overturn. As possible pathways to counterbalance this negative outlook, we have argued that strengthening overall diversity in the space, strengthening the value of decentralization beyond technological considerations, and reaffirming Web3's commitment to creatively re-imagine institutional arrangements are promising paths to hedge against the carnival's end. In illustrating the tension through various examples and highlighting possible ways to navigate it, we have also attempted to make the more subtle point that for Web3 to be different, we must focus on people and the stories that bind them together, perhaps even more than focusing primarily on Web3's underlying technologies.

REFERENCES

Beckert, J. (2010). Institutional isomorphism revisited: Convergence and divergence in institutional change. *Sociological Theory*, 28(2), 150–166. https://doi.org/10.1111/j.1467-9558.2010.01369.x

Brody, A., & Couture, S. (2021). Ideologies and imaginaries in blockchain communities: The case of Ethereum. *Canadian Journal of Communication*, 46(3), 543–561. https://doi.org/10.22230/cjc.2021v46n3a3701

Buterin, V. (2021, March 21). *The most important scarce resource is legitimacy*. https://vitalik.ca/general/2021/03/23/legitimacy.html

Colbert, Z. (2022, August 18). *The BlackRock Trust: Crypto legitimacy or the beginning of the end for Bitcoin?* https://www.coindesk.com/layer2/2022/08/18/the-blackrock-trust-crypto-legitimacy-or-the-beginning-of-the-end-for-bitcoin/

DAOhaus. (n.d.). *DAOhaus*. Retrieved December 27, 2022, from https://daohaus.club/

David, R. J., Tolbert, P. S., & Boghossian, J. (2019, December 23). *Institutional theory in organization studies*. Oxford Research Encyclopedia of Business and Management. https://doi.org/10.1093/acrefore/9780190224851.013.158

Deephouse, D. L. (1996). Does isomorphism legitimate? *Academy of Management Journal*, 39(4), 1024–1039. https://doi.org/10.5465/256722

De Filippi, P., Mannan, M., Henderson, J., Merk, T., Cossar, S., & Nabben, K. (2022). *Report on blockchain technology & legitimacy* [Technical report, European University Institute]. https://doi.org/10.2870/34617

DiMaggio, P. J., & Powell, W. W. (1983). The iron cage revisited: Institutional isomorphism and collective rationality in organizational fields. *American Sociological Review*, 48(2), 147–160. https://doi.org/10.2307/2095101

Dixon, C. (2021, October 7). *Why Web3 matters*. Future. https://future.com/why-web3-matters/

Dylan-Ennis, P., Kavanagh, D., & Araujo, L. (2022). The dynamic imaginaries of the Ethereum project. *Economy and Society*, 52(1), 1–23. https://doi.org/10.1080/03085147.2022.2131280

Frumkin, P., & Galaskiewicz, J. (2004). Institutional isomorphism and public sector organizations. *Journal of Public Administration Research and Theory*, *14*(3), 283–307.

FTX.com. (2022). Retrieved August 30, 2022, from https://about.ftx.us/

Graham, S. (2022, March 5). *What the devil are Moloch DAOs, and why should you care?* https://daohaus.mirror.xyz/U_JQtheSzdpRFqQwf9Ow3LgLNG0WMZ6ibAyrjWDu_fc

Hannan, M. T., & Freeman, J. (1977). The population ecology of organizations. *American Journal of Sociology*, *82*(5), 929–964. https://doi.org/10.1086/226424

Hoefer, R., & Ha, S. E. (2022a, April 30). *Are DAOs organizations with a shared onchain bank account? Maybe not*. The DAO Book. https://www.thedaobook.io/are-daos-organizations-with-a-shared-onchain-bank-account-maybe-not/

Hoefer, R., & Ha, S. E. (2022b, April 12). *What is the difference between product DAOs and community DAOs?* The DAO Book. https://www.thedaobook.io/product-daos-and-community-daos-and-progressive-decentralization-mvc-mvp-pd/

Kastrenakes, J. (2021, December 21). *Jack Dorsey says VCs really own Web3 (and Web3 boosters are pretty mad about it)*. The Verge. https://www.theverge.com/2021/12/21/22848162/jack-dorsey-web3-criticism-a16z-owners-hip-venture-capital-twitter

Laul, M. (2022, February 16). *Isomorphism in DAO governance*. Medium. https://mariolaul.medium.com/isomorphism-in-dao-governance-43abb7a546d8

Marlinspike, M. (2022, July 1). *My first impressions of web3*. https://moxie.org/2022/01/07/web3-first-impressions.html

Maurer, B., Nelms, T. C., & Swartz, L. (2013). "When perhaps the real problem is money itself!": The practical materiality of Bitcoin. *Social Semiotics*, *23*(2), 261–277. https://doi.org/10.1080/10350330.2013.777594

Meyer, J. W., & Jepperson, R. L. (2000). The "actors" of modern society: The cultural construction of social agency. *Sociological Theory*, *18*(1), 100–120. https://doi.org/10.1111/0735-2751.00090

Meyer, J. W., & Rowan, B. (1977). Institutionalized organizations: Formal structure as myth and ceremony. *American Journal of Sociology*, *83*(2), 340–363. https://doi.org/10.1086/226550

Ooki DAO. (2022, September 22). *CFTC imposes $250,000 penalty against bZeroX, LLC and its founders and charges successor Ooki DAO for offering illegal, off-exchange digital-asset trading, registration violations, and failing to comply with bank secrecy act*. https://www.cftc.gov/PressRoom/PressReleases/8590-22

OpenSea. (2022). *Careers*. Retrieved August 30, 2022, from https://opensea.io/careers

Quittner, D. J. (2021, October 24). *Why do you think it's called discord?* Decrypt. https://decrypt.co/84049/why-do-you-think-its-called-discord

rationalaussie. (2022, June 1). https://twitter.com/rationalaussie/status/1478983282226122756. Twitter. https://twitter.com/rationalaussie/status/1478983282226122756

Roose, K. (2022, March 18). What is web3? *The New York Times*. https://www.nytimes.com/interactive/2022/03/18/technology/web3-definition-internet.html

Rosati, P., Lynn, T., & Fox, G. (2021). Blockchain: A technology in search of legitimacy. In S. Patnaik, T.-S. Wang, T. Shen, & S. K. Panigrahi (Eds.), *Blockchain technology and innovations in business processes* (pp. 17–32). Springer. https://doi.org/10.1007/978-981-33-6470-7_2

Siebert, A. (2021, August 16). Regulating crypto is essential to ensuring its global legitimacy. *TechCrunch*. https://techcrunch.com/2021/08/16/regulating-crypto-is-essential-to-ensuring-its-global-legitimacy/

Stackpole, T. (2022, May 10). What is Web3? *Harvard Business Review*. https://hbr.org/2022/05/what-is-web3

Still, D. (2021, November 15). *Introduction to Web 3.0* [Substack newsletter]. Growth Investing Newsletter. https://davidstill.substack.com/p/introduction-to-web-30

Strang, D., & Meyer, J. W. (1994). Institutional conditions for diffusion. In R. W. Scott & J. W. Meyer (Eds.), *Institutional environments and organizations: Structural complexity and individualism* (pp. 100–111). Sage.

Suchman, M. C. (1995). Managing legitimacy: Strategic and institutional approaches. *The Academy of Management Review*, *20*(3), 571. https://doi.org/10.2307/258788

Swartz, L. (2018). What was Bitcoin, what will it be? The techno-economic imaginaries of a new money technology. *Cultural Studies, 32*(4), 623–650. https://doi.org/10.1080/09502386.2017.1416420

Teodoro, M. P. (2014). When professionals lead: Executive management, normative isomorphism, and policy implementation. *Journal of Public Administration Research and Theory, 24*(4), 983–1004.

Tolbert, P. S., & Zucker, L. (1983). Institutional sources of change in the formal structure of organizations: The diffusion of civil service reform 1880–1935. *Administrative Science Quarterly, 30*, 22–39.

Walden, J. (2020, January 9). *Progressive decentralization: A playbook for building crypto applications*. Andreessen Horowitz. https://a16z.com/2020/01/09/progressive-decentralization-crypto-product-management/

What is Web3 and why is it important? (n.d.). Ethereum.Org. Retrieved April 2, 2024, from https://ethereum.org/en/web3/

HASH, BASH, CASH: HOW CHANGE HAPPENS IN DECENTRALIZED WEB3 CULTURES

Paul Dylan-Ennis

University College Dublin, Ireland

ABSTRACT

A Web3 lifeworld consists of an imaginary and a shared commons. A Web3 imaginary is shown to include most, if not all, of the following: (i) the stated goal or purpose of the community, (ii) the behavioral norms, (iii) the lore or history, and (iv) what is opposed. A typical Web3 commons is shown to involve three elements: hash (technical), bash (social) and cash (finance). When changes come in Web3, the response is enacted using an available lever from the hash, bash, cash model of decentralized organization, but the response must not be in friction with the community's imaginary, or it will most likely grind to a halt. Effective response to change becomes part of the Web3 lifeworld's toolkit.

Keywords: Ethereum; Web3; decentralized autonomous organizations; decentralized finance; non-fungible tokens

WEB3 CULTURES

Culture, rather than finance or technology, drives change in Web3. Before there is a blockchain or a token, there is a cultural drive to create them. When the blockchain has a hiccup, it is culture Web3 communities fall back to.

Culture is understood here as the "lifeworld" of the community (Carr, 1970). The lifeworld is what a community takes to be self-evident at a "slice of time." It is not meant as a cultural essence people are imbued with. Instead, the lifeworld is self-evident, but also always evolving little by little, constantly negotiated with (Williams, 1989, p. 13). Culture is the currently accepted self-evident context held by a community.

The concept of the lifeworld is introduced to first help put form on Web3 culture and second to explain how change is enacted in Web3 cultures using the hash, bash, cash model of decentralized organization.

Let's start with the first goal, putting form on Web3 cultures. A typical Web3 culture consists of an *imaginary* (or imaginaries) and a *commons*. Taken together, these form a Web3 lifeworld.

Charles Taylor provides a broad summary of an imaginary:

> [...] a sense of the normal expectations that we have of one another, the kind of common understanding which enables us to carry out the collective practices that make up our social life. This incorporates some sense of how we all fit together in carrying out the common practice. This understanding is both factual and "normative"; that is, we have a sense of how things usually go, but this is interwoven with an idea of how they ought to go, of what missteps would invalidate the practice. (Taylor, 2002, p. 106)

In the social science literature on cryptocurrencies, imaginaries have played an important role. At first, the concept was implicit. Maurer et al. (2013) highlighted the paradox of how the Bitcoin community is sustained by a social discourse about removing the social and political dimensions from money (p. 274). Dodd (2018), Schneider (2019), and Caliskan (2022) consolidated this argument, and all claim Bitcoin's proposed asocial system of money is, in practice, sustained by its sociality. Lustig and Nardi (2015) showed how users of Bitcoin had become aware of these social paradoxes of Bitcoin over time, but still valued its core principles.

As Bitcoin matured, the literature turned to the question of whether its commitment to decentralization had been delivered upon. Böhme et al. (2015) were the first to comprehensively chart the complicated nexus of stakeholders present in the Bitcoin system and how in its practical implementation Bitcoin was full of centralized chokepoints. De Filippi and Loveluck (2016) went further and proposed that Bitcoin's governance can be divided between a visible blockchain infrastructural layer and an invisible developer management layer that shapes it, suggesting the developers sometimes operate in an undemocratic manner. A later article by Reijers and Coeckelbergh (2018) calls this the distinction between on-chain and off-chain governance, in contrast to the Bitcoin rhetoric that emphasizes only the former.

It is in the work of Swartz (2018) that the association of Bitcoin with imaginaries was consolidated. She argued that Bitcoin's culture emerged from a blend of crypto-anarchism and cypherpunk. Crypto-anarchism is expressed in Bitcoin through the imaginary of digital metallism, which proposes Bitcoin as a sound money alternative to state-controlled fiat currencies. Bitcoin is scarce digital gold, controlled not by the state but by algorithmic code (in theory). In turn, the cypherpunk imaginary is infrastructural mutualism, which draws on the free software tradition concerned with privacy and online surveillance.

Kow and Lustig (2018) focused on the distinction between the *abstract* imaginaries guiding Bitcoin culture (decentralization, removal of intermediaries) and the *concrete* imaginaries (the actual implemented software solutions) that move the project forward. They found that tensions between the abstract and the concrete were productive and forced different stakeholders to converge or "crystallise" a solution (p. 225). Husain et al. (2020) uncovered three imaginaries operative in the wider ecosystem: crypto-libertarians, crypto-commonists, crypto-governmentalisms, while recognizing they shared a prefigurative *ethos* (see also Nabben, 2023). Most recently, Brody and Couture (2021) argued that when it comes to imaginaries, Ethereum "is best characterized as a space where different ideological horizons cohabitate while leaning decidedly toward the left" (p. 14) (see also Dylan-Ennis et al., 2022).

WEB3 IMAGINARIES

Adapting to local conditions, a Web3 imaginary includes most, if not all, of the following: (i) the stated goal or purpose of the community, (ii) the behavioral norms, (iii) the lore or history, and (iv) what is opposed.

Let's apply this to four examples within the broader story of cryptocurrency and Web3.

Bitcoin: (i) Bitcoin's (current) purpose is to be digital gold. (ii) It is expected this will be achieved in a decentralized manner. (iii) This is in keeping with the early ideals of its missing founder Satoshi Nakamoto. (iv) Bitcoin opposes the inherited fiat monetary system. Note the purpose has evolved over time. Originally, Bitcoin was presented as an electronic cash with gold-like features, but this conception of Bitcoin has changed over time, now leaning more to the gold motif than cash.

Ethereum: (i) Ethereum's purpose is to be a world computer. (ii) It is expected that this will be achieved in a decentralized manner. (iii) This ideal has been negotiated among influential leaders and members over time. (iv) Ethereum opposes the centralization characteristic of Web 2.0.

Decentralized autonomous organization (DAO) culture: (i) DAOs allow distributed online communities to self-organize. (ii) It is expected this will be achieved in a decentralized manner. (iii) DAOs were once set up to be purely algorithmic (see DuPont, 2017) but were forced to change by *The DAO* hack, enabling a new social conception of DAOs. (iv) DAOs oppose traditional hierarchical forms of organization, such as corporate models.

Decentralized finance (DeFi) culture: (i) DeFi allows for permissionless finance. (ii) It is expected that this will be achieved in a decentralized manner. (iii) DeFi exploded during DeFi summer, amid the pandemic. (iv) DeFi opposes traditional financial institutions, such as banks and Wall Street.

Non-fungible Token (NFT) culture: (i) NFTs enable the creative ownership economy. (ii) It is (somewhat) expected that this will be achieved in a decentralized manner. (iii) NFTs exploded in popularity through the creation of profile picture collections such as CryptoPunks. (iv) NFTs present an alternative to the established art world.

Most researchers will naturally be operating at a more granular level and tell us about the imaginaries of say *Uniswap* or *Bored Ape Yacht Club*. Grounding a project as a Web3 imaginary helps put cultural form on Web3 projects. It tells us what is important to the specific community but rooting this importance within the wider Web3 meta-culture. For example, it becomes readily apparent when performing analyses of Web imaginaries that decentralization is the most consistent meta-principle, but just as much that each community spins the meaning of decentralization their own way: reinventing money, reinventing the Web, reinventing art, etc.

Imaginaries are the cultural bedrock underlying these Web3 worlds, but imaginaries are in a constant negotiation with both their inner and outer worlds. When an imaginary is prodded, it responds. Responses are usually habitual, built on accumulated know-how, but also each new event is adding to that know-how, an update. On occasion, the prod will be major and may occasion major reflection and reinvention.

The situation at any moment is akin to Heidegger's workshop (Dreyfus, 1990). In this scene, the tradesman is hammering away without a thought in the world. For Heidegger, we are most at home when we are in the unconscious flow of doing or when things are ready-to-hand. Readiness-to-hand means a state when the context recedes from view and everything is working without friction.

Then there is a knock on the door, there is a phone call, the hammer breaks. When the flow-state is broken, we enter a state of conscious reflection, where things appear present-at-hand. In this more abstract and theoretical mindset, we seek to fix the situation in order to get back to the flow of readiness-to-hand.

In contemporary technology studies, Heidegger's ready-to-hand/present-at-hand model has been transfigured onto infrastructural terms by Star and Ruhleder (1996). In this translation, infrastructures that work well disappear from view and conscious thought. When the infrastructure breaks, such as the Internet suddenly not working, it emerges starkly in view as present-at-hand, a problem to be fixed.

Unlike the slow-and-steady examples that populate Heidegger or Star and Ruhleder, Web3 infrastructure does not recede from view most of the time. Infrastructure is called up early and often prodded by a teenage, angsty ecosystem constantly on the edge of chaos. It is therefore necessary for Web3 cultures to have highly distributed and well-known mechanisms that the community can leverage, *quick*!

THE HASH, BASH, CASH MODEL OF DECENTRALIZED ORGANIZATION

In Web3, this model soon becomes apparent to those immersed in it (or those who observe as academic researchers). It does not have a native term. There is not often reflection on the model or how it works. Instead, the model exists as a prefigurative praxis that can be called upon at any moment. I call it the hash, bash, cash model of decentralized organization (Dylan-Ennis, 2021).

Let's take Ethereum as a meta-example of a Web3 culture. When Ethereum needs to enact change, this change must flow through its technical (hash), social (bash), and financial (cash) spaces. These three spaces are *the commons*, the second dimension of a Web3 lifeworld.

Every Web3 culture has a commons, a shared space each community member cares for, albeit to different degrees. I use the word "care" here carefully. It is meant in Heidegger's sense as investment in a world. Investment in the broadest possible sense: psychological, social, empathetic, financial, etc. Not everything is financial, not even in Web3.

In our Ethereum example, we find a community that cares about a shared digital commons that comprises three spaces: hash, bash, cash.

Hash refers to the technical dimension of a Web3 project. It usually involves core infrastructure such as a blockchain, smart contracts, voting tools (like Snapshot), etc. Web3 communities imbue on-chain decisions with a true decisiveness because what happens on-chain is as close to the truth as one can get. On-chain is truth-adjacent. In Ethereum's case, the technical dimension is the Ethereum blockchain as the canonical state of the "world computer."

Bash refers to the social dimension of a Web3 project. It usually involves a set of community discussions outlets, such as Reddit, a Discord server, Twitter, governance forums, etc. The social world is the town hall where the community generates chatter about the latest drama but also where community consensus organically emerges. It is the "eye test" where debates occur a little ad hoc, but slowly people begin to gain a sense of the popularity of certain ideas. When these ideas gain a backing – qualitatively sensed, not quantitatively measured – they will often be formalized and put into proposals, such as Ethereum's Ethereum Improvement Proposal system.

Cash refers to the financial dimension of a Web3 project. It typically concerns the relevant micro-economy impacting community members. It can be a native blockchain token (like Ether), a token built on another blockchain (like Shiba Inu built on Ethereum), or it might mean the community treasury overseen by a DAO. As in the real world, economic concerns diminish during the good times, known as bull runs, but then become contentious in the bad times, known as bear markets or Crypto Winter. In the case of Ethereum, the cash dimension relates to the management of the native currency Ether, but the Ether price also acts as a barometer for the overall health of the Web3 ecosystem.

HOW CHANGE HAPPENS IN DECENTRALIZED WEB3 CULTURES

Internal and external shocks to the system are routine in Web3 cultures. Change, volatility, and chaos are the norm. Stability is an unusual, suspicious event, like the calm before the storm. Let's take a look at a classic DeFi internal shock, courtesy of SushiSwap.

SushiSwap is a protocol for swapping tokens on Ethereum. It originated in 2020 out of an infamous "vampire attack," where SushiSwap copied the codebase of the established token-swapping protocol Uniswap but added an extra token as incentive for users to migrate their liquidity over to SushiSwap's liquidity pools.

In terms of its *imaginary*, SushiSwap contains all the traits of a pure DeFi project, arguably even its paradigmatic case. It allows for permissionless finance, its community believe that this is to be achieved in a decentralized manner, its lore is deeply rooted in the original 2020 DeFi summer, and it takes a populist stance against traditional financial institutions.

In terms of its *commons*, SushiSwap is a smart contract protocol for token swapping. It is run as a DAO through blockchain governance (hash), a community that organizes on a dedicated Discord and Telegram, with a governance forum (bash) and finally a community treasury, currently $17 million in various crypto assets (cash).

Yet, SushiSwap almost collapsed before it even got going. Back in September 2020, its leader, known only by the pseudonym Chef Nomi, decided to transfer $14 million worth of Ether from the SushiSwap "developer fund" to a personal wallet. In this early era of DeFi culture, it was not uncommon for a founder to have unilateral power to do this. This is about as internal a shock as it gets; the founder has stolen the community treasury!

How to enact the appropriate response in a decentralized Web3 culture like SushiSwap? Response travels through the commons. Not linearly, of course, but messily, allowing emergent consensus within the chaotic conditions of a distributed online culture.

In SushiSwap's case, the job was to get the *cash* (the community "developer fund") back into the *hash* (an Ethereum wallet under the control of the community, ideally now a multisig or multi-person wallet). The solution can only arise from within the community since there is no central authority who could intervene on their behalf.

In Web3 cultures, the difficulty of the response's travels through the commons depends on how much friction it generates with the imaginary. This is the key to understanding how change happens in decentralized Web3 cultures. Too many sparks and a response grinds to a halt.

The successful response within the SushiSwap community came from the *bash* part of the commons. The solution could not be technical because – per the DeFi imaginary – it is not possible to simply reverse the transaction through centralized mechanisms. They don't exist. Instead, the community applied pressure where it could, socially.

The SushiSwap community first started to dig into the identity of Chef Nomi. This did not result in a clear answer but made apparent to Chef Nomi that his (or her or their) life would be one of the fugitive, with the community constantly on their tail.

This pressure caused Chef Nomi to transfer the money over to cryptocurrency exchange owner Sam Bankman-Fried, who then helped migrate the funds over to a multisig wallet, restoring the old order. From *bash* to *hash*.

This solution traveled through the commons frictionlessly because it did not violate any of the core principles of the DeFi imaginary. Contrary to popular conception, Web3 cultures do not suddenly become inert when faced with the lack of a technical solution. Or the lack of a centralized mechanism. Instead, they are content to evoke social solutions so long as they are not in contradiction with their cultural beliefs, their imaginary.

CONCLUSION: WEB3 LIFEWORLDS

A Web3 lifeworld consists of an imaginary and a shared commons. To the community, the life world is a self-evident slice of time, but it's also an evolving world, usually incrementally.

When changes come in Web3, as it constantly does, the response is enacted using an available lever from the hash, bash, cash model of decentralized organization. This shared commons of tools, techniques, and methods (the know-how) must not be in friction with the community's imaginary, or it will most likely grind to a halt.

Once the response has flowed through the commons without friction, the habitual know-how is updated and refined. When the issue is settled, the community went back to unconscious flow.

The accumulated know-how is deepened. Next time the SushiSwap community needed it, the *bash* tool box includes social pressure based on crowdsourced investigation.

REFERENCES

Böhme, R., Christin, N., Edelman, B., & Moore, T. (2015). Bitcoin: Economics, technology, and governance. *Journal of Economic Perspectives*, 29(2), Article 2. https://doi.org/10.1257/jep.29.2.213

Brody, A., & Couture, S. (2021). Ideologies and imaginaries in blockchain communities: The case of Ethereum. *Canadian Journal of Communication*, 46(3), Article 3. https://doi.org/10.22230/cjc.2021v46n3a3701

Caliskan, K. (2022). The rise and fall of Electra: Emergence and transformation of a global cryptocurrency community. *Review of Social Economy*. https://www.tandfonline.com/action/showCitForMats?doi=10.1080%2F00346764.2022.2039404

Carr, D. (1970). Husserl's problematic concept of the life-world. *American Philosophical Quarterly*, 7(4), 331–339.

De Filippi, P., & Loveluck, B. (2016). The invisible politics of Bitcoin: Governance crisis of a decentralised infrastructure. *Internet Policy Review*, 5(3), Article 3.

Dodd, N. (2018). The social life of Bitcoin. *Theory, Culture & Society*, 35(3), Article 3. https://doi.org/10.1177/0263276417746464

Dreyfus, H. L. (1990). *Being-in-the-world: A commentary on Heidegger's being in time, division I*. MIT Press.

DuPont, Q. (2017). 'Experiments in algorithmic governance: A history and ethnography of "The DAO," a failed decentralized autonomous organization'. In M. Campbell-Verduyn (Ed.), *Bitcoin and beyond: cryptocurrencies, blockchains, and global governance* (pp. 157–177). Routledge. https://doi.org/10.4324/9781315211909-8

Dylan-Ennis, P. (2021). Teaching cryptocurrencies as cryptocultures. *Journal of Applied Learning and Teaching*, 4(2), Article 2. https://doi.org/10.37074/jalt.2021.4.2.12

Dylan-Ennis, P., Kavanagh, D., & Araujo, L. (2022). The dynamic imaginaries of the Ethereum project. *Economy and Society*, 52(1), 1–23. https://doi.org/10.1080/03085147.2022.2131280

Husain, S. O., Franklin, A., & Roep, D. (2020). The political imaginaries of blockchain projects: Discerning the expressions of an emerging ecosystem. *Sustainability Science*, 15(2), 379–394. https://doi.org/10.1007/s11625-020-00786-x

Kow, Y. M., & Lustig, C. (2018). Imaginaries and crystallization processes in Bitcoin infrastructuring. *Computer Supported Cooperative Work (CSCW)*, *27*(2), Article 2. https://doi.org/10.1007/s10606-017-9300-2

Lustig, C., & Nardi, B. (2015). Algorithmic authority: The case of Bitcoin. In *2015 48th Hawaii international conference on system sciences* (pp. 743–752). https://ieeexplore.ieee.org/xpl/conhome/7068092/proceeding

Maurer, B., Nelms, T. C., & Swartz, L. (2013). "When perhaps the real problem is money itself!": The practical materiality of Bitcoin. *Social Semiotics*, *23*(2), Article 2. https://doi.org/10.1080/10350330.2013.777594

Nabben, K. (2023). Web3 as 'self-infrastructuring': The challenge is how. *Big Data & Society*, *10*(1). https://doi.org/10.1177/20539517231159002

Reijers, W., & Coeckelbergh, M. (2018). The blockchain as a narrative technology: Investigating the social ontology and normative configurations of cryptocurrencies. *Philosophy & Technology*, *31*(1), Article 1. https://doi.org/10.1007/s13347-016-0239-x

Schneider, N. (2019). Decentralization: An incomplete ambition. *Journal of Cultural Economy*, *12*(4), Article 4. https://doi.org/10.1080/17530350.2019.1589553

Star, S. L., & Ruhleder, K. (1996). Steps toward an ecology of infrastructure: Design and access for large information spaces. *Information Systems Research*, *7*(1), Article 1.

Swartz, L. (2018). What was Bitcoin, what will it be? The techno-economic imaginaries of a new money technology. *Cultural Studies*, *32*(4), Article 4. https://doi.org/10.1080/09502386.2017.1416420

Taylor, C. (2002). Modern social imaginaries. *Public Culture*, *14*(1), 91–124.

Williams, R. (1989). *Culture*. Fontana Press.

PART 2

VAUDEVILLE

POLITICAL ECONOMY OF THE CRYPTO-ART CRAZE

Geert Lovink

Institute of Network Cultures, The Netherlands

ABSTRACT

This paper explores the rise of non-fungible tokens (NFTs) and their impact on the art world. By examining the esthetics and political economy of crypto art and its relationship to online pop culture, it questions the value of NFTs and whether they truly represent a source of income for artists or simply contribute to the speculative nature of crypto investments. This paper concludes by asserting that the world of crypto art is dominated by right-wing libertarians and black box algorithms, and that a radical redistribution of wealth is necessary to address the issues of power, race, and gender within the industry.

Keywords: Crypto; criticism; arts; media theory; blockchain; NFTs

"Every time I think I've sorted out my life, capitalism collapses." Juliet – "One character asks the other what he likes. The answer is money. 'I can't believe you like money too!' the first character says without irony, 'We should hang out!'" Idiocracy – "My ultimate dream job is to trade labor for capital." Darcie Wilder – "Which artist was the wealthiest in Renaissance Florence? Neri di Bicci. Second wealthiest? Andrea di Giusto Manzini. Heard of either of them?" @hravg – "If you have a problem, use blockchain. Now you have two problems and a right-libertarian fan club." Aral Balkan – "Money is a meme and now that memes are money we don't need money, we just need memes." @punk4156 – "If you don't get it, have fun being poor." Bitcoin sayings.

When the Homer Pepe non-fungible token (NFT) sold for $223,000, Barry Threw cheered: "The art world is a software problem now." Let's return to the early 2021 crypto art wave. Here, newly created speculative "assets"[i] are financed with lavish amounts of "funny money," superfluous cash that is spent on even more speculative ventures. The choice of the young crypto-millionaires not to stash their profits away in investment funds or real estate is the most likely explanation for the NFT boom.[ii] In line with 1990s start-up values, the newly acquired wealth should not be invested in fine art paintings or laudable charities but continue to circulate inside the tech scene itself. The only aim of the virtual is to further expand the virtual: a boom that fuels the next boom. What else should one purchase after the Miami condo and the Lambo? It's easy, *épater les bourgeois*: refuse to be patrons. Unlike colonial and carbon money, the information technology (IT) rich are not interested in living forever and becoming esteemed supporters of avant-garde fine arts, architecture, or classical music. The surprising twist here is their sudden interest in digital arts.

D. Gerard (2021) explains how the hype, commonly known as Web3, started:

> Tell artists there's a gusher of free money! They need to buy into crypto to get the gusher of free money. They become crypto advocates and make excuses for proof-of-work. Few artists really are making life-changing money from this! You probably won't be one of them.

As Brett Scott (2021) explains, crypto-hype promises artists they are destined for market greatness. But such hype, driven by males, can only take off if everyone buys into it. "Far from saving you from bullshit jobs, trading is a bullshit job, and the only way to temporarily win at it is not to throw yourself into battle against 'the market.' It's to collaborate in swarms." The moment the hype takes off is the ultimate reward for the struggling pioneer. As Chelsea Summers (2021) quips: "There is nothing as sweet as professional vindication after years of people rejecting your work, underestimating your value, and generally dismissing you. And by you I mean me. And by professional vindication I mean money."

Take Hashmasks and Cryptopunk, fixed number of storage places that make it easy to buy, sell, and compare similar images ("collectables"). Here, the speculative game is most obvious. The top 10 images sold on Cryptopunk during the February–April 2021 hype period were priced between $1.46 and $7.57 million, proving Mazzucato's thesis that value had become subjective.[iii] It is telling that online details about the transactions fail to mention a description of the works, let alone their esthetics, reducing the artworks to numbers such as #7804 or #3396. While "famous" NFT artworks may be handpicked by Sotheby's experts, gallerists, critics, and curators, it is not (yet) clear where buyers can go to resell such works. While the details are lacking, the overall logic is clear: artworks are stored value, that value is expected to rise, and these staggering prices will continue to be designated in fiat currency. While bitcoin (BTC) or Ethereum (ETH) may rise and fall and the blockchain could vanish altogether, the scheme assumes this will never happen and that these "rare" digital artworks will keep their value.

"Art history will be seen as before and after NFTs," says @Hans2024. What is art at the crossroads of the game, virtual reality (VR), bitcoin, and social media experience? For some, there is an element of magic in buying a piece of "rare art." For others, like Sybil Prentice, NFTs have a garage sale vibe: leftovers of an accelerated online life in which image production and consumption happens at a relentless pace

(@nightcoregirl, 2021). Yet whether positive or negative, it's clear that crypto art and NFTs alter the landscape of art. As Derek Schloss and Stephen McKeon (2020) state, "in a natively digital medium, art takes on a more expansive role, intersecting with virtual worlds, decentralized finance, and the social experience." Before digging into the tale of NFTs, let's look at the broader narrative around blockchain, crypto, and the future of digital money.

We can define crypto art as rare digital artworks, published onto a blockchain, in the form of NFTs. Crypto art is not just any image but comes with a distinct style, a particular esthetic that goes with the territory. Let's therefore study the esthetics of the pioneers back in 2014. The common cultural references here are not New York's *Artforum* or Berlin's *Texte zur Kunst* but the online pop culture of imageboards: memes, anime, Pokémon cards, and the like. Jerry Saltz (2021): "Most NFT so far is either Warhol Pop-y; Surrealism redux; animated cartoon-y; faux-Japanese Anime; boring Ab-Ex abstraction; logo swirling around commercial; cute/scary gif; glitzy screensaver; late Neo-conceptual NFT about NFT-ism. All Of those are NFT Zombie Formalism." In short, what's striking is the overall retrograde style, as if we're stuck in a loop, forever repeating *Groundhog Day*. The settings are copy-pasted from American science-fiction films and comic books and projected into today's game environment.

NFTs are based on the assumption that scarcity is a good thing that needs to be reintroduced. Scarcity creates the possibility of value skyrocketing and speculation, which may in turn attract investors. The fatal destiny of the artwork is to become unique. Ours is an anti-Benjamin moment when digital art in the age of technical reproduction makes its big leap back into the 18th century. At the same time, we need to remind ourselves that "decentralized finance" is an alternative reality, driven by libertarian principles, fed by a temporary abundance of specific free money and a religious belief in technology that will save humankind. Digital reproduction and "piracy" are no longer the default. Those who disagree with this premise would need to become hackers (again), cracking the code in order to enjoy the artwork. Is this the only way of making a living, to become "rare" again?

Back to the screen; @lunar_mining's tweets are refreshing. "I love stormy days when the market is dumping. Feels healthy and cathartic – as natural as the seasons." I contacted @lunar_mining because of a critical tweet:

> NFTs =! digital art. NFTs replicate the mechanics of the art marketplace, but I've yet to see an NFT with meaning or soul or abyssal depth. There's an emptiness to NFT trading, a nihilism: it is a marketplace without ideas.

The person behind the address is the artist and former CoinDesk editor Rachel-Rose O'Leary. I asked her opinion about crypto art. Rachel-Rose: "There's a low-level boyish signaling out there but also some nuance that is emerging. For example, you can see the early stages of meme culture fusing with collectibles, which is potentially a powerful combination."

For Rose, art ended with Sol Lewitt, who said that the idea becomes the machine that makes the art. This realization contains the key to art's exit from itself. Crypto is an idea turned into a machine. It is the crystallization of ideas into architecture. By binding narrative to a machine, crypto has the potential not simply to describe the world but to actively shape reality. "In a world of unprecedented political urgency, contemporary art has retreated into subjective delusions. In contrast, crypto offers a powerful regenerative vision. That's why I'm expending my energy here rather than the art world." She observes a hollowing out of culture in general. "Art on the art market shares the same overpriced, pop-culture feel as the current NFT market, related to a declining culture industry and the behavior of markets than NFTs or crypto culture itself."

Is the essence of art that it should appeal to (crypto)investors? "NFT platforms aren't competing with the auction house or gallery – they're competing with Patreon," tweets Tina Rivers Ryan. Are these patrons the medieval cardinals of today? Here we see how the perverse logic of the art market can become internalized into the mind of the artist. According to Robert Saint Rich (2020),

> the influence of social media has created a perspective in artists that they need to produce masterful quality works in a large enough quantity so that they can be shared on an almost daily basis. This is an impossible standard that forces artists to create uninspired work.

Artists create banal artwork for banal tastes, hoping to give their pieces popular appeal. But paradoxically, the aim of investors was never to collect art pieces. The crypto art system is a financial system, putting creators into peer-to-peer contact with the nouveau riche of today: the crypto millionaires. While we may critique this situation, it cannot be undone. A return to "normal" is no longer on the cards. This is a digital world; we've passed the point of "newness." Crypto art belongs to that moment in the history of contemporary arts when both painting and conceptual art forms are becoming impossible.

Let's define what we encounter here as "admin art" that solely exists on a ledger. While there was no Excel art that we know of as a genre, there was net.art, video art, new media art, sound art, electronic arts …. It is in fact the ledger that defines the art form, not cryptography as such. Admin art fits into that cloud of temporary buzzwords. However, for the sake of the argument, let's stick to this misnomer called crypto art: meta-tagged online images, defined by their desire to become a record, to obtain a timestamp, to embody a digital unit of value. The value is inscribed inside the work, readable by machines. Crypto art is retrograde in that it wants to put the genie back in the bottle and create digital originals. Its innovation claims to fix past structural mistakes. What it shares with the avant-garde is its initial unacceptability. The discontent of crypto arts lies in the perverse obsession to get onto the ledger.

Admin art is what art becomes when it is defined by geeks. These geeks dress up as notaries and play-act at being lawyers, fastidiously policing "authenticity records." At the center of all this is the notion of ownership and the promise of being "securely stored on the blockchain" (Connor, 2021). How is an artwork purchased and ownership transferred? First you need to setup a digital wallet on a smartphone and purchase some cryptocurrency (usually Ethereum in the case of crypto art). Then, we visit the website with the art pieces. The interface is structured in typical fashion, with "top sellers" and "top buyers" conforming to the established "most viewed" influencer logic. We then have recently added works, followed by a section where you can "explore" the cheapest or highest priced NFTs.

As in the case with any platform these days, the user design is profile centric. Only after creating a profile, one is able to purchase and "mint" an artwork. Either there will be an instant sale price or one set by an auction.

The most obvious issue one has to deal with is connectivity to the internet. But alongside this, there is a stack of necessities, from cloud services to browsers, operating systems, the Ethereum currency, the blockchain, the wallet, and platforms like Opensea and Foundation, each with their own layers of services, networks, and transaction fees. So where exactly, in this soup of platforms and protocols, is the token ID?

If the production and distribution costs of digital art works tend toward zero, what does it feel like to produce worthless works? What are the mental costs, the "creative deficit" if one can freely copy-paste, steal motifs, and quote without consequences? While some celebrate the infinite number of possible combinations, others lament the culture of indifference this entails. This culture is driven by the promise of opportunity, the excitement of being in on the game. We're on the payment train. Instead of underground esthetics that need to be experienced firsthand, the focus of the artistic endeavor has shifted to storing value.

So, the excitement for crypto art is fed by an unspoken desire to disrupt the old Silicon Valley order and its outdated obsession with free things and free ideas. However, what remains is the central role of the market, which is run by a handful of platforms and managed by curators. Jargon like "hotbids" and "drops" seem to come from nowhere. This is by no means a move away from post-digital art (or post-internet art values, for that matter). Crypto art is material as hell. It cannot exist outside of data centers, undersea cables, servers, wallets, and the handheld devices of its traders. A substantial number of crypto artists draw on paper. The maker's ideology and practice is never far away.

In the debates, NFTs claim to be possible sources of income that fight mass precarity among artists and creative workers. Selling crypto art as unique works (or in limited series) is claimed to be an additional income stream for most producers. The demand of a Universal Basic Income will remain in place though. Highflying artists Beeple and Pak are the exception to the rule. Overinflated prices during a short hype cycle merely say something about the Tulipomania state of crypto, the wealthy that need to stash their money somewhere, creating a new right-wing libertarian class of under 30 crypto millionaires as a spin-off. Marketplaces for crypto art are, all too often, ways to temporarily store "funny money" elsewhere. What's prevented at all times is a sustainable financial solution. The ideology of speculative cryptocurrency hoarding and the demand of artists for a living wage are inherently incompatible.

Ledger technologies are, at their core, boring, administrative procedures. There is no artistic potential in them, other than the "art and money" engagement described by Max Haiven (2018) in his *Art After Money* book, which plays around with concepts such as the gift, exchange value, and symbolic exchange. The blockchain is, in essence, a follow-up to the excel sheet. There's no Excel Art – and for that the world can be thankful. We suffer enough from the bookkeeper logic. In the end, the NFT saga centered around a brief encounter between art and crypto start-ups. While in the past decades it was mostly real estate and other technologies that were used as objects of speculation, in this rare case, it was image board game-like images that were the privileged victims. For the blockchain, crowd art was just a test scenario. The platforms end up doing it for technology and money sake, without any interest in the life and works of artists – let alone in place of NFTs in art history.

Early 2021, the Italian art critic Domenico Quaranta (2022) wrote an NFT book, in Italian. A year later, he wrote an interesting update for the English translation, *Surfing With Satoshi – Art, Blockchain and NFTs*. The book is surprisingly balanced due to his insider's view and historical awareness of the burning issue how electronic artists are going to be paid in the digital age. In the historical chapter, he provides early examples of artists who experimented with certificates such as Yves Klein, Piero Manzoni, Sol LeWitt, and the Artist's Reserved Rights Transfer and Sale Agreement from 1971, drawn up by Seth Siegelaub and Robert Projansky. Via Hito Steyerl's *Duty Free Art* (2017), Quaranta arrives at issue how the market for new media/digital artworks is (not) operating. Despite the large sums paid in overvalued crypto-currencies (reaching its highest valuation early November 2021), the author questions if there is such a thing as "crypto art" – a safe bet after the crypto "market" lost two-thirds of its value.

This leaves us with the question of 99% of works circulating on exchanges like Nifty Gateway, SuperRare, Foundation, OpenSea, and others. Quaranta provides the reader with a quick overview of NFTs prehistory and early days of Jennifer and Kevin McCoy, rare Pepes, CryptoKiddies, and CryptoPunks that found their use in the Metaverse avatar profile market. But what about the rest? The long tail remains largely unresearched. What can be observed are ties to dreamy, dark anime esthetics and earlier image boards, varying from 4Chan and Reddit, Flickr, LiveJournal, Imgur to Pinterest. The shared culture consists of social media, memes, and image boards, not the contemporary arts gallery.

"Bitcoin is what you get when you'd rather see the world burn than trust another human being ever again," says Aral Balkan. Black box algorithms and right-wing libertarians are hegemonic givens here. Despite all the "democratic" promises, the crypto business is anything but decentralized and deeply dominated by racist right-wing techno-libertarians. This is out there, in the open, for everyone to see. Unless this is properly addressed, nothing will move on, certainly not in the art world. If the crypto community cannot discuss its own power, race, and gender issues, then why bother? The world is not in need of more billionaires but is instead crying out for a radical redistribution of wealth. Unless crypto starts to sabotage its own speculative dream machines such as decentralized finance (DeFi), decentralized autonomous organizations (DAOs), Web3, and its unholy alliance with metaverse will inevitably collapse, time and again.

NOTES

i. As Finn Brunton (2019) describes it, "it is a project of making the future into an object of knowledge" (p. 12).

ii. Read about the possible collapse scenarios for crypto art hype here: https://twitter.com/DCLBlogger/status/1365651253422776321. Market data can be found here: https://cryptoart.io/data.

iii. According to Mariana Mazzucato (2018), value became what consumers were prepared to pay. "All of a sudden, value was in the eye of the beholder. Any goods or services being sold at an agreed market price were by definition value-creating." A particular NFT may sell at auction for 100 USD or 100,000 USD, both valuations are real.

REFERENCES

Brunton, F. (2019). *Digital cash: The unknown history of the anarchists, utopians, and technologists who created cryptocurrency*. Princeton University Press.

Gerard, D. (2021, March 11). *NFTs: Crypto grifters try to scam artists again*. https://davidgerard.co.uk/blockchain/2021/03/11/nfts-crypto-grifters-try-to-scam-artists-again/

Haiven, M. (2018). *Art after money, money after art: Creative strategies against financialization*. Pluto Press.

Mazzucato, M. (2018). *The value of everything: Making and taking in the global economy*. PublicAffairs.

@nightcoregirl. (2021, April 18). *NFTs have a #GARAGESALE vibe rn* [Tweet]. Twitter. https://twitter.com/nightcoregirl/status/1383654340674547715

Quaranta, D. (2022). *Surfing with Satoshi: Art, blockchain and NFTs*. Aksioma.

Rich, R. (2020, December 26). *The influence of social media has created a perspective in artists that they need to produce masterful quality works in a large enough quantity ...* [Tweet]. Twitter. https://web.archive.org/web/20210520084016/https://twitter.com/fatherrich_/status/1343000927448535043

Saltz, J. [@jerrySaltz]. (2021, April 15). *Most NFT so far is either Warhol Pop-y; Surrealism redux; animated cartoon-y; faux-Japanese Anime; boring Ab-Ex abstraction; logo swirling around commercial; ....* [Tweet]. Twitter. https://twitter.com/jerrysaltz/status/1379056028969488390

Schloss, D., & McKeon, S. (2021, July 7). *You're sleeping on crypto art* [blog]. Collab+Currency. https://medium.com/collab-currency/youre-sleeping-on-crypto-art-7df920ec038e

Scott, B. (2021, January 30). The real lesson of the GameStop story is the power of the swarm. *The Guardian*. https://www.theguardian.com/commentisfree/2021/jan/30/gamestop-power-of-the-swarm-shares-traders

Steyerl, H. (2019). *Duty free art*. Verso.

Summers, C. (2021, October 7). Confessions of an angry middle-aged lady. *Oldster*. https://oldster.substack.com/p/confessions-of-an-angry-middle-aged

WHEN DIGITAL CARNIVAL? DISTRIBUTED CONTROL OF THE METAVERSE ASSET LAYER TO ENABLE CREATIVE DIGITAL EXPRESSION TO FLOURISH

Eric Alston

University of Colorado Boulder, USA

ABSTRACT

This paper argues that a coordinated network of independent producers is crucial in creating an immersive metaverse. A digital asset layer that is beyond the control of any single counterparty, along with reliable definition and exchange of fungible and non-fungible digital objects, is important for individual digital creative expression to flourish. Non-fungible digital objects are essential in creating an asset layer for a metaverse that approximates the full range of independent human creative expression. The development of non-fungible tokens (NFTs) alongside cryptocurrencies, governed by distributed and transparent control, can create an intermediation layer that is separate from the control of a platform intermediary.

Keywords: Digital governance; cryptocurrency; blockchain; NFTs; metaverse

A carnival is a beautiful expression of the human tendency to celebrate on a massive scale. It involves complex individual and coordinated human expression that far exceeds that of similar human tendencies to party among friends. Governing these large celebrations or festivals involves coordinating independent activities, which can also influence the extent and form of the independent activity that is possible. By necessity, some amount of independent bargaining power is essential for creative artisanal production to flourish. That is, for any metaverse to be immersive like a carnival or festival, it will need to involve independent creative input from many producers on a massive scale.

This paper discusses the importance of independent creative input from many producers on a massive scale to create an immersive metaverse like a carnival or festival. Pursuant to this aim, a digital asset layer that coordinates a network of independent producers should ideally be beyond the control of any single counterparty. This paper highlights that the reliable definition and exchange of fungible and non-fungible digital objects is necessary to enable digital creative expression to flourish.

Furthermore, non-fungible digital objects will play a necessary role alongside fungible tokens in creating an asset layer for a metaverse that approximates the range of independent human creative expression in the real world. However, the current applications of non-fungible tokens (NFTs) have considerable problems in achieving their intended functions beyond signifying ownership within a group that values formal recognition. Despite how far they have to go in terms of development, NFTs alongside cryptocurrencies can ideally create a more complete asset layer for digital contexts. Together with governance innovations surrounding distributed and transparent control of this asset layer, this stack of institutions and technology can create an intermediation layer that is at least partly independent from the control of a platform intermediary.

CREATIVE, LARGE-SCALE HUMAN CELEBRATIONS

Carnival – an instance of merrymaking, feasting, or masquerading; an organized program of entertainment or exhibition.

Festival – a time of celebration marked by special observances (1a); an often periodic celebration or program of events or entertainment having a specified focus.[1]

The formally celebrated carnival is typically associated with countries that have an extensive history, including colonial, with Roman Catholicism (Abreu & Brasil, 2020). However, historians of the now-global phenomenon attribute the wanton celebration of carnival to earlier pagan traditions of Bacchanalia, Saturnalia, and Lupercalia (Cudny, 2016). In a typical act of syncretism, carnival came to be celebrated prior to the period of fasting associated with Lent in the Catholic tradition (Cudny, 2014). But there is likely something much more universally human in this celebration. China, India, and the Arab world each have similar traditions of coming together to celebrate effusively, often until well after midnight. Whether it's the Chinese New Year, Diwali, or Eid Al-Fitr (to name just a few cherished non-Western celebrations!), periods of effusive communal celebration are part and parcel of the human tradition (Cudny, 2016). None of this is meant to belittle the fact that these distinct traditions are celebrating very different reasons or beliefs underlying the specific date of a given celebration. Instead, it is to suggest that the carnival tradition is an expression of something more integrally human. Where the Catholic tradition of carnival did not spread, county and state fairs, rodeos, and even festivals like Burning Man represent a similar effusive space for human interaction.

What do carnival attendees around the world have in common? They tend to express their creativity individually and communally, resulting in a range of artistic output from music to food to dance to costuming and parades (Frost, 2016). This eruption of creative expression is frequently concentrated into a single context. It's a necessarily chaotic synergy of individual and community expression into a greater ordered whole. The cultural ubiquity of celebration becomes exponential when spanning generations, cultural groups, and wide geographic regions.

A proper festival involves exuberant, vibrant, creative production, both individual and cooperative. This can include lavish and ornate costumes, dance troupes, floats, and musicians (Riggio, 2004). Moreover, these periodic acts of extensive and coordinated yet independent human celebration contain an element of the irrepressible. For example, the tradition of Venetian masks during the carnival was associated with a period in which celebration was prohibited, and revelers disguised their identity to escape public recognition (Johnson, 2011). The fact that carnivals have long involved pseudonymity and anonymity through costume and masking (Twycross & Carpenter, 2017) provides an interesting analogy to the current context of pseudonymity and anonymity that distributed networks afford their users.

What do festival periods that convulse entire counties, countries, and cultures have in common? They tend to extend far beyond the level at which any one participant can be familiar with all others involved. In fact, in festivals that span cities or take place across an entire nation, the celebration exceeds any individual's ability to participate in or even perceive all the human activity that a given celebration encompasses (Ogundeji & Fasehun, 2021). A celebration thus involves the coordination of many intrinsically personal spheres of human interaction within and around one another. Thus, institutionalized governance emerges in the space between the spheres of our relationships that are governed by personal knowledge and bonds (Alston et al., 2018).

As the police in any city where a large festival has occurred can attest, certain kinds of crimes emerge from the sheer volume of individuals who have been brought together by the communal act of celebration (Slaughter, 2013). Therefore, the way that a given celebration of human creative expression and production is governed is a central determinant of the extent of this output that a given complex human social order can sustain. Governance can therefore be understood as a mechanism that operates as a scalar mechanism in human social orders, which means governance has an integral role in human celebrations above a certain size as well.

For example, Burning Man, which started as a voluntarist, communitarian, and even anarchist community, has come to involve considerable organizational definition (St John, 2020). This includes defining rules for camp placement in subsequent years, selling tickets, accepting donations, and interfacing with federal and state authorities. The need for governance thus persists as human orders scale beyond the personal. And if we're being honest, any good festival is one that has more than just your friends present – otherwise it's just a great party.

Governance requires rules, and applying such rules can lead to unpopular decisions, often by those directly affected. While this is inevitable, it is not catastrophic (DuPont, this volume). Not everyone can have the best camp locations in Black Rock City, but different people may want different locations for various reasons. Resolving these demands, which can be complementary or conflicting at times, is the essence of governance (Alston, 2022). For festivals to occur at the scale they do, governance is necessary (Getz, 2009), particularly if the festival happens annually for days or even weeks.

Governance raises the question of how to achieve the group's objectives and who should make the decisions. If a camp at Burning Man loses its long-held location due to poor clean-up or other infractions, they must understand the reasons for the decision and be informed of the rules for cleaning up matter-out-of-place (St John, 2019). These characteristics of notice and transparent process are hallmarks of governance in modern liberal societies (Effron, 2020). Individuals who wield power within a system are crucial, and if this power becomes too concentrated or unchecked, it can lead to various well-understood problems associated with more autocratic governance (Gilley, 2003).

POLYCENTRICITY IN FESTIVALS AND CARNIVALS

Festivals and carnivals are complex events that are influenced by various spheres of private and public authority, making them polycentric (Aligica & Tarko, 2012). Different stages at a single music festival are often managed separately, with each performing artist having their own manager. Food trucks, merchandise booths, and other outlets are also managed independently, allowing attendees greater choice at a particular event (Getz et al., 2006). However, for the average ticket holder, food truck vendor, and lesser-known artist, the terms of their contracts are fixed and standardized. These terms reflect the comparative scale of the parties involved in the transaction. Unless a rock star is involved, centrally managed events tend to reflect the relative scale of attendees and vendors in the terms offered. As a result, many stages of output become routinized and standardized, such as the use of brutalist metal grilles to channel crowd flows at large urban music festivals (Earl et al., 2004).

Contractual terms and space management reflect the standardization that centralized governance at scale tends to produce. The prevalence of brutalist architecture in the former Soviet republics under limited budgets and centralized governments can be understood as a direct result of this reality (Crowley & Reid, 2002). Centralized output at scale requires reliably uniform output (Strijbos, 1997). Financing to obtain this scale similarly tends to require centralized governance to credibly commit to creating this uniformity and scale of output. For example, the products in big box stores are incredibly uniform compared to the variance in products at a farmers' market. While farmers' markets offer more idiosyncratic choice and individual esthetic variance, reliable uniformity of product tends to obtain at scale in economic production and governance, even if this reliability in production comes at the cost of variance in individual esthetic (Folta & Klee, 2016).

However, not all forms of governance tend toward centralization. Farmers' markets are a great example of how individual production from many distinct individuals and groups is often integral to the very existence of a market. If a single agricultural conglomerate tried to sell as wide a range of products as is available at a farmers' market, it is unlikely they would attract customers who could just as easily obtain those goods (alongside many others) at a large grocery store chain. To put it simply, having a single producer would destroy the intended reasons for a farmers' market in the first place (Dodds et al., 2014). Some markets remain integrally local, while others scale to a global level, and have varying levels of production and supply chain arrangements.

ARTISANS, BARGAINING POWER, AND CREATIVE PRODUCTION

Will creative production inevitably fall before the grist mill of production for a global economy? There are reasons to suspect otherwise. Consider the wine industry as an example of highly individualized artisanal production. Specific producers still command considerable price premiums relative to producers from the same region using techniques that, to the uninformed observer, look identical (Goldstein et al., 2008). In industries where refined creative output commands a large premium, such as wine or art, the bargaining power still resides with the producer. This may be less common today, given the increasingly global wine production of many countries and the ways in which the digital age has disrupted traditional art markets. However, certain producers in Bordeaux, Napa, and Piedmont command prices that far outstrip their competitors (Benfratello et al., 2009). While the producers at the very top of price lists may not produce a per-dollar amount of quality that justifies their price (Goldstein et al., 2008), compared to the need for Michelin-starred restaurants and rising billionaires to have the absolute best in their cellars, price reflects quality in locally specialized production of wine and art in ways that many products no longer do (Poulsen & Mønsted, 2020).

Is it possible to have both artisanal variation and esthetic vision in a global market? The examples discussed so far suggest a path forward, but they rely on creative producers maintaining bargaining power and consumers having a choice among many independent producers, which creates beneficial governance incentives.

Moreover, the examples mentioned so far assume a certain level of luxury, such as being able to shop at a farmer's market or patronize an art gallery regularly. Is there a way for individual creative expression to reach a global audience at an affordable level for the average consumer? Music, video, and other audio-visual techniques can be duplicated digitally, which is not possible for physical media. This is not to say that reproducing digital information is costless for digital artists or software producers, but it does emphasize the transformative ability of the digital age for a single creator to reach an audience of millions at a marginal cost of production of which wine producers and painters can only fantasize (Poort et al., 2010).

If the existing models of digital marketplaces do not provide a clear path forward, how can individual artistic expression be maximally facilitated in the digital context? The answer lies in the means of reliably securing unique digital objects, which is necessary for artistic digital expression to become economically valuable. In most economically significant contexts for producing scarce digital objects (or NFTs), the predominant economic value has not derived from securing a digital asset layer in a system of distributed governance (Bamakan et al., 2022).

For instance, in video games, players collect in-game items or experiences that are valuable because they are rare (Lehdonvirta & Ernkvist, 2011). However, if every player has all the items or experiences, then there is no reason for players to keep playing or make more purchases. This means that game developers may not need a distributed network to prove the rarity of their in-game assets, as other players can see how rare they are by observing the game's communication and interaction (see also Arjalies & Compain, this volume).

NFTs have initially been applied to secure ownership recognition of a particular piece of digital art, whether it is an image, a video, or an audio file. However, the term "recognition" here displays the intrinsic limitation of NFTs. While they can secure a piece of art, it will ultimately be reproduced locally, and likely at high fidelity if the purchaser cares enough about digital art to spend hundreds or thousands of dollars on the work (Rockett, 2021). The technology does not secure against unauthorized reproduction of the digital art – it only prevents replication of the token that signifies ownership of that art for users of a particular network.

In the first case, decentralized governance of in-game purchases of scarce digital objects is not integral due to the alignment of the game producer's incentives to create sufficient scarcity in fungible currency and non-fungible digital objects like skins or other character-specific attributes. In the latter case, the NFT only signifies ownership, rather than securing it, which does not ameliorate many of the problems inherent in ensuring ownership of reproducible digital objects.

BARGAINING POWER IN THE METAVERSE

So why did I start talking about a carnival if I only came to throw cold water all over it? Put differently, if the initial applications of unique digital objects (individually tokenized) do not solve human coordination problems within our increasingly digital organizations, then what's the point? However, the combination of these two classes of digital objects (fungible and non-fungible) creates the basis for a digital asset layer beyond the control of any one counterparty in a digital environment with many independent producers. A metaverse will inherently be a network of coordinated yet independent human social activity (Hadi et al., 2024), such that digital objects will necessarily be native to this same network – the question becomes, who controls the asset layer on which these digital object reside and are exchanged?

Currently, platforms control access to the ecosystems of applications and content that will one day become the metaverse. If the same single producers (or conglomerates of content, intellectual property (IP), and finance) control the contractual terms for independent creatives' production, this will be a metaverse whose creative margins are predominantly determined by the central platform authority (Atrakchi-Israel & Nahmias, 2022). Although a user may get to choose their hair color and outfit, all avatars are still constrained to a certain uniformity of dimensions (Dupre, 2022).

A metaverse that surpasses the dystopian visions of virtual reality to date is one in which independent producers maintain a healthy share of bargaining power against the singular network on which they all coordinate and compete. When a consumer devotes their attention and/or tokens to one digital boutique or gallery, they do not do so for another competing boutique. However, the independence of these boutiques and their ability to pursue competing creative visions depends, in part, on an asset layer around which they can all coordinate without a single actor capturing the lion's share of the rents. An open metaverse is one in which individual creators will still find it costly to compete for global attention. Nevertheless, independent producers of some of the finest aspects of human creative expression manage to do so globally today. In a digital context, any metaverse that hopes to encourage the same levels of human creative expression must credibly enable that creative expression to flourish free from the strictures of centralized governance that result from market power imbalances between the network layer on which all independent producers must coordinate and the size of any one producer.

While NFTs are still in their early stages, successful networks that recognize digital ownership as valuable to other members may persist in transformative ways. To view tokens with a unique digital identity tied to instances of human creative expression as limited to their current applications is to misunderstand the way in which fungible and non-fungible property instruments form the lifeblood of human economic interactions. In truth, human ownership claims exist on a continuum of fungibility (Marinotti, 2021; Sheldon, 2006), just as some NFTs are one-offs, while others entitle the holder to a claim among several to many other such claims. This variation has its precedent in artist prints and limited-issue sports cards.

Innovation around reliably unique (or limited and tied to specific within-network privileges or content) tokens provides a necessary complement to the reliably scarce digital units of account that have given rise to networks fully devoted to cryptocurrency applications. Distributed governance of networks that facilitate the specification and exchange of fungible and non-fungible digital objects creates an asset layer for the future digital economy that is more like a farmers' market than a Costco. For a metaverse to ever come close to realizing the unpredictable and beautiful cacophony of human creative expression that is a carnival, it will need a digital asset layer that facilitates coordination and preserves bargaining power in the hands of creators. While any such metaverse is further away than many advocates make it out to be, innovation in this space is a major prerequisite to realizing the digital artisanal vision I have briefly sketched herein.

NOTE

1. Throughout, I use these words interchangeably to refer to large-scale human celebrations involving individual and coordinated creative expression among many independent groups. These definitions are taken from Merriam-Webster's dictionary (2024, https://www.merriam-webster.com).

REFERENCES

Abreu, M., & Brasil, E. (2020). Toward a history of carnival. *Oxford research encyclopedia of Latin American history*. Retrieved April 6, 2024 from https://oxfordre.com/latinamericanhistory/view/10.1093/acrefore/9780199366439.001.0001/acrefore-9780199366439-e-820

Aligica, P. D., & Tarko, V. (2012). Polycentricity: From Polanyi to Ostrom, and beyond. *Governance*, 25(2), 237–262.

Alston, E. (2022). *Governance as conflict: Constitution of shared values defining future margins of disagreement*. MIT Computational Law Report.

Alston, E., Alston, L. J., Mueller, B., & Nonnenmacher, T. (2018). *Institutional and organizational analysis: Concepts and applications*. Cambridge University Press.

Atrakchi-Israel, B., & Nahmias, Y. (2022). Metaverse, competition, and the online digital ecosystem. *Minnesota Journal of Law, Science & Technology*, 24, 235.

Bamakan, S. M. H., Nezhadsistani, N., Bodaghi, O., & Qu, Q. (2022). Patents and intellectual property assets as non-fungible tokens; key technologies and challenges. *Scientific Reports*, 12(1), 2178.

Benfratello, L., Piacenza, M., & Sacchetto, S. (2009). Taste or reputation: What drives market prices in the wine industry? Estimation of a hedonic model for Italian premium wines. *Applied Economics*, 41(17), 2197–2209.

Crowley, D., & Reid, S. E. (Eds.). (2002). *Socialist spaces: Sites of everyday life in the Eastern Bloc* (Vol. 1). Berg.

Cudny, W. (2014). The phenomenon of festivals: Their origins, evolution, and classifications. *Anthropos*, 109(2), 640–656.

Cudny, W. (2016). The concept, origins and types of festivals. In *Festivalisation of urban spaces: Factors, processes and effects* (pp. 11–42). Springer Nature

Dodds, R., Holmes, M., Arunsopha, V., Chin, N., Le, T., Maung, S., & Shum, M. (2014). Consumer choice and farmers' markets. *Journal of Agricultural and Environmental Ethics*, 27, 397–416.

Dupre, M. H. (2022). *Zuckerberg's lifeless metaverse avatar is comically different from the one he advertised*. Futurism. https://futurism.com/the-byte/metaverse-different-advertised

Earl, C., Parker, E., Tatrai, A., & Capra, M. (2004). Influences on crowd behaviour at outdoor music festivals. *Environmental Health*, 4(2), 55-62.

Effron, R. J. (2020). The invisible circumstances of notice. *The North Carolina Law Review*, 99, 1521.

Folta, K. M., & Klee, H. J. (2016). Sensory sacrifices when we mass-produce mass produce. *Horticulture Research*, 3, 16032.

Frost, N. (2016). Anthropology and festivals: Festival ecologies. *Ethnos*, 81(4), 569–583.

Getz, D. (2009). Policy for sustainable and responsible festivals and events: Institutionalization of a new paradigm. *Journal of Policy Research in Tourism, Leisure and Events*, 1(1), 61–78.

Getz, D., Andersson, T., & Larson, M. (2006). Festival stakeholder roles: Concepts and case studies. *Event Management*, 10(2–3), 103–122.

Gilley, B. (2003). The limits of authoritarian resilience. *Journal of Democracy*, 14, 18.

Goldstein, R., Almenberg, J., Dreber, A., Emerson, J. W., Herschkowitsch, A., & Katz, J. (2008). Do more expensive wines taste better? Evidence from a large sample of blind tastings. *Journal of Wine Economics, 3*(1), 1–9.

Hadi, R., Melumad, S., & Park, E. S. (2024). The Metaverse: A new digital frontier for consumer behavior. *Journal of Consumer Psychology, 34*(1), 142–166.

Johnson, J. H. (2011). *Venice Incognito: Masks in the serene republic*. University of California Press.

Lehdonvirta, V., & Ernkvist, M. (2011). *Knowledge map of the virtual economy*. World Bank.

Marinotti, J. (2021). Possessing intangibles. *The Northwestern University Law Review, 116*, 1227.

Ogundeji, P. A., & Fasehun, M. A. (2021). Insights from festivals and carnivals. In A. Akinyemi, T. Falola (Eds.), *The Palgrave handbook of African oral traditions and folklore* (pp. 105–118). Palgrave Macmillan.

Poort, J., Rutten, P., & Van Eijk, N. (2010). Legal, economic and cultural aspects of file sharing. *Communications and Strategies, 77*, 35–54.

Poulsen, C., & Mønsted, M. (2020). Identity markers for wine producers: Terroir and beyond. *Journal of Wine Research, 31*(3), 194–217.

Riggio, M. C. (Ed.). (2004). The carnival story – Then and now 1: Introduction to part I. In *Carnival* (pp. 39–47). Routledge.

Rockett, C. (2021). The real disruption is coming. *Boulder Weekly*. https://boulderweekly.com/entertainment/the-real-disruption-is-coming/

Sheldon, D. P. (2006). Claiming ownership, but getting owned: Contractual limitations on asserting property interests in virtual goods. The UCLA Law Review, *54*, 751.

Slaughter, P. (2013). Of crowds, crimes and carnivals. In R. Matthews & J. Young (Eds.), *The new politics of crime and punishment* (pp. 178–198). Willan.

St John, G. (2019). At home in the big empty: Burning man and the playa sublime. *Journal for the Study of Religion, Nature & Culture, 13*(3), 286–313.

St John, G. (2020). Ephemeropolis: Burning man, transformation, and heterotopia. *Journal of Festive Studies, 2*(1), 289–322.

Strijbos, S. (1997). The paradox of uniformity and plurality in technological society. *Technology in Society, 19*(2), 177–194.

Twycross, M., & Carpenter, S. (2017). *Masks and masking in medieval and early Tudor England*. Routledge.

WEB3 AS DECENTRALIZATION THEATER? A FRAMEWORK FOR ENVISIONING DECENTRALIZATION STRATEGICALLY

J. P. Vergne

UCL School of Management, UK

ABSTRACT

Web3's raison d'être *is decentralization. Quite problematically, however, few industry analysts can articulate what "decentralization" really entails; whether it differs at all from the notion of "distribution," and how either construct can be measured with observable data to enable a meaningful analysis of the industry's core promise. Instead, Web3 is akin to a decentralization theater in which archetypical characters, who resonate with the likes of Hamlet and Godot, enact decentralization based on fictitious narratives. After critically reassessing these narratives about decentralization, this paper offers a fresh perspective to evaluate, less theatrically and hopefully more rigorously, future claims about "being decentralized." I argue that the crucial issue lurking behind the decentralization narrative is the dispersion of authority within blockchain platforms, which consists of two fundamental dimensions, namely the dispersion of information and of decision-making. The value proposition of Web3 will not be taken seriously until the industry can provide reliable indicators of authority dispersion and demonstrate that the latter affects strategic outcomes for blockchain platforms, including innovation, growth, and value creation.*

Keywords: Decentralization; blockchain; digital platform; distributed; authority

INTRODUCTION

The Web3 community is characterized by a collective obsession with the notion of "consensus" and, at the same time, by a lack of consensus around what Web3 actually refers to. The term "Web 3.0," spelled with a dot followed by a zero, used to refer to the "semantic Web," a standardization initiative aimed at making Web data readable by machines. This concept is only loosely related to the current "Web3" moniker – typically spelled without a space between "Web" and "3." Over the years, the term "Web3" has gradually supplanted "Web 3.0" in the industry buzzword race, as suggested by the Ngram search below (see Fig. 10.1), to eventually achieve dominance in 2019.

In the following, I critically examine Web3's claim to fame, namely that Web3 provides a "decentralized" alternative to existing web platforms. To illustrate my arguments, I leverage short blogs posted by Web3 builders, funders, analysts, and critics on "crypto Twitter," which often acts as the main stage for Web3's decentralization theater.[i]

WEB3 = THE DECENTRALIZED WEB?

Defining Web3 (Fig. 10.2) can be about as controversial as using pineapple as a pizza topping. Some attempts at capturing its essence include the following.

A common thread across definitions is the idea that (1) Web3 is both decentralized and distributed; (2) Web3 enables users to co-own blockchain platforms and to exchange value peer to peer using self-managed (cryptocurrency)

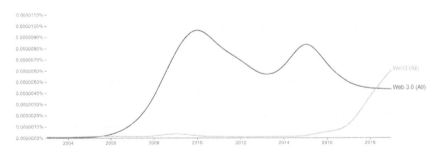

Fig. 10.1. Increasing Usage of the "Web3" Term (Google Ngram, 2024).

Fig. 10.2. Definitions of Web3.[ii]

wallets. Both features are premised on the ability to design a network of nodes that can seamlessly connect any user to any other user, without Web traffic having to be routed through trusted intermediaries. If blockchain is to be the foundation of Web3, then the decentralized software applications (known as "dApps"), which generate the data filling the blocks of the chain, will effectively become its core substance. Decentralization has been hailed by the Web3 community as both a mission and organizing principle, which is why we need more than a superficial understanding of decentralization to make sense of this emerging industry.

DECENTRALIZATION IS THE NEW DISRUPTION

To achieve respectability in the golden age of Web 2.0, a startup had to "disrupt" some industry. Cofounders sometimes accompanied this mission statement with an injunction for the startup to "disrupt itself." Nowadays, to achieve respectability in the age of Web3, a founding team has to "decentralize" some industry. Founders often accompany this mission statement with an injunction for the project to "decentralize itself." The meaning of these guidelines remains vague enough to prevent rigorous evaluation of whether the project has ultimately succeeded. Has Instacart disrupted groceries retailers? Has Bitcoin decentralized banking? Questions of this type have no obvious answers because it is unclear what exactly was being asked in the first place.

Before this paper offers a fresh perspective on decentralization, it takes stock of prior attempts at delineating the concept. In keeping with the spirit of this publication, I propose to view the Web3 community as a *decentralization theater*, namely, a fictitious space whose performers are enjoined to enact decentralization to preserve the coherence of the play. In Web3's decentralization theater, the standard script is known to all – take a traditional digital business that is commonly believed to be "centralized" and build a "decentralized" version of it. Since decentralization allegedly brings valuable benefits (e.g., privacy, openness, security), it should also confer a competitive advantage – or, put differently, a decentralized version of a digital business is just a *better* business. If examples of this gameplay abound, as illustrated below in Fig. 10.3, very few have reached the tipping point of becoming mass-market as of the time of writing.

To decentralize traditional business models, Web3 entrepreneurs are expected to rely on a toolkit that includes decentralized cryptocurrency (e.g., Ether), decentralized blockchains (e.g., Ethereum), decentralized protocols (e.g., 0x), decentralized applications (e.g., The Sandbox), decentralized marketplaces (e.g., LooksRare), decentralized digital assets (e.g., ape NFTs), and decentralized governance (e.g., Aragon). But how do we know exactly that any given Web3 ecosystem is decentralized – or at least, *more* decentralized than the Web2 model it is meant to outcompete? (Schneider, 2019). This is where the rubber does not meet the road quite yet.

Some see decentralization as the middle ground between centralization and distribution, as was initially proposed by Paul Baran (see Panel 1 in Fig. 10.4) (Baran, 1964). Others see distribution as the middle ground between centralization and decentralization, as proposed by Ethereum community contributors

Fig. 10.3. Decentralized Web3 Version of Popular Web 2.0 Businesses.

(see Panel 2 in Fig. 10.4; essentially the same as Panel 1, only after swapping the terms "distributed" and "decentralized"). Yet others see the terms "decentralized" and "distributed" as synonymous. Notwithstanding a potential nuance between decentralization and distribution (Vergne, 2020), very few industry insiders can provide a clear definition of either term when prompted. A predictable outcome, given these divides, is that the two terms are poorly defined, let alone measurable with any sort of consistency. How can we tell, then,

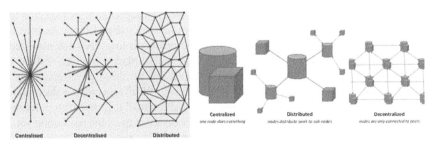

Fig. 10.4. Depictions of Centralization and Distribution (on the Left: Baran, 1964 and on the Right: Ethereum Stackexchange, 2020).

whether Bitcoin is more (or less) decentralized (or distributed) than Ethereum? Or that Audius is indeed a more decentralized (or distributed) music platform than Spotify?

POPULAR CHARACTERS IN THE DECENTRALIZATION THEATER

In the decentralization theater, popular characters embody different ways to think about the decentralization of Web3. This section portrays four of them, namely Hamlet, Godot, Bucket, and Figaro, and discusses the limitations of their act.

The "Hamlet" of Decentralization: To Be or Not to Be ... Decentralized

According to proponents of a Hamlet definition of decentralization, an entity is either centralized or decentralized, period. One typically relies on a simplistic criterion to arrive at such a binary determination. For instance, if an entity has a CEO, it is centralized; if it doesn't have one, then it is decentralized (Fig. 10.5).

Hamlet definitions certainly have the benefit of simplicity, but they overlook crucially important dimensions. Can't an organization run by a CEO be located along a continuum of centralization, depending, for instance, on the extent to which decisions are delegated to middle managers? Wouldn't the dispersion of ownership – and owners' ability to swiftly remove a poorly performing CEO change the "centralization" the story? And what if an organization is not incorporated, does not have a CEO, yet depends on just a handful of agents to operate? Would that necessarily make it more decentralized that a CEO-run corporation with dispersed ownership, frequent CEO turnover, and substantial amounts of authority (Kavanagh & Ennis, 2020) delegated across hundreds of middle managers (see Bakos et al., 2021, for related arguments in the context of permissioned vs permissionless ledgers)?

The "Godot" of Decentralization: To Wait Indefinitely for an Attack to Succeed

For some, a system is decentralized when it has so many points of failure that it simply cannot fail amid adverse circumstances, for any attacker would have to simultaneously attack on too many fronts to be successful. From this perspective,

If your blockchain has a CEO then it's not decentralized.

Companies are NOT decentralized.
Opensea is a company. Binance is a company.
M3t@mask is a company. Twitter is a company!
I think thousands of people here do not understand this simple concept. We are not decentralized. That world is far off. But now you know why we need it!

Fig. 10.5. Twitter Commentators on Corporate Control and Decentralization.

decentralization makes a system resilient in perpetuity – and adversaries end up waiting indefinitely for their attacks to reach their objective (like the characters in Beckett's *Waiting for Godot*, who end up waiting indefinitely for the elusive Godot). A limitation of this view is that it is often trivial to identify a meta-system that encompasses most of the focal system's agents (or nodes) and could therefore represent a central point of failure. Take a computer that runs an arbitrary large number of independent virtual machines; sadly, the hardware that hosts them all represents a single point of failure. Similarly, a state can decentralize political authority across an arbitrarily large number of elected representatives; but when they all meet in person to pass laws inside the parliament building, that building represents a single point of failure (e.g., a bomb could kill them all at once).

Some blockchain networks get criticized for heavily relying on Infura and Amazon Web Services to host nodes, thereby creating, de facto, central points of failure. One might argue that heavy reliance on computer chips manufactured by Intel or on rare earth materials from China might also represent single points of failure for any computing network (Gochhayat et al., 2020). If we pushed this line of reasoning to the limit, any system whose nodes are located on Earth has a single point of failure, for a massive solar flare could cause an electromagnetic superstorm and knock out all computers in one go (see Fig. 10.6 for related commentary). Likewise, in at-risk countries, unfettered climate change could lead most businesses to fail, however decentralized they claim to be.

Any system can be argued to be part of a broader meta-system which, out of logical necessity, will represent a single point of failure, but to avoid the risk of infinite regress that comes with this perspective, it is crucial to limit our analyses of decentralization to the boundaries of the focal system. The blockchain software run by node operators, for instance, clearly falls within the system's boundaries; the location where node operators store their off-chain data, possibly; but who supplies the rare earths for the computers that run node software, probably not.

The "Bucket" of Decentralization: To Decentralize Is to Remove Inequality

Charlie Bucket, before visiting Willy Wonka's chocolate factory, lived in extreme poverty. But this kind of economic inequality would not exist in a truly decentralized system, according to proponents of Bucket definitions of decentralization. The latter argue that only in a centralized system can cryptocurrency tokens be concentrated in the hands of a happy few. Yet, by equating economic inequality with token ownership concentration and, by extension, with centralization, Bucket definitions can be quite misleading. First, the wealth of any given

Build a rocket company to launch satellites to create decentralized internet. Either that or become space pirates and take over spacex starlink system with spaceships equipped with lasers.

Web 3 will no longer be decentralized if we can't run our own nodes. Metamask is down because infura is down

Fig. 10.6. Twitter Commentators on Web3's Reliance on Centralized Infrastructure.

individual is determined by the sum of the value of all the assets they own – not just by the value of their holdings in one specific asset (here, cryptocurrency). Thus, to measure the dispersion of, say, bitcoin cryptocurrency across users and call it a measure of inequality is about as informative as counting the dispersion of Lamborghinis across the residents of Italy to evaluate inequality in the country. As it turns out, some wealthy individuals may have a strong preference for holding real estate rather than luxury cars, or for driving Ferraris rather than Lamborghinis. Put differently, the dispersion of Lamborghinis (or of bitcoin cryptocurrency) does not say as much about wealth inequality as it does about wealthy individuals' *preferences for holding certain assets over others.* A second issue, perhaps even more problematic, is the underlying assumption, made in Bucket conceptualizations, that the dispersion of Lamborghini ownership is a reasonable proxy to capture the decentralization of the Lamborghini *car company.* Which amounts to conflating the internal organization of a corporation with the size of its product's user base. As such, to claim that bitcoin is not decentralized because the top 1% bitcoin holders own most of the bitcoin network's supply is missing the point altogether.

There is one situation, however, where the dispersion of token ownership is very informative – and that is when token ownership gives substantial decision rights over the system. But the tokens themselves, in such a context, are just how the dispersion of decision rights can be observed. In other situations, it may be that the dispersion of computing power, the existence of backdoors and master passwords, or the presence of supernodes with special privileges end up mattering much more than token ownership concentration. Put simply, we should not conflate the construct (decision-making dispersion) with its context-specific measurement (token ownership concentration).

The "Figaro" of Decentralization: To Decentralize Is to Disintermediate

Figaro was first featured in three plays by Beaumarchais and later in countless opera performances, perhaps most famously in Mozart's *Marriage of Figaro.* In the story, feisty Figaro acts as the quintessential intermediary – between prospective lovers, between aristocratic families, and between social classes. In the Beaumarchais trilogy, every aspect of the plot unfolds thanks to the introductions and connections that Figaro is making between other characters. Quite ironically, Figaro likes to be called "Anonymous" by others, in order to keep his intermediating role as discreet as possible. In Web3, decentralization is commonly associated with disintermediation, namely, with the removal of all the trusted Figaros that would normally intermediate transactions between agents. But what makes an intermediary? Do anonymity and pseudonymity alter the fundamental nature of intermediaries (Caliskan, 2020; Swartz, 2018)?

An ongoing controversy in Web3 is whether network validators, such as miners in proof-of-work blockchains, represent intermediaries. Since miners cannot screen users to allow or disallow access to a blockchain network, they do not constitute traditional financial intermediaries (and should not be regulated as such). However, a block of transactions cannot be added to the main chain without a miner proposing to add the block. At the same time, miners are equivalent and substitutable to the extent that they enforce the same rules written in open-source code and do not have to exercise subjective judgment. So, are they intermediaries at all? The answer depends on the level of analysis. A transaction between two Bitcoin users on the main chain does require a miner – in that sense, there is intermediation when considering the transaction level. However, at the level of the Bitcoin network, it makes sense to regard miners as falling within the boundaries of the organization – in fact, miners are just a special type of users, rather than a third party. The exchange of data within the organization's boundaries does not represent, strictly speaking, a form of intermediation – or else we would be claiming that the network is intermediating itself. Importantly, the above discussion emphasizes a crucial difference between disintermediation and decentralization. The former really is a matter of role definition (third-party intermediary or not?), whereas the latter regards the dispersion of the role's performance (many miners available to perform the task or just a handful?) (Nabben, 2021). As a result, the decentralization theater should take distance from Figaro's character and instead refocus on theorizing what matters more fundamentally to the dispersion of authority within system boundaries.

THE DECENTRALIZATION OF WHAT?

Our brief (and incomplete) review of the characters that commonly embody decentralization in the Web3 theater has highlighted three desirable features that a robust conceptualization of decentralization should have:

- Decentralization is not a one or zero but is best conceptualized alongside a continuum.
- Discussing decentralization presupposes identifying system boundaries.
- Decentralization must be distinguished from related notions, such as inequality and disintermediation.

Besides, a robust definition of decentralization must focus on the what of decentralization before discussing the how of its measurement. Lengthy debates, indeed, have focused on whether decentralization would be best captured with a Gini coefficient of inequality, a Herfindahl index of concentration, or a Shannon measure of entropy. All these measurements capture, in their own valid ways, the dispersion of something – but of what exactly? That is the question.

To tackle the "what?" question upfront, I argue that decentralization concerns authority dispersion within an organization, a system, a digital platform, or a network (typically, blockchains are these four things all at once; Davidson et al., 2018). For our purposes, I envision authority as consisting of two components: (1) The ability to access information and (2) the ability to contribute to decision-making. Indeed, it is easy to see why an agent without any access to information nor any say in decision-making would have little authority. Perhaps less intuitive is the recognition that information access and decision-making do not necessarily go hand in hand.

Blockchain data may be accessible to agents but do not give them decision rights. Likewise, agents with decision rights sometimes do not have access to the information that is relevant to making a given decision. As a result, it is wise to consider as two separate dimensions the dispersion of information access, on the one hand, and of decision-making, on the other hand, when unpacking authority dispersion.

To flesh out this two-dimensional framework, consider the following illustration. In the United States, the entire population (335 million) has access to information regarded as "public"; about 3.5 million people have access to information classified as "confidential" and about 1.5 million to information classified as "top-secret" (owing to the supply of specific security clearances). Given these data, how dispersed is information access in the United States? One can intuitively understand that information dispersion would be minimal if only one person (e.g., the president) could access non-public information and maximal if everyone could access all three types of information. It follows that dispersion should increase when more people are granted access to confidential and/or top-secret information. Intuitively, one can also see why maximizing information dispersion is not necessarily desirable, nor an end in itself; rather, information dispersion is a system property whose optimal value depends on system objectives (DuPont & Maurer, 2015), among other things (e.g., if the objective is "national security," when might it be optimal to give everyone access to top-secret information?). Importantly, one does not need to look at the precise mathematical definition of dispersion indices (e.g., Gini's, Herfindahl's, and Shannon's) to make these determinations. Provided that a dispersion index correctly captures the minimum, the maximum, and *what* exactly needs to be measured, it will do a good-enough job at measuring information dispersion, independently of the exact shape of the underlying function.[iii] Any good-enough index can be used to compare similar systems (e.g., countries, organizations, and blockchains) and indicate which ones have more information dispersion than others. As well, it should be usable to capture the evolution of dispersion over time.

Importantly, a good-enough index of information dispersion should be deployed within appropriate system boundaries. Picture a blockchain with 300 special nodes who, unlike regular nodes, can see all the information. How dispersed would information be in that system? Well, it depends entirely on the total number of nodes. If there are 300 nodes in total, then every node is "special," and information is maximally dispersed. However, as the user base grows to, say 1,000 users and later to 1,000,000 users, the ratio of special-to-total nodes shrinks rapidly (down from 100% to 30% and later 0.03%). Any organization that grows its user base while holding constant the number of agents with special privileges is bound to become more "centralized" over time. A good-enough index of dispersion should thus be implemented in a way that accounts for this reality – by always considering the number of frontline users as the base layer in the measurement breakdown (just like we acknowledged, earlier, that all the 335 million US residents can access "public" information).

To capture the dispersion of decision-making, which represents the second component of authority, a very similar process can be implemented. In the United States, every citizen over 18 years old can contribute to deciding who their

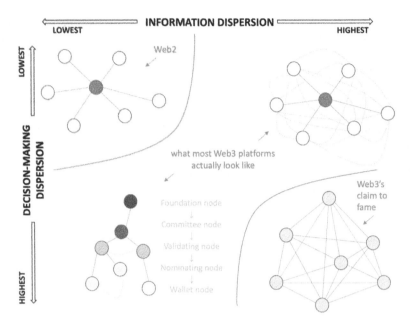

Note. Blue nodes contribute to decision-making, white nodes do not. The darker the blue, the higher the level of the decision-maker. Curvy dotted lines indicate information exchange. Straight lines indicate information exchange and, additionally, influence of decision-makers on others. Adapted from Vergne (2020).

Fig. 10.7. Variation in an Organization's Decision-Making and Information Dispersion.

representatives shall be through voting (roughly 200 million US citizens); about 500 representatives then decide on the law (Congressmen and women) and one person only can decide to implement executive orders (the president). If choosing representatives, passing new laws, and implementing executive orders were the only three types of decisions that mattered, then we could use the same metric for measuring the dispersion of decision-making as we used for information dispersion. With a standardized metric, every organizational system under scrutiny could be placed on a map of the kind depicted in Fig. 10.7.

TAKING DECENTRALIZATION SERIOUSLY AND STRATEGICALLY

Our proposed perspective need not star Hamlet, Godot, Bucket, or Figaro to tell the story. Instead, it moves beyond decentralization as an elusive narrative to offer authority dispersion as a tractable construct that can be defined and measured rigorously with real-world data. To take this perspective to the next level, we should delineate the types of information and decisions that matter to blockchain platforms and evaluate, for each type, what proportion of nodes are actually involved. For example, with Bitcoin, hosted wallets can only access information about unspent transactions outputs; light nodes can, additionally, access information about block header history; but only full nodes can access, on top of that, the entire history of transactions contained in prior blocks. The number of wallets, light nodes, and full nodes will thus affect the extent of information dispersion. If, over time, the number of wallet users increases but the number of full nodes does not, it should (in theory) and will (in practice) decrease authority dispersion.

Web3 entrepreneurs, investors, and developers need to take "decentralization" seriously if they are to leverage it strategically and not just rhetorically (Faustino, 2019; Vergne & Swain, 2017) – often as part of clumsy public relations (PR) claims that risk getting increasingly ridiculed by skeptics. As long as Web3 community managers make baseless claims about their network being "very decentralized" or "more decentralized" than others, the industry will face major roadblocks. Furthermore, Web3 builders need to gain a clear understanding of what level of authority dispersion they need to achieve and why, given their platform's objectives. It is likely that most individual users do not care about "decentralization" any more than they care about privacy. However, to be successful, a digital platform must match users to complementors (e.g., dApp developers), who bear a platform-specific risk when they commit resources to building on top on an architecture they do not control (e.g., recall how facebook.com killed video-sharing platform Vine by suddenly revoking its network access). A crucial implication is that a platform's authority dispersion mitigates risk for third-party complementors, thereby making the platform relatively more appealing to them than its more "centralized" counterparts.

The strategic value of authority dispersion is perhaps best understood when taking a historical perspective. For instance, in the early days of radio broadcasting, state monopolies, such as the BBC, were able to prevent the free diffusion of content by adding locks to radio receivers (Johns, 2010). Competition emerged (illegally) with pirate radio, which sought to promote diversity and creativity in programming. Unlike state monopolies, who favored live broadcasting, pirate radio pre-recorded chunks of content to enable others to design modular programming (decision-making dispersion). These programs were then aired from multiple locations onto unlocked receivers, whose designs were shared widely, so anyone could build them and listen in (information dispersion). Avant-garde record labels, specializing in jazz and rock "n" roll, found pirate radio appealing owing to authority dispersion and censorship resistance (quite literally, as state monopolies would often censor non-religious radio programming before the 1960s). Eventually, the superiority of the pirate model ended the radio monopolies (e.g., the BBC's ended in 1967) and innovations introduced by pirate radio diffused rapidly in the industry afterward (Durand & Vergne, 2013).

Authority dispersion may well be a powerful draw for complementors and, as a result, a powerful driver of network effects for digital platforms (e.g., complementors attract users, who attract more complementors, and so on). Once we measure rigorously both information and decision-making dispersion across blockchains, we will finally be able to unpack the elusive notion of "decentralization" and study its effects on a variety of strategic outcomes, including innovation

Replying to @nlw

The cryptoasset space is also plagued by 'decentralisation theater' - the urge to make an effectively centralised system look decentralised by masquerading the centralising elements.

If your users aren't running their own nodes, your blockchain is just decentralization theater.

Jameson Lopp
@lopp

It is easier for a camel to pass through the eye of a needle than for a centralized project to decentralize itself.

nic carter
@nic__carter

Mostly, cryptocurrencies indulge in "decentralization theater." They cosmetically look decentralized – through globally dispersed nodes and some form of distributed block production, but ultimately they are controlled by a single entity and can be stopped arbitrarily.

Fig. 10.8. Decentralization Theater ... or Circus?

(Wang & Vergne, 2017), growth (Chen et al., 2020), and value created (Hsieh et al., 2017). This will likely reveal a contrasted picture and encourage entrepreneurs and venture capitalists to use more nuance in their discourse. Without a more pragmatic comprehension of authority dispersion going forward, Web3's decentralization "theater," as healthy skeptics sometimes call it (see Fig. 10.8), runs the risk of becoming a circus.

NOTES

i. The paper refers to "Twitter" throughout since, at the time of writing, the social media platform had not yet been renamed "X."

ii. All tweet URLs can be found in the References list. As per the publisher's policy, account handles verified by Twitter are deemed to be controlled by public figures, and as a result, corresponding handles have not been blurred.

iii. Indeed, pairwise correlations among 10 different dispersion metrics examined by Gochhayat et al. (2020) across seven scenarios range between 0.83 and 0.99, indicating substantial convergence between Fairness, Gini, Entropy, Distance, and Cosine Similarity metrics (see Table 3 in their paper).

REFERENCES

Bakos, Y., Halaburda, H., & Mueller-Bloch, C. (2021). when permissioned blockchains deliver more decentralization than permissionless. *Communications of the ACM, 64*(2), 20–22.

Baran, P. (1964). *On distributed communications: I. Introduction to distributed communications networks.* RAND Corporation. https://doi.org/10.7249/RM3420

Caliskan, K. (2020). Data money: The socio-technical infrastructure of cryptocurrency blockchains. *Economy and Society, 49*(4), 540–561. https://doi.org/10.1080/03085147.2020.1774258

Chen, Y., Pereira, I., & Patel, P. C. (2020). Decentralized governance of digital platforms. *Journal of Management, 47*(5), 1305–1337. https://doi.org/10.1177/0149206320916755

Davidson, S., De Filippi, P., & Potts, J. (2018). Blockchains and the economic institutions of capitalism. *Journal of Institutional Economics, 14*(4), 639–658. https://doi.org/10.1017/S1744137417000200

DuPont, Q., & Maurer, B. (2015). *Ledgers and law in the blockchain.* https://www.kingsreview.co.uk/essays/ledgers-and-law-in-the-blockchain

Durand, R., & Vergne, J.-P. (2013). *The pirate organization: Lessons from the fringes of capitalism.* Harvard Business Review Press.

Ethereum Stackexchange. (2020). *Question on the terms 'distributed' and 'decentralised'.* Retrieved January 28, 2024, from https://ethereum.stackexchange.com/questions/7812/question-on-the-terms-distributed-and-decentralised.

Faustino, S. (2019). How metaphors matter: An ethnography of blockchain-based re-descriptions of the world. *Journal of Cultural Economy, 12*(6), 478–490. https://doi.org/10.1080/17530350.2019.1629330

Gochhayat, S. P., Shetty, S., Mukkamala, R., Foytik, P., Kamhoua, G. A., & Njilla, L. (2020). Measuring decentrality in blockchain based systems. *IEEE Access, 8*(November), 178372–178390. https://doi.org/10.1109/ACCESS.2020.3026577

Google Ngram. (2024). *Search results for "Web3.0, Web3."* Retrieved January 28, 2024, from https://books.google.com/ngrams/graph?content=Web+3.0%2CWeb3&year_start=2003&year_end=2019&corpus=en-2019&smoothing=0&case_insensitive=true

Hsieh, Y.-Y., Vergne, J.-P., & Wang, S. (2017). The internal and external governance of blockchain-based organizations: Evidence from cryptocurrencies. In M. Campbell-Verduyn (Ed.), *Bitcoin and beyond: Cryptocurrencies, blockchains, and global governance.* (pp. 48–68). Routledge. https://doi.org/10.4324/9781315211909

Johns, A. (2010). *Death of a pirate: British radio and the making of the information age.* W.W. Norton.

Kavanagh, D., & Ennis, P. J. (2020). Cryptocurrencies and the emergence of blockocracy. *Information Society, 36*(5), 290–300. https://doi.org/10.1080/01972243.2020.1795958

Nabben, K. (2021). Blockchain security as "people security": Applying sociotechnical security to blockchain technology. *Frontiers in Computer Science, 2,* 62. https://doi.org/10.3389/FCOMP.2020.599406/BIBTEX

Schneider, N. (2019). Decentralization: An incomplete ambition. *Journal of Cultural Economy, 12*(4), 265–285. https://doi.org/10.1080/17530350.2019.1589553

Swartz, L. (2018). What was Bitcoin, what will it be? The techno-economic imaginaries of a new money technology. *Cultural Studies, 32*(4), 623–650. https://doi.org/10.1080/09502386.2017.1416420

Twitter. (2017–2022). *URLs listed by order of appearance.* Retrieved July 3, 2022, from
- https://twitter.com/Syntropynet/status/1534899649420701697
- https://twitter.com/dabit3/status/1496609480905302024
- https://twitter.com/ArthurB/status/1444614479078170628
- https://twitter.com/SuhailKakar/status/1531161044428673025
- https://twitter.com/CryptoHustle/status/906521152289419269
- https://twitter.com/CoinSeer/status/1499741734670110722
- https://twitter.com/TolulopeAjayii/status/1517572747781627905
- https://twitter.com/Arthur_MacLeod_/status/1462204338961620996
- https://twitter.com/jimbocoin/status/1443180809540755462
- https://twitter.com/lopp/status/1277693301378953217
- https://twitter.com/nic__carter/status/1008419215479574528
- https://twitter.com/mrauchs/status/1039900187920084993

Vergne, J.-P. (2020). Decentralized vs. distributed organization: Blockchain, machine learning and the future of the digital platform. *Organization Theory, 1*(4), 1–26. https://doi.org/10.1177/2631787720977052

Vergne, J. P., & Swain, G. (2017). Categorical anarchy in the UK? The British media's classification of bitcoin and the limits of categorization. In R. Durand, N. Granqvist & A. Tyllström (Eds.), *Research in the sociology of organizations* (Vol. 51, pp. 185–222). Emerald Publishing Limited. https://doi.org/10.1108/S0733-558X20170000051005

Wang, S., & Vergne, J.-P. (2017). Buzz factor or innovation potential: What explains cryptocurrencies' returns? *PLoS ONE, 12*(1), e0177659. https://doi.org/10.1371/journal.pone.0169556

THE RISE OF BLOCKCHAIN EGREGORES

Primavera de Filippi[a], Morshed Mannan[b] and Wessel Reijers[c]

[a]*Harvard University, USA*
[b]*European University Institute, Italy*
[c]*Paderborn University, Germany*

ABSTRACT

This paper explores the emergence of cryptocurrencies like Dogecoin and Shiba Inu in the "crypto-carnival" and their ties to the Trickster archetype. It discusses the concept of tokens and the surge of tokenization in the crypto-summer of 2020–2021. This paper explains how Shiba Inu became a purely recursive token with no external measure of value. It also explores the creation of egregores, which are created intentionally or unintentionally by groups of people who share a common belief or interest. Finally, this paper discusses how digital assets born out of a countermovement may eventually fall prey to the same system they were trying to escape from, using the carnivalesque to trigger the emergence of an egregore that brings monetary value to worthless objects.

Keywords: Blockchain; memes; egregores; cryptocurrency; altcoins; Dogecoin

Imagine a world in which money grows from cybernetic trees. Anyone can enter the digital land of plenty, plant a tree, and go about handing money to all who want it – from the poor beggar to the richest person in the land. The latter might even use his or her giant virtual megaphone to spread the word among the people, from up high in his mighty castle. Yet, beware of the rogue who challenges your charm! He might dump all his money on the poor, accusing you of blasphemy. For, in which carnivalesque world do you think you live – you fool! – in which nothing is what it seems; even when the code is writ large on the walls.

Though seemingly surreal, this imagined land is not all that different from actual reality, in which we are faced with a burgeoning "crypto-carnival." In the last heat wave of the crypto-summer (2020–2021), there was a surge of tokenization: the creation of digital tokens for the sake of generating economic value. For outsiders, the universe of tokens might seem simply bizarre. Take the events surrounding the crypto token "Shiba Inu." Built on the Ethereum blockchain, Shiba Inu was presented by its anonymous founder Ryoshi as the "Dogecoin killer." It takes its name from the Japanese dog breed that famously figured as the logo of Dogecoin.

Dogecoin is a cryptocurrency created as a joke in 2013, in honor of the Doge meme featuring a Shiba Inu dog surrounded by broken English sentences. It quickly gained a cult following on the internet, especially after Elon Musk started "pumping" the cryptocurrency on social media. Despite its facetious origins, Dogecoin today enjoys a large community of crypto-enthusiasts and is regarded as one of the most popular cryptocurrencies (in terms of fame, not market cap). The cryptocurrency is used as a tip currency on social media platforms and has been leveraged to raise funds for several charitable causes, including the construction of water wells in Kenya (Rizzo, 2023). Yet, Dogecoin does not have any intrinsic value, except that which the speculative crypto-market gives it.

Just like Dogecoin, Shiba Inu is a purely recursive token: it does not refer to any external measure of value like a particular asset, it simply refers ... to itself. One way in which its value has been raised is through so-called "airdrops," which means that tokens are given out for free to generate a sense of attachment (or simple economic opportunism) among their new owners, which as a magical psychological "sauce" increases the value of the coin. This highly volatile situation is fueled by speculations of rich and powerful people (influencers), in this case, Elon Musk, whose comments on Dogecoin during a TV program had a positive impact on the value of Shiba Inu. The Shiba Inu community also tried to raise its token's value by giving half of the supply of tokens to Vitalik Buterin, the founder of Ethereum, the decentralized platform on which Shibu Inu operates. Buterin, however, did not want to hold on to his coins (in crypto language: HODL), but instead "burned" 90% of his SHIBU tokens (at the time worth $6.7 billion; Crawley, 2021) and donated a large sum of tokens to the India Covid Relief Fund in 2020 (at the time worth $1.2 billion; Seward, 2021). He was unwilling to take on the personal power that came with his holding of tokens.

There is much that is carnivalesque about this narrative, in particular to people who are unfamiliar with the crypto universe, its language, and its customs. First, there is something carnivalesque, or even absurd, about the sense of value involved in the Shiba Inu case, which seems, on the one hand, a mere figment of the imagination but, on the other hand – at least theoretically – the equivalent of an amount of hard cash that for most people seems unfathomable. In this latter sense, Buterin's donation was one of the largest charitable donations in history. Second, there is a great sense of make-believe in the Shiba Inu story. Its value is not tied to an asset perceived to have intrinsic value, but it is made through networks of communication, speculation, and storytelling, on platforms like Reddit and Twitter. In this flow of information, there is an unstable and fleeting idea of what is true and what is false. Shiba Inu's white paper (called "Woofpaper"), for instance, speaks of lofty ideals like community-based decentralization, a highly capitalist form of value creation through tokenization, and it calls Buterin a "friend" of Shiba Inu despite his actions at the same time leading to a sharp drop in its token's value.[1] Third, Shiba Inu's tokenization is surrounded by a meme-fueled carnivalesque culture. By carnivalesque, we do not only refer to carnivals, that is, either traveling amusement parks and fairs or the festivities that accompany significant dates in the Christian liturgical calendar. The term encompasses a wider array of collective activities where the established order is symbolically and playfully inverted and an opening is provided to imagining alternative orders (Godet, 2020, p. 3). For instance, the Shiba Inu community (or "SHIBArmy") generates a constant stream of memes that are seldomly taken seriously by the outside world, while some of the community members engage in social media pranks. They have posted fake "news" about celebrities (e.g., Elon Musk or Jack Dorsey) buying or advocating for Shiba Inu (Kiran, 2022). They have also created a series of petitions advocating for Shiba Inu to become an accepted form of payment by platforms such as Amazon or Paypal,[2] or a tradable asset on platforms like Coinbase or Robinhood (the latter of which received over 480,000 signatures).

The Shiba Inu story can be seen as a broader microcosm of the crypto world. In many ways, it is an extreme example of the carnivalesque – a world that is turned upside down and where the rules of the game are constantly being rewritten. It is a world where anything is possible and where, as one popular meme put it, "to the moon" is not just a dream but a destination.

While Dogecoin and Shiba Inu might have started as jokes, they have nonetheless managed to tap into a real community of people, who are looking for alternatives to the traditional financial system. Although many people may still choose to describe both of the cryptocurrencies as scams, the community that has emerged around them indicates that there is more to the story; just as there is more to the carnival experience than mere escapism. Indeed, while Dogecoin and Shiba Inu may not be traditional investment assets, they have nonetheless provided a way for people to explore the inner workings of the traditional financial system and discover new market manipulation techniques which are usually hidden from view, only available to the professional con men who present themselves to the world as financiers and qualified investors. And they manage to do so while participating in a community that is built on humor, creativity, and a shared love of dogs.

SHIBA THE TRICKSTER

This is anathema to the traditional financial system. After all, money and finance are serious business, greased and underwritten by suited professionals. Unlike the carnival, where everything short of violence is permitted (Robinson, 2011), the monetary system corrals and limits the possibilities for alternatives beyond those offered by the system itself.[3] The issuance of new forms of money and the minting of coins are either the prerogative of sovereign states or this monetary policy sovereignty is expressly mandated by states to a supranational body (Bodin, 1992, p. 78; Van Riet, 2016, p. 3). In contrast, in the crypto-carnival, as with earlier carnivals in which Jesters or Tricksters were elected king, this prerogative is subverted altogether. Unlike complementary currencies, which do not seek to replace legal tender but supplement them by catering to the needs of communities that are underserved by legal tender (Dini & Kioupkiolis, 2019), cryptocurrencies allow for the imagining of alternative monetary orders. In the crypto-carnival, anyone can issue or mint new currencies – with the aspiration of it serving the functions of money – and not bow before any political sovereign. If anything, for certain cryptocurrencies like Dogecoin and Shiba Inu, it is the image and mental construct of the hunter-dog that rules supreme in the communities that use them.

In a sense, Dogecoin and Shiba Inu embody the Trickster archetype, one that is present in the mythology of many cultures and ages (Jung, 2003). A Trickster, in general terms, has several conflicting traits: they are clever in some ways, while still being oafish in other respects (e.g., crude habits and proclivities). They can be self-serving but still achieve a "culture-hero" status for their capacity to challenge the status quo, to create, and usher in new cultures (Carroll, 1981). A myth about the coyote as a Trickster provides an illustrative example: a coyote, after a hunt, wished to drink water but found that the water body was entirely owned by frogs. The frogs exclusively controlled access and control to the water as it was behind their dam. In exchange for a large shell that the coyote obtained during its hunt, the frogs allowed him to have a large drink of water. The frogs became increasingly worried that the coyote had his head beneath the water for an extended period and drank a large quantity of their water, asking him repeatedly why he was drinking so much. The coyote repeatedly said that it was merely thirsty. Once it had finished drinking, the dam collapsed – because the coyote had been slowly dismantling it underwater! The frogs were furious that their water had been taken, to which the coyote responded: "It's not right that one people have all the water. Now it is where everyone can have it" (Erdoes & Ortiz, 1984, pp. 335–356).

As Salinas (2013) argues, this myth shows the dual nature of the Trickster: he is a hero for democratizing access to a lifesaving resource, while also being flippant and sneaky. Dogecoin and Shiba Inu, similarly, embody the traits of a noble rogue (Hynes & Doty, 1997). They promise to democratize finance and achieve forms of community ownership that appear out of reach of most people (due to the vigilant efforts of suited frogs perhaps!), yet they do so in a manner that is humorous (e.g., the deliberate use of broken English, often in Comic Sans font) and occasionally duplicitous (e.g., sharing fake news). Part of this humor plays on qualities attributed to the hunter-dog, its charm, good nature, openness, and seeming lack of guile, while still being bold (Holden, n.d.). It is still early days, but the Shiba Inu dog might find itself among the coyote, the raven, and the hare among the Trickster figures in the pantheon of North American mythology (Carroll, 1981). At the same time, the Trickster archetype also calls for the observer to look closer, to look at the deeper meaning behind their funny form or antics (Campbell & Moyers, 1991).

SHIBA THE EGREGORE

Yet, things that were born in the carnivalesque realm – that of jokes, pranks, and jests – may evolve into more serious things, with real stakes attached to them. This is when the tricksters take on a life of their own and evolve into an *egregore*, a spirit that manifests itself in the collective imagination of a group of people. The egregore, which has its origins in ancient Greece, is a "thought-form" that develops over time and can be described as a collective, unconscious entity that is shaped by the imaginations of the people in a group (i.e., a mental construct that is created through the power of thought). In some cases, an egregore can be created intentionally by a group of people to achieve a specific goal. For example, Satoshi Nakamoto – the mysterious entity that published the Bitcoin whitepaper in 2008 – is an egregore that was intentionally created by a person (or a group of persons) to steward the development of Bitcoin while retaining total anonymity. In other cases, an egregore can be created unintentionally by a group of people who share a common belief or interest, through memetic evolution and consolidation. Santa Claus and, to continue with the animal realm, the Easter Bunny are examples of the latter. Santa Claus is a figure that is known and loved by millions of people around the world. He is a jolly, fat man who brings presents to good little girls and boys. Santa Claus is an egregore because he was created by the collective imagination of humanity. He is a product of our collective unconscious. Irrespective of whether egregores are created intentionally or unintentionally, their power is that they can be "invoked" to influence people's behavior in real life. "If you misbehave, Santa Claus will not bring you any presents this year" is perhaps one of the most common invocations of the Santa Claus egregore, whose mission is to convince kids to behave well.

Becoming an egregore is the dream of every meme, joke, prank, trickster, and prankster. This is the culmination of their career, as these conceptual entities manage to trespass into the real world, entering into the minds of people and acting through them. An egregore is fed by the attention and energy that people give to it. The more attention and energy an egregore gets, the stronger it becomes. And the stronger it becomes, the more influence it has over the people who believe in it.

But how does a mere concept or an idea turn into an egregore? We are all familiar with the notion of the "meme" – a concept that was popularized by Richard Dawkins in his 1976 book *The Selfish Gene* to demonstrate how ideas develop and disseminate by contaminating the minds of people and then using these people to spread further into other people's minds. Memes turn into an egregore when they coalesce around a distinct and recognizable entity, which is collectively recognized by a larger community of people and, as such, can be used to influence in turn the thoughts and actions of these people. A meme is the atomic unit of culture, often taking the form of a single image or phrase that is passed from one person to another.

Memes are typically created to be funny or entertaining. Conversely, an egregore is a cultural entity that is created by a group of people, and that eventually acquires power over these people. The egregore is the collective consciousness of a group. It is an entity that is created and sustained by the collective beliefs, thoughts, and energy of that group.

Perhaps the best example of a meme turning into an egregore is Dogecoin, as the figure of the Doge and the coin itself have taken on a life of their own. The Doge meme started as a picture of a Shiba Inu, with the text "Doge" accompanied by a variety of broken English sentences written in Comic Sans. While the point of the meme was merely to be goofy and funny, with Dogecoin, the meme has taken off and has become a force to be reckoned with, an egregore with a real impact in the world. While maintaining its carnivalesque features – perhaps even leveraging them – Dogecoin has become an instrument for people, like Elon Musk, to influence other people's behavior to accumulate power (and money). But was Elon Musk really the one in power, or was he being instrumentalized by the egregore of Dogecoin to expand its own reach?

There are many other examples of carnivalesque entities and memes that have turned into egregores, also thanks to blockchain and cryptocurrencies. Take Pepe the Frog: a green frog taken from a comic book and turned into an Internet meme, which eventually became one of the most popular memes of 4chan – home of many prominent Internet memes, such as lolcats, rage comics, and Wojaks. In 2016, the first digital collectibles of the meme were created, as a collection of rare Pepes were recorded on the Bitcoin blockchain (Unchained, 2023). Soon after, the first crypto-art market platform was developed, specifically designed to trade and exchange these collectibles. The value of these Rare Pepes was initially very low but quickly rose to significant amounts as the crypto-art community began recognizing the value of these digital assets. After one of these Rare Pepes was purchased for US$38,500 in a first New York City-based live auction, and later sold three years later for US$312,000, more and more people started buying and holding these digital assets, to resell them at a later time (Mapperson, 2021). Today, in the aftermath of the second non-fungible token (NFT) craze, some of these Rare Pepes have reached a market value of over half a million dollars.

While the egregore (and therefore the value) of Dogecoin and Rare Pepe emerged out of the love and enthusiasm of a distributed network of meme-lovers and geeks, others – more commercially-oriented initiatives – took inspiration from these communities to develop a more "serious" marketing strategy, leveraging the notion of community as the main lever by which to create value out of thin air – or rather, thin memes.

If you haven't heard of the Bored Apes Yacht Club (BAYC), you're probably not enough of a "cool kid." BAYC is a collection of 10,000 NFTs, each representing a somewhat different kind of bored ape. These NFTs can be purchased for several hundred thousand dollars (sometimes even a few million dollars) to become part of an exclusive community of cool kids, who get to hang out in some of the most glamorous venues together with their fellow apes. Since its launch in April 2021, the BAYC NFT collection has generated over 2.7 billion dollars of trade volume (Khatri, 2022). And since 10,000 Bored Apes were not enough to satisfy the greed of the crypto-art world, derivative collections of these apes were created through memetic engineering. New NFT collections, such as the Mutant Ape Yacht Club or the Bored Ape Kennel Club, were made available for free to the owners of a Bored Ape so that they could further disseminate to whoever they deem are the worthiest of these new apes. An uninterested gift as a generous sign of appreciation? More like a marketing campaign, as every sale of these NFT collections comes along with a royalty payment to the initiators of the collection. Besides, giving these NFTs away to the Bored Apes owners contributed to increasing the value of the original Bored Apes, and automatically created a new market for all these derivative apes. Most importantly, this contributed to turning the Bored Apes into an egregore, a collective and autonomous entity, powered by the collective (un)consciousness of the crypto-art world.

CONCLUSION

We have shown how, in this carnivalesque world, things that start as obvious jokes and potential scams might evolve into powerful egregors, turning frivolous jokes and facetious pranks into more serious entities with memetic power, which may eventually acquire real value because of the community that builds around them. Dogecoin and Rare Pepe are two examples of how things born out of a countermovement, aimed at exploring alternative realities beyond the status quo, can eventually fall prey to the very same system that they were originally trying to escape from – using the carnivalesque as a tool to trigger the emergence of an egregore that will be able to bring monetary value to digital assets that have no value in and of themselves. Similarly, the Shiba Inu and Bored Ape Yacht Club initiatives are examples of how egregores can be intentionally designed – for the best or the worst – using marketing strategies that take advantage of the power of communities to bring value to otherwise worthless objects. In both cases, the community, as memetic nodes which can comprise the networked instantiation of an egregore, is essential to create value where there was none before. Once launched into the wild, these egregores are no longer directly under our control, they will continue to evolve to please the crypto-finance and crypto-art world, on which they ultimately feed.

NOTES

1. See https://shibatoken.com/.
2. See https://www.change.org/t/shiba-inu-coin-en-us.
3. In this narrower sense, bankers can also be considered to have traits of the Trickster archetype, as they practice their own alchemy in creating new financial products and creatively exacting rents from financial transactions. See Kelsey (2017).

REFERENCES

Bodin, J. (1992). *Bodin: On sovereignty*. Cambridge University Press.
Campbell, J., & Moyers, B. (1991). *The power of myth*. Anchor.

Carroll, M. P. (1981). Lévi-Strauss, Freud, and the trickster: A new perspective upon an old problem. *American Ethnologist, 8*(2), 301–313. https://doi.org/10.1525/ae.1981.8.2.02a00050

Crawley, J. (2021, September 14). *Vitalik Buterin burns $6B in SHIB tokens, says he doesn't want the 'power.'* CoinDesk. https://www.coindesk.com/markets/2021/05/17/vitalik-buterin-burns-6b-in-shib-tokens-says-he-doesnt-want-the-power/

Dini, P., & Kioupkiolis, A. (2019). The alter-politics of complementary currencies: The case of Sardex. *Cogent Social Sciences, 5*(1), 1–21. https://doi.org/10.1080/23311886.2019.1646625.

Erdoes, R., & Ortiz, A. (1984). *American Indian myths and legends*. Pantheon.

Godet, A. (2020). Behind the masks. *Journal of Festive Studies, 2*(1), 1–31. https://doi.org/10.33823/jfs.2020.2.1.89

Holden, J. (n.d.). *An introduction to the Shiba Inu (part 1)*. https://www.shibas.org/newstand/intro_to_shiba_part1.pdf

Hynes, W., & Doty, W. (1997). Introducing the fascinating and perplexing trickster figure. In W. J. Hynes & W. G. Doty (Eds.), *Mythical trickster figures: Contours, contexts, and criticisms* (pp. 1–12). University of Alabama Press.

Jung, C. (2003). *Four archetypes*. Routledge.

Kelsey, D. (2017). *Media and affective mythologies: Discourse, archetypes and ideology in contemporary politics*. Palgrave Macmillan.

Khatri, Y. (2022). *Bored Ape NFT floor price hits record high above $430,000*. The Block. https://www.theblock.co/post/144399/bored-ape-nft-floor-price-hits-record-high-above-430000

Kiran, S. (2022, March 14). *Did Elon Musk really attend a Shiba Inu live event? Here's the truth*. Watcher Guru. https://watcher.guru/news/did-elon-musk-really-attend-a-shiba-inu-live-event-heres-the-truth

Mapperson, J. (2021, 3 March). Rarest Pepe – 'Most important NFT in art history' – Sells for 205 ETH. *Bitcoin Insider*. https://www.bitcoininsider.org/article/106699/rarest-pepe-most-important-nft-art-history-sells-205-eth

Rizzo, P. (2023, March 6). *Dogecoin foundation to raise $50k for Kenya's water crisis*. CoinDesk. https://www.coindesk.com/markets/2014/03/11/dogecoin-foundation-to-raise-50k-for-kenyas-water-crisis/

Robinson, A. (2011, January 11). In theory Bakhtin: Carnival against capital, carnival against power. 2012. *Ceasefire Magazine*. https://ceasefiremagazine.co.uk/in-theory-bakhtin-2/

Salinas, C. S.-R. (2013). *Trickster dialogics: A method for articulating cultural archetypes from 'Q' to performance art* [PhD dissertation, Arizona State University].

Seward, Z. (2021, September 14). *Vitalik's regift of unsolicited DOGE knockoffs sends memecoin prices plunging*. CoinDesk. https://www.coindesk.com/markets/2021/05/12/vitaliks-regift-of-unsolicited-doge-knockoffs-sends-memecoin-prices-plunging/

Unchained. (2023, July 7). *Rare Pepe NFTs: A brief introduction*. Unchained. https://unchainedcrypto.com/rare-pepe-nfts/

Van Riet, A. (2016, May). *Safeguarding the euro as a currency beyond the state* [Occasional Paper No. 173, ECB]. https://doi.org/10.2139/ssrn.2797259

CRYPTO PERSONALITIES AS CARNIVALESQUE JESTERS

Alesha Serada

University of Vaasa, Finland

ABSTRACT

In this paper, I discuss the personalities of several representative crypto YouTube celebrities and Bitcoin aficionados, such as George Tung from CryptosRUs, Mike Jenkins (Guy) from Coin Bureau, Lark Davis, Andreas M. Antonopoulos, and Richard Heart. I look closely at their online performances to reveal the character of a trickster, the ambivalent mythological figure that symbolizes chaos, creativity, and disruption. Based on the core literature on the subject, I trace how the figure of a trickster has transformed into the jester in medieval times, and then into the adventurer in the new modern times, and how this transformation is relevant for today. A variety of examples demonstrates that the jester, the trickster, and the adventurer all reveal themselves in different facets of crypto influencers' performances. However, the most popular YouTubers are also comparatively tame: they produce educational content on cryptocurrencies and blockchain, as compared to "get rich quick" schemes, which are typically presented with a higher degree of tricksteriness. There are also crucial differences and omissions: crypto influencers do not demonstrate queerness, which is inherent to the trickster, and they do not balance praise with abuse, as jesters do. The modern type of an adventurer is more fitting, although it is mostly found in the virtual Wild West of blockchain entrepreneurship, rather than on the most popular YouTube channels.

Keywords: Trickster; jester; adventurer; celebrity culture; YouTube; trust

TRICKSTER, JESTER, ADVENTURER: HOW TO DIAGNOSE A CRYPTO PERSONALITY

My intention here is to bring up a curious case that fits a variety of interpretations of tricksteriness, that is, crypto YouTubers in 2020–2022 (as ironically depicted in a collective sketch in Fig. 12.1). The particularities of differences between different traditions related to tricksters are up to debate. In different contexts, crypto celebrities can be interpreted as tricksters, jesters, or adventurers, which provides slightly different angles for understanding their role in contemporary society.

First, I refer to Radin's (1956) characterization of the Winnebago Trickster, which is one of the oldest recorded traditions coming from Native Americans. For a more specific Western angle, I use the conceptualization of a carnivalesque

Fig. 12.1. An Image Generated in DALL·E 2 on June 13, 2022, Based on the Text Prompt "crypto YouTuber."

jester by Mikhail Bakhtin (1984), which he crafted by studying the culture of Western Europe against his personal background of the tumultuous Soviet ordinary life. I refer to the English translation of the book, but my main source is the expanded Russian edition (Бахтин, 1990). To introduce the contemporary version of the modernist trickster, I turn to the figure of the European adventurer (French: "l'aventurier"), or opportunist, exemplified in the celebrity persona of Giacomo Casanova, and I turn to Alexandre Stroev for in-depth cultural analysis (Stroev, 1997; Строев, 1998). I refer to the authorized Russian edition of his book which was first published in French and then, slightly extended, in Russian.

THE TRICKSTER, NOW ON BLOCKCHAIN

A trickster can be found in many cultures. The educated Western audience is best familiar with the Winnebago Trickster Cycle, described in the classical ethnographic research by Paul Radin (1956).[i] The myth about the trickster may be universal, due to the similar challenges that humanity encountered in its development across continents (Radin, 1956, p. 134). In the myths of Native Americans, as well as in other cultures, a trickster is the agent of chaos but also the discoverer of new things. He causes harm to others but also always brings it on himself. The original Trickster is obsessed with sexual desires: "lust is his primary characteristic" (Radin, 1956, p. 136). He (or them, as they can be whoever, physically, and procreate with all genders) is inherently queer, bisexual, and gender-fluid. The Trickster's "... sex life, indeed, his whole physical life, is for him still something of a wild phantasmagoria" (Radin, 1956, p. 138), similar to carnal manifestations of "Rabelaisian humor" in European Middle Ages. For instance, the original Winnebago Trickster Wakdjunkaga cannot even place his genitals correctly on his own body, and he requests assistance from forest animals to make his penis the right size (Radin, 1956, p. 141). Later, and in a different culture, Gargantua will domesticate his genitals with his famous codpiece, the luxurious accessory meticulously crafted to support the "erective virtue" of his "natural member" (Rabelais, 1955, p. 21). Speaking of crypto YouTubers, we may hear the echo of this ancient tricksteriness in Richard Heart's comparison of his penis to a Red Bull can (Heart, 2022).

The Trickster embodies the becoming of a human: he is neither a deity nor a fully formed person. He is the outlier in a stable order and the exception in any categorization. Finally, the Trickster is the subject of unbelievable stories and hilarious anecdotes for people's enjoyment and entertainment. This may be everything a crypto YouTube personality would want to be.

However, most watched crypto personalities do not qualify for original tricksters: their performance is typically safely straight. Excessive mating behavior, prominent in the original Trickster, is also absent, if we leave out the most adventurous ones such as the late John McAfee or the very much alive Richard Heart. Those blessed ones who are not immersed in the blockchain discourse as a part of their job may be surprised to find out that the majority of top crypto YouTubers, for the most part, create the impression of incredibly smart and humorous people, fun to be around, at least, as virtual entertainers. They keep up with the latest news beyond their trade, make light-hearted jokes that are never too risky, and carefully maintain the facade of cool self-awareness. A regular crypto YouTuber is surprisingly discreet, albeit always ready for a little transgression. For example, George Tong from CryptosRUS jokes about creating an account at OnlyFans, and Guy from Coin Bureau complains about the perils of dating. Behind this facade, we may even catch a hint of an "authentic" and, in a good sense, unremarkable life (Coin Bureau, 2022a) – in sharp contrast with Richard Heart (2022).

There is one mantra, though, that breaks the immersion for a critically thinking audience member: every crypto YouTuber will tell you that Bitcoin shall go to the moon, no reasonable explanation needed. Bitcoin aficionados retain their beliefs in certain properties of cryptocurrencies even when reality proves otherwise (Knittel et al., 2019; Vidan & Lehdonvirta, 2019). It may be that these inconsistencies in the worldview of a "true Bitcoiner" are rooted in the well-familiar archetype of a trickster, who embraces absurdity and controversy.

> Bear markets are tough. But don't give in to the crazy bears who say that everything is going to go to zero. We probably have a lot more pain and sideways action to come for the crypto, but crypto is not going to zero – it is not going away. And, just to show my belief in that, I bought some more Bitcoin today. I keep averaging in every single week. (Davis, 2022)

There is one important feature that is specific to blockchain-based entrepreneurship, as opposed to the tech startup scene in general, or even generic "not-financial advice" on YouTube: tricksteriness is an inherent quality of the crypto discourse, even in its tamest forms. Generally, the job of crypto personalities is to generate trust in Bitcoin and blockchain and to maintain this trust despite the many crushes of the market and daily broken promises of the technology. This task is made almost impossible by the fragility of their own status and the extreme volatility of their subject. By the nature of their job, a crypto personality is someone "who dupes others and who is always duped himself" (Radin, 1956, p. ix), just as the classical North American trickster.

This carnivalesque spirit still dwells even in the least chaotic of crypto personalities. We may find such an example in Andreas M. Antonopoulos, a notable "bitcoiner" and a top crypto YouTuber (probably one of the most popular ideologists of Bitcoin on YouTube, which generally favors more practical content over ideology). His presentation rarely takes the elaborate forms of a staged and edited YouTube video; Antonopoulos mostly records and publishes talks in a more traditional form of on-stage performance. And yet, he also has the Trickster in him. The Trickster performs the "two-fold function of benefactor and buffoon" (Radin, 1956, p. 124). He brings chaos and destruction, but he may also, mostly accidentally, bring culture to the people.

> International wire transfers have always been kind of an Achilles heel of traditional finance. They are slow, insecure, expensive, full of delays and uncertainty, you never know if it's going to get there in an hour or three weeks. And you stumble up across all of this patchwork of regulation anytime you try to do an international wire transfer. And this is the area where cryptocurrency shines. (Biz Jet TV, 2020)

In the real world, everything that Antonopoulos said about wire transfers is true for cryptocurrencies, while wire transfers, in fact, "shine" and mostly do their job as they should.[ii] However, Antonopoulos is still a trickster (this is how he can perform a complete inversion of the real world's state of things, wide-eyed and with a straight face). Being the trickster that he is, he accidentally makes a surprisingly reasonable claim that blockchain can be useful to create immutable records of maintenance and flight logs in aviation.

> The ability to immutably record maintenance logs and, perhaps, even flight logs, because these are documents that are often critical in post-accident forensic investigation. (Biz Jet TV, 2020)

Not everything that a trickster says is colorful exaggeration and (self-)deception. This is how tricksters gain trust, but also, this is why they are not taken seriously. Misunderstood and punished tricksters have been a staple of every mythology, and the reason to punish them was almost always "not knowing their place." In sheer numbers, probably the most popular character of this kind is the legendary Chinese monkey trickster Sun Wukong, known in popular culture for causing "havoc in Heaven" and being locked up for that. The European Loki would come second, recently also popularized in the United States by Marvel Comics and their TV series. We should, however, critically re-evaluate the role of a trickster in the current times, when material safety is in much shorter supply than utopian disruption.

THE CRYPTOCARNIVALESQUE JESTER

While other authors of this book have already covered the concept of cryptocarnival, here I will focus on the concept of a jester. Radin (1956), who is also familiar with the European tradition, suggests that the medieval European jester has inherited many of the Trickster's traits (p. ix): a jester is disruptive, he is comical, he turns the world upside down. The jester and the king are two interchangeable symbolic figures of the carnival, where one inevitably turns into another: "The king's attributes are turned upside down in the clown; he is the king of a world, 'turned inside out'" (Bakhtin, 1984, p. 370). Performing "the king of the world" is very common on celebrity YouTube; however, many popular and trusted crypto YouTubers present themselves as down-to-earth, ordinary people with a bit of tricksteriness up their sleeve. They generate trust by alternating between a charming madcap and even more relatably as "just your average Guy." This is why George Tung from CryptosRUs starts his streams with a catchphrase: "I am George, we're all George."

> I try to be modest, I try to live a modest lifestyle, but I've attained that life-changing wealth. What I've been telling you guys about dollar cost average, and hodling, and achieving life-changing wealth, – I have achieved it. And I have achieved it not through some prestigious job or some prestigious business, – I've attained it by buying low and hodling. (Tung, 2021)

The jester is an inherently democratic figure: he is out in public for everyone to see, and he performs for the poor and the rich alike. Same as jesters of the past, crypto YouTubers constantly mock the authorities, speak against oppression of the impoverished and the unbanked (which is just a rhetorical figure in this context), and provide surprisingly competent emotional support in the times of fear when the market is "bearish." This becomes a routine performance, as the cryptocurrency market undergoes a major crash almost every year.

> I'm not selling. I'm not selling at all. Some people have claimed that I run the biggest "hopium" channel, and I only talk about what's coming, and I never really focus on the downs and stuff. I do, I do tell you guys that the best time to buy is when the things are down, right? but people claim that "hey, you know what, you've been wrong." I have been wrong. I am a human. I am not God. If I was God, I would have all the money in the world already, or I wouldn't even need money – that's really silly, right? (Tung, 2021)

Folk masses would eagerly trust the jester because he was the opposite of power, oppression, and fear. He heralded the alternative kind of truth, joyous and improper, that helped to resist the hypocrisy of the powerful through carnivalesque laughter (Bakhtin, 1984, pp. 93–94). The liberating potential of folk laughter recognized no authority, and nothing was sacred. In fact, the main purpose of the carnival is to swap around the sacred and the profane. This is how trust was gained at the medieval marketplace, at least, in Bakhtin's carnivalesque: the unofficial folk truth treats seriousness as a sign of deception.

In this scheme of the world, the figure of a jester (fool) is closely related to the concept of "praise-abuse": a public verbal performance that simultaneously praises and verbally abuses its subject. For instance, in Gargantua's prologue, it is passionately described as "the cry of the barker, the quack, the hawker of miracle drugs, and the bookseller" (Bakhtin, 1984, p. 167) – a subversive sales pitch that could be heard at the medieval marketplace.

We may find a rather tame equivalent of "praise-abuse" in the performance of Crypto Guy, the character created by Mike Jenkins. Every video on his "The Coin Bureau" channel starts with the announcement that Guy is not a financial advisor, which is legally required in the media that discuss financial issues. Early in his career, Jenkins started embellishing disclaimers to avoid repetition; sometimes he rhymes them, as a jester would do; in other cases, he creates a different comical character who delivers the "praise-abuse." For instance, in one of such sketches, the character based on Tony Montana from De Palma's (1983) *Scarface* mocks Guy for being unqualified as a financial advisor but praises him for delivering high-quality educational content. Both characters are played by Jenkins.

> (In the character of Tony Montana): "'F you came here for financial advice, 'en forget it. You little friend Guy ain't no financial advisor, he's just some punk on the internet, making his videos for education and entertainment ...." (Coin Bureau, 2022b)

One might point at the slightly cringeworthy hyperperformativity of this character; Jenkins is obviously clowning, not acting, in this role. The other character of Guy is not so obviously carnivalesque, but it is used as a persona that Jenkins wears even in his unscripted performances, when he keeps his inner jester concealed. In this regard, being a celebrity persona in general is very much like the job of a jester: "... they were not actors playing their parts on a stage ... but remained fools and clowns always and wherever they made their appearance" (Bakhtin, 1984, p. 8). This also begs the question whether we may treat one's performance in a video as ordinary life. However, in 2020–2022, to many of us, and especially YouTube celebrities, streaming has been the prevailing form of performing social interaction, and the line between mediated and unmediated life has almost disappeared.

Especially in the times of COVID-19, mediated online performance of a crypto jester can be compared to the later form of carnivalesque, the Romantic grotesque that was mostly mediated through literature: "an individual carnival, marked by a vivid sense of isolation" (Bakhtin, 1984, p. 37). In this derivative, and hopelessly modern, form, mediated through Romantic literature, "laughter was cut down to cold humor, irony, sarcasm" (Bakhtin, 1984, p. 38). Irony is relatively rare in crypto discourse in general (although its level increases during "crypto winters," at least, judging by the amount of self-deprecating memes on Twitter). Top crypto YouTube personalities rarely take risks by making ironic statements, which can easily be misinterpreted by their fan base, but certain elements of the grotesque carnivalesque reveal themselves in the professionally scripted, staged, and cut broadcasts of The Coin Bureau. Its host Guy still retains some of his joyousness as a crypto trickster; it is hard to tell, however, how "authentic" this joyousness is. Again, to a critical viewer, this performance becomes melancholic, almost tragic, when Guy reluctantly makes his obligatory joke about not being a financial advisor at the beginning of each video. It feels almost as if he swore to be funny and original about unfunny and mundane things twice a week until the end of his crypto career.

THE BLOCKCHAIN AFICIONADO AS AN ADVENTURER

For the goals of our study, the main difference between the trickster, the jester, and the adventurer can be found in how much courage and weirdness would be required for them to signify radical social disruption. The degree of recklessness and absurdity seems to diminish, as society moves from more conservative and traditional to open and innovative regimes of operation. Despite its many failures, contemporary Westernized society has provided the highest level of social mobility so far; in the meantime, everyone can become a "visionary" and an "innovator," even if just for 15 minutes on YouTube. In comparison, traditional society would require turning the world upside down, symbolically, for someone to even imagine changing one's social status. The figure of the European adventurer is representative of such transformation of the social system from rigid and closed to fluid and open; this is also the most recognizable type among blockchain entrepreneurs in real life. On YouTube, we may find the most iconic example in Richard Heart, and the most obvious sign of his adventurer-like personality is his "largest cut diamond" that he showcases. Let us find out why.

As feudal society was disintegrating in Europe throughout the 17th century, so did the folk laughter culture (Bakhtin, 1984, p. 33). New capitalist relationships were emerging across Europe, and going "from rags to riches" was now, at least, imaginable, if not particularly probable. This is how the concept of "life-changing wealth" entered fictional and real-life narratives, which typically featured the character of an adventurer, during the Enlightenment. Initially, a French "l'aventurier" signified social mobility, which was unthinkable in a traditional society.

An adventurer is a person of unknown social status, but most likely, the impoverished lower middle class, who is able to infiltrate the upper class by all means necessary. A typical adventurer exhibits exotic tastes and conspicuous consumption; he may be covered with jewelry, even though some of it is fake (Строев, 1998, p. 19). In high society, he is the agent of chaos and a magnet for misfortune, which he is still able to use to his own benefit (Строев, 1998, p. 18). Same as the Winnebago Trickster, the adventurer "... possesses no values, moral or social, is at the mercy of his passions and appetites, yet through his actions all values come into being" (Radin, 1956, p. ix). The best example here is the famous adventurer Giacomo Casanova, best remembered for his mastery as a pickup artist with the impressively long list of women (and men) whom he seduced.

While the adventurer may take up the role of the "king of the carnival" in some narratives of its epoch, he is different from a carnivalesque jester. Unlike jesters, adventurers would rarely perform in public. European adventurers of the 18th century had the luxury of a private life when they could be their "authentic selves" (even in prison). They mostly addressed their painstakingly crafted performances directly to the elites, especially the aristocracy and the nobility, from whom they extracted money by borderline unlawful means. Today, a crypto adventurer performs for investors, rather than for the public, like crypto jesters.

The *ethos* of an adventurer and a blockchain aficionado is generally the same. They both support their lifestyle by collecting investments into elaborate financial schemes and innovative technologies. There is one particular shared belief, acquired in early modernity, that is almost uncanny: both the adventurer and the blockchain adopter passionately wish to delegate governance to the machine (see Rohr, 2019). Alexandre Stroev dissects this passion of the late 18th century adventurers in the chapter "The Ideal State of the Lottery." The adventurer "turns the Fortune of Fortune into the tool for selection of people and redistribution of wealth, in order to build the ideal society ..." (Stroev, 1997, p. 191, my translation from Russian).

Casanova was not even the first believer in the "code is law" principle. This honor belongs to the influential Enlightenment thinker Diderot, who proposed the project of the state lottery that would serve as progressive taxation and presumably decrease inequality in French society. Eventually, none other than the adventurous Casanova established the state lottery in France, motivated not so much by profit (which appeared to be quite substantial), as by his fascination with cryptography and mathematics (Строев, 1998, p. 200). Casanova also practiced less conventional sciences: for instance, he staged alchemic rituals in attempt to help his "friend with benefits," the fellow adventurer Madame d'Urfé, to be reborn in the body of a young boy (Строев, 1998, p. 174) – speaking of suppressed queerness on the startup scene almost three centuries ago. Tragically, we have yet to find a crypto YouTube celebrity that queer (please send tips).

CONCLUSION: CRYPTO, YOU ARE NOT BEING WEIRD ENOUGH

Is cryptocarnival the true carnival, at least, as represented by its YouTube spokespersons? Even though YouTube lacks the sociality and physical presence of the historical carnival culture, crypto influencers still utilize several important elements of this culture. These elements include disruption of social order, reversion of social roles and meanings, and creation of the utopian second world where everything is possible. However, this is not enough to employ the carnivalesque to the full extent. At large, the crypto community lacks in laughter, queerness, and grotesque. This is why the face of crypto is boredom, not laughter. Its community is united not by the visceral joy of collective celebration, but by the populist sentiment of "us against them." Such illusion may create the illusion of overcoming fear and doubt but also can be used to cultivate fanaticism and idolatry. Sadly, these are the exact things against which the trickster and the jester were fighting.

The stories of a trickster, a jester and, to some extent, of an adventurer, prove that productive social disruption is incompatible with financial motivation. In the latter case, instead of joyful and inherently humane carnival, we observe a "society of the spectacle" (Debord, 1983), an illusion produced by circulation of the already accumulated capital. The purpose of this spectacle is to extract value from the consumers, rather than liberate them from the consumerist ways of living. At the beginning of the previous "crypto winter," Richard Heart promised salvation to all his fans, which, of course, comes at the price of buying into his own Ethereum-based coin HEX. The examples of Heart and McAfee demonstrate how tricksteriness transforms into adventureness when a crypto personality has a financial interest in the form of their own project or a coin. Such examples have mostly remained out of scope of this brief review, which has focused on the most popular crypto YouTubers. It is notable, however, that the most popular videos on crypto YouTube are still basic explanations of how Bitcoin and blockchain work, which demonstrates that their popularity is driven by curiosity and information foraging of the most general audience. Crypto YouTubers who are also entrepreneurs and/or scammers typically have smaller but more devoted audiences, and their performance is far more chaotic, but this should be the subject for another research.

How can we escape the rule of the old Capital and launch our own Carnival? In order to qualify as fully carnivalesque, crypto personalities should be cursing Bitcoin just as much as they are praising it. The jester is allowed to speak freely, delivering "praise-abuse," even at the king's court. Of course, this regime of truth is not without consequences: it can also be directed back to the jester himself. To add injury to insult, verbal abuse would turn easily into physical abuse at the real-life carnival. Naturally, this kind of disruption creates an occupational hazard for the Jester-King. According to Bakhtin (1984), "... The king is the clown. He is elected by all the people and is mocked by all the people. He is abused and beaten when the time of his reign is over ..." (p. 197). In the crypto-adjacent community, the best example of the sacrificial jester is the late John McAfee; in addition to being a notorious trickster, he had been involved in a truly Rabelaisian sex scandal

(I will leave the essence of the scandal for curious readers to research themselves). This eccentric episode still makes sense when viewed through the prism of the carnivalesque: it perfectly embodies "the destroying and renewing force of the material bodily lower stratum" (Bakhtin, 1984, pp. 266–267), transgressing the boundaries between the body and the earthly matter. Regardless of the true cause of his death, McAfee was just too much of a trickster for this world.

NOTES

i. This trope has been popularized by Carl Jung, who described the Trickster as one of cultural archetypes, although Jung's work should not be treated as credible or scientific but rather a cultural appropriation, conveniently adapted for Western readers.

ii. Here, I could speak about the countries under sanctions and the unbanked, sadly, from my personal experience, but to put it very, very shortly, cryptocurrencies are the absolute last means that the unbanked would use, precisely because they are extremely "slow, insecure, expensive, full of delays and uncertainty" as compared to other relatively legal underground money networks. If sanctioned by the state, they are also very prone to state-level corruption.

REFERENCES

Bakhtin, M. M. (1984). *Rabelais and his world*. Indiana University Press.
Biz Jet TV. (Director). (2020, July 25). *Bitcoin, blockchain & private aviation* [Video]. YouTube. https://www.youtube.com/watch?v=-usR_cqBMxQ
Coin Bureau. (Director). (2022a, January 21). *Macey discusses her portfolio!!* 🚀 [Video]. YouTube. https://www.youtube.com/watch?v=GP6CrZnQddc
Coin Bureau. (Director). (2022b, February 13). *Behind the scenes: Scarface disclaimer!* 👑 [Video]. YouTube. https://www.youtube.com/watch?v=1UmYQBEpjZY
Davis, L. (Director). (2022, June 13). *Here's why Bitcoin, Ethereum, & crypto are crashing today* [Video]. YouTube. https://www.youtube.com/watch?v=zZIY9wlw6uc
Debord, G. (1983). *Society of the spectacle* (K. Knabb, Trans.). Black & Red.
De Palma, Brian (Director). (1983). *Scarface*. Universal Studios.
Heart, R. (Director). (2022, May 17). Playboy model learns about finance with Richard Heart. How to get rich in the bull market and bear! [Video]. YouTube. https://www.youtube.com/watch?v=p_xj2SlZZ7A
Knittel, M., Pitts, S., & Wash, R. (2019). "The most trustworthy coin": How ideological tensions drive trust in Bitcoin. *Proceedings of the ACM on Human–Computer Interaction*, *3*(CSCW), 1–23. https://doi.org/10.1145/3359138
Rabelais, F. (1955). *Works*. Tudor.
Radin, P. (1956). *The trickster: A study in American Indian mythology*. Philosophical Library.
Rohr, J. (2019). Smart contracts in traditional contract law, or: The law of the vending machine. *Cleveland State Law Review*, *67*, 23.
Stroev, A. (1997). *Les aventuriers des lumières*. FeniXX.
Tung, G. (Director). (2021, May 30). *Bitcoin capitulation is coming – Why I'm not selling*. CryptosRUs. [Video]. YouTube. https://www.youtube.com/watch?v=EYWO-CIo0OY
Vidan, G., & Lehdonvirta, V. (2019). Mine the gap: Bitcoin and the maintenance of trustlessness. *New Media & Society*, *21*(1), 42–59. https://doi.org/10.1177/1461444818786220
Бахтин, М. (1990). Творчество Франсуа Рабле и народная культура Средневековья и Ренессанса. Художественная литература.
Строев, А. (1998). "Те, кто поправляет фортуну": Авантюристы Просвещения. Новое литературное обозрение.

WEB3: THE GENTRIFIED CARNIVAL?

Donncha Kavanagh

University College Dublin, Ireland

ABSTRACT

Web3 reflects and instantiates the "ludic turn" of the last few decades, where identity is increasingly forged through play and games rather than through work. The ludic is especially evident in the Bitcoin ecosystem, where the elements of the carnivalesque – play, anarchy, dissimulation, vulgar language, and excessive consumption – are pervasive. These elements may also be divined in Web3, though they are less ubiquitous, which suggests that Web3 is perhaps best seen as a gentrified *carnival.*

Keywords: Carnivalesque; Bitcoin; gentrification; dissimulation; Web3

Carnival, then, does not describe freedom, or even a new authority, but rather the process by which one authority replaces another through the temporary institution of madness in society. (Dowling, 2020, p. 54)

In his classic book, *The Grasshopper*, Bernard Suits (1978) argues that playing games is the supreme good, for the simple reason that in a Utopia, we would play games rather than work. And while a workless, playful world might still be fanciful – despite talk about how artificial intelligence will make work redundant (Danaher, 2019) – the latter part of the 20th century has certainly seen a shift from a work to a play ethic. For instance, membership of trade unions has decreased as people increasingly build their identity on play rather than work (union membership in the United States has dropped from over 20% of the civilian labor force in 1983 to 10% in 2021 (US Bureau of Labor Statistics, 2022)), while political parties, like the Labour Party in the United Kingdom, have found it difficult to frame a political ideology centered on work and employment. In contrast, individuals are increasingly forging their identities around play rather

---

Defining Web3: A Guide to the New Cultural Economy
Research in the Sociology of Organizations, Volume 89, 147–154
Copyright © 2024 by Donncha Kavanagh
Published under exclusive licence by Emerald Publishing Limited
ISSN: 0733-558X/doi:10.1108/S0733-558X20240000089013

than work: two-thirds of US adults and three-quarters of children under 18 play video games weekly (Entertainment Software Association, 2021); the principal web forum for board games, boardgamegeek, which was founded in 2000, has a database of some 140,000 table-top games; while the global sports market is estimated to be worth over US$500 billion (Wood, 2022). This empirical reality has, since 2000, been accompanied by a flood of journal articles and books about play and games, which contrasts with the whole of the 20th century when relatively few books on the subject were published on the subject (e.g., Caillois, 1961; Huizinga, 1949).

Crypto reflects and instantiates this turn to the ludic. The mining of cryptocurrencies is designed as a competitive game of chance and resources, with the winner obtaining a prize (a block reward or coins of the cryptocurrency). Mining is also a cooperative game where the game design incentivizes miners to work together to ensure the game is not hijacked by "bad" actors. For many in the domain, cryptocurrencies are just speculative gambles, the latest installment of what Strange (1986) calls "casino capitalism" but with a novel, digital twist. Thus, a particular branch of crypto, decentralized finance (DeFi), can be understood as just a development of conventional finance, which is itself infused with algorithms from game theory and advanced mathematical techniques for optimizing rewards in games of chance.

But crypto is about more than play and games. Hence, in an earlier paper, I proposed that cryptocurrencies, but Bitcoin in particular, exhibit many of the attributes associated with the medieval carnival (Kavanagh & Miscione, 2019). However, Bitcoin and Web3 are not the same, and so the issue I address in this paper is the degree to which Web3 exhibits the same attributes of the carnival. In short, is Web3 a form of carnival and to what extent can the metaphor help us understand the nature of Web3? In some ways, Web3 is even more of a carnival than Bitcoin in that a vast panoply of very different games exist on the various blockchains that underpin Web3. Unlike Bitcoin, which was designed with a specific, but limited purpose, the Ethereum blockchain was designed as a digital infrastructure into which one could "plug-and-play" many types of activities, with smart contracts prescribing the "rules of the game." This diversity of forms of play and games, reflecting independent creative output from many producers, mirrors the diversity of the traditional carnival with its multiplicity of games and activities. Moreover, just as one must pay money – often in the form of tokens – to play many of the carnival games, so too it is in Web3's token economy.

In the carnival, things are often not what they appear to be. It is a place of make-believe, misrepresentation, and dissimulation: what you see is *not* what you get. Identity is also disguised, which is why the mask is the carnival's iconic image. Hiding identity has been a long-standing ambition in the crypto world – though less so in Web3 – going back to the cypherpunk movement of the 1980s, which was dedicated to building anonymous systems on the Internet, including anonymous digital money (Lopp, 2016). Fittingly, the identity of Satoshi Nakamoto, who wrote the original Bitcoin white paper, is still unknown to this day. More broadly, cryptographic algorithms are the tool of choice as they ensure anonymity while their own inner workings are axiomatically unknowable.

But facilitating anonymity has opened up the crypto world to all sorts of hustles, scams, rug pulls, and trickery, usually designed to prey on the newcomer's desire to make a quick dollar (Mackenzie, 2022). Trickery and dissimulation are consistent with the ethos of the carnival, but in the crypto world, it manifests as outright criminality on a significant scale. The deceit and duplicity go back at least to the Mt Gox collapse in 2011, with the loss of 850,000 bitcoins, worth more than $450 million at the time, but scams, hacks, "pump and dump," and Ponzi schemes have continued unrelentingly since then. In 2021, cryptocurrency-based crime hit an all-time high when illicit addresses received $14 billion, up from $7.8 billion in 2020 (Grauer et al., 2022, p. 3).

Even the carnival cannot tolerate this level of crime, and so there has been a concerted effort to address the criminal opportunities inherent in a system that valorizes anonymity. Hence, the cypherpunk obsession with privacy is much less central to Web3 than it is to Bitcoin, and instead significant work has been put into creating Sybil-resistant identity systems, decentralized proof-of-personhood and reputation systems, and new initiatives such as non-transferable soul-bound tokens (Weyl et al., 2022). However, as Ford (2020) has argued, these systems of digital personhood will be inadequate unless they are also coercion-resistant, which would require creating digital versions of the privacy booths used in in-person voting. Creating such systems presents technical and security/privacy challenges that will almost certainly conflict with the cypherpunk/Bitcoin desire for anonymity. These initiatives, which are still very much in progress, suggest that the carnival metaphor needs to evolve along with the evolution of the crypto world from Bitcoin to Web3. One way of conceptualizing this evolution is to say that Web3 has *gentrified* the Bitcoin carnival.

In his seminal book on play, *Homo Ludens*, Huizinga (1949) argued that play was foundational to both festival (as in carnival) and ritual. Indeed for Huizinga (1949), "there is no formal difference between play and ritual, [and] so the 'consecrated spot' cannot be formally distinguished from the play-ground" (p. 10). History supports this position as the carnival has always had a strong religious dimension – carnival was the Catholic festive period before the liturgical and fasting season of Lent. If Lent was a period of abstinence, commemorating the 40 days Jesus spent fasting in the desert, carnival was a period of indulgence, excessive consumption, public entertainment, social satire, grotesque bodily displays, vulgarity, and a general reversal of social norms – the word carnival is derived from the Latin phrase *carne levare*, which means "remove meat." Today, we tend to be unaware of or ignore the carnival's association with religion, consumption, and fasting, but it can still be useful as we grapple with defining Web3.

In an insightful paper, Faustino et al. (2021) describe and analyze the quasi-religious nature of the crypto-community toward blockchain technologies, and they explore how myth, faith, and ritual work in this context to translate contemporary anxieties around the financial crisis and the centralization of power. For them, the mysterious creator of Bitcoin, Satoshi Nakamoto (2021), is analogous to the legendary King Arthur, in that "Nakamoto embodies the reputation of a noble altruist in the crypto-community, offering salvation from a crisis by introducing decentralisation as a new ruling power: a round table of equals rather than of a despotic sovereign" (p. 6). Thus, Nakamoto's (2008) white paper has now been accorded the status of a "sacred text" from which Bitcoin maximalists seem loath to deviate, though in practice they have accepted innovations in the Bitcoin ecosystem.

The Irish author, Brendan Behan, reputably quipped that the first item on the agenda of any new Irish political party was "the Split." And so it has been with crypto, with its forks in existing blockchains, new blockchains, Civil Wars, and new labels for communities within an ecosystem (e.g., solarpunks and lunarpunks). Crypto is certainly full of variety, but at a high level, it is worth contrasting the cult of Bitcoin and the cult of Ethereum. If Nakamoto is Bitcoin's mythical quasi-religious leader – giving birth to Bitcoin through a cryptographic version of immaculate conception – Ethereum's mythological equivalent must be Vitalik Buterin, who authored the original Ethereum white paper and has continued to play a Christ-like role in the Ethereum community. Tellingly, when the first popular decentralized autonomous organization (DAO) – The DAO – came unstuck due to an exaggerated belief in the rational authority of smart contracts, the decision to fork the blockchain was largely due to his intervention and charismatic authority (DuPont, 2017). On the darker side, Moloch, an ancient Carthaginian demon, has been repurposed within Web3 as the "demon" responsible for those coordination failures that occur when individual incentives are misaligned with globally optimum outcomes (the prisoners' dilemma and the tragedy of the commons are good examples). Ethereum, its disciples argue, provides the means, through DAOs, to slay this god of coordination failures, Moloch (Hoffman, 2020; Soleimani et al., 2019).

As well as having a pantheon of quasi-religious deities, crypto cults also appropriate other religious practices, such as rituals, sacred texts, shared worldviews, ethics, and the like. Here, I will just focus on the religious aspects of the carnival, specifically the carnival's association with excessive consumption as a counter to the abstinence of Lent. In the case of Bitcoin, the excess is most obviously manifest in its consensus mechanism's obscene consumption of energy (its annualized consumption was estimated at 95TWh in September 2022, which is more than what the Philippines consumes (Cambridge Centre for Alternative Finance, 2022). That excess contrasts with the engineered *scarcity* of bitcoins, where the number of bitcoins is deliberately limited. In contrast, Web3's political economy is defined by *surplus* – as an endless number of tokens can be produced and there are no material constraints – rather than the scarcity of traditional capitalism. Moreover, Ethereum's move to proof-of-stake means that the excessive consumption associated with proof-of-work has now been eliminated. So, with Bitcoin, tokens are scarce and energy consumption is excessive, while Web3's trajectory is in the opposite direction: there is an excess of tokens, while energy consumption is minimal.

The carnival metaphor sheds further light on how Web3 differs from Bitcoin in terms of its attitude to authority. The medieval carnival exhibited two elements related to power structures. First, the carnival created a space and time where all participants are considered equal, where hierarchy and status are suspended, and where there is free contact between those who might normally be separated by profession, property, caste, or age. This produces a temporary social unity, like the unity of an enclave. We find this ideology of equivalence in both Bitcoin and Web3 as both systems are designed around the idea of bringing people together in a digital world of equality. Moreover, this pursuit of equality underpins the commitment to privacy that is a feature of both systems, even if that commitment is stronger in Bitcoin.

The carnival's second power dimension centers on how it enables and encourages authority to be contested. We see this in the inversions – such as a commoner playing the role of a king – which can be seen as the lower orders challenging the dominant social hierarchy (Bakhtin, 1968, p. 109). Similarly, the carnival enables forms of illegal behavior – such as prostitution, violence, drunkenness, stealing – to be temporarily allowed, even expected. But the challenge to authority is not always benign, and carnivals can also be a potential locus for revolt. This mix of fun, creativity, and rebellion is well captured in this stanza from *The Humours of Donnybrook Fair*, a song about an annual fair held in Donnybrook, Dublin, founded by charter of King John in 2014:

To Donnybrook steer, all you sons of Parnassus

Poor painters, poor poets, poor newsmen, poor knaves

To see what the fun is that all fun surpasses

The sorrow and sadness of green Erin's slaves

The song dates from at least the early 19th century as Croker (1839, pp. 184–189) includes it in his collection. Parnassus is a metaphor for arts and learning, while the mention of "green Erin's slaves" alludes to the long history of Irish uprisings – especially the rebellions of 1798 and 1803 – against English rule. Donnybrook Fair was always associated with "rough merriment," and indeed, the word "donnybrook" has entered the dictionary as meaning "rowdy brawl" or "scene of chaos." Bitcoin instantiates this rebellious version of the carnival, as it feeds on the cryptopunk/crypto-anarchist ideology that explicitly seeks to subvert the existing social order, especially the power of the state and banks.

The authorities' response to the carnival can be ambivalent. One approach is to license social protest as a way of containing potential rebellion and confirming the existing social order (Burkert, 1985; Sales, 1983). Alternatively, the carnival can be heavily regulated or subdued. For instance, from the early 19th century, the evangelicals sought to end Donnybrook Fair, which they saw as an affront to moral rectitude. Along with the evangelists, the state, the police, and the temperance crusaders worked to abolish the fair, but it took their combined forces some 60 years to succeed, as the annual fair continued up to 1868, even though for most of the 19th century, the fair was "woefully quiet, almost respectable" (D'Arcy, 1988).

The authorities have been similarly ponderous in their attempts at regulating Bitcoin. Some 13 years after the first bitcoins were minted, the regulatory bodies are still only getting to grips with how to govern cryptoassets and cryptocurrency markets. Initially, the authorities largely ignored cryptocurrencies, taking the reasonable view that they don't regulate private gambling or sales of the Linden dollar, the virtual currency used in Second Life. In recent years, they have become more active in response to the rising value of cryptoassets and the proliferation of scams, rug pulls, and the like. However, a comprehensive regulatory regime is still not in place, partly because the domain is so novel and dynamic and because the regulators want to foster innovation and, at the same time, ensure the field is robust, fair, and resilient.

At the same time, and not unlike the "civilization" of Donnybrook Fair, much of Web3 has now forgotten, ignored, or been unaware of the anti-state ideology that animated Web3's origins in Bitcoin, the cypherpunks and crypto-anarchists. This may be because, notwithstanding the rhetoric of equality, what we have in Web3 is a *gentrified* carnival, devoid of Bitcoin's rebellious anti-statism but retaining the carnival's playfulness and creativity (Ennis, 2017). There are still scams and illegal behavior, but these are best understood as individual money-making rackets rather than a collective attempt to create a new social order (Campbell-Verduyn & Hütten, 2019).

While Bitcoin exhibits many of attributes of the medieval carnival – perceived equality, dissimulation, token-based games, play, ritual, mythology, excess consumption, subversion of authority – in the case of Web3, it seems better to see the carnival as gentrified, denuded of the excesses, criminality and anti-statism that characterize Bitcoin. And while I have not conducted a detailed content analysis of Web3 and Bitcoin discourse, my sense is that Web3 is not characterized by the vulgar and crude language that, in our earlier paper, we found in the online chatter about bitcoin and which Bakhtin identified as a special, generative form of communication associated with the carnival (Kavanagh & Miscione, 2019). Instead, Web3 appears to debate issues in a more genteel manner, befitting its concern with funding public goods and maintaining the ecosystem's infrastructure.

Another important feature missing from the cryptocarnival – in its Bitcoin and Web3 manifestations – is ilinx, one of Caillois' (1961) four forms of play. Ilinx, or vertigo, is a play that consists "of an attempt to momentarily destroy the stability of perception and inflict a kind of voluptuous panic upon an otherwise lucid mind" (Caillois, 1961, p. 23). In the carnival, ilinx occurs any time there is a rapid whirling or falling movement that might cause dizziness, such as in the various vertigo-inducing contraptions that feature in fairgrounds and amusement parks. But Web3 has no swings or merry-go-rounds, no ilinx. More broadly, Web3 is a virtual environment, separate from the physical world and hence devoid of ilinx. The physical world is sometimes referred to as "meatspace," and perhaps, there is nothing more meaty than the carnival, given that the word "carnival" is derived from the Latin *carnis*, meaning "meat." Web3 is thus beyond the realm of what Loïc Wacquant terms "carnal sociology" or a "sociology of flesh and blood," which, at its core, contains a carnal conception of the agent, at odds with the neo-Benthamite, utility maximizing agent (homo economicus), and the neo-Kantian symbolic animal of cultural anthropology (Wacquant, 2015). The challenge, then, for Web3 is to, em, flesh out its carnival, engaging much more with "meatspace," the physical world. Indeed, this is already happening as we see in the regen movement and in new initiatives such as Chainlink (chain.link) which seeks to expand the capabilities of smart contracts by enabling access to real-world data.

In this short paper, I have explored how the carnival metaphor might help us answer the question, "What is Web3?" The metaphor is useful in that so much happens in the carnival, and we can certainly identify many elements of the carnival in Bitcoin. But the metaphor seems to work less well in Web3, or at least it might be better to see Web3 as a gentrification of the Bitcoin carnival, as there is much less concern about overthrowing the state or the banking system and more focus on the genteel practice of building public goods and a decentralized, resilient digital infrastructure. Or maybe even that is going too far, as Web3 lacks the giddiness, the meatiness, the smells, the vulgarity, the pains, the grotesque, and the visceral experiences of the carnival. But then again, that might be just another layer of trickery: misrepresenting Web3 as a cryptocarnival when it is anything but.

REFERENCES

Bakhtin, M. (1968). *Rabelais and his world*. Indiana University Press.
Burkert, W. (1985). *Greek religion: Archaic and classical*. Harvard University Press.
Caillois, R. (1961). *Man, play and games*. Thames and Hudson.
Cambridge Centre for Alternative Finance. (2022). *Cambridge Bitcoin electricity consumption index (CBECI)*. Cambridge Bitcoin Electricity Consumption Index. https://ccaf.io/cbeci/index/comparisons
Campbell-Verduyn, M., & Hütten, M. (2019). Beyond scandal? Blockchain technologies and the fragile legitimacy of post-2008 finance. *Finance & Society*, 5(2), 126–144.
Croker, T. C. (1839). *Popular songs of Ireland*. Colburn.
Danaher, J. (2019). *Automation and utopia: Human flourishing in a world without work*. Harvard University Press.
D'Arcy, F. A. (1988). The decline and fall of Donnybrook fair: Moral reform and social control in nineteenth century Dublin. *Saothar*, 13, 7–21.
Dowling, C. (2020). Bakhtin and the free state in at swim-two-birds. In R. Borg & P. Fagan (Eds.), *Flann O'Brien: Gallows humour* (pp. 48–60). Cork University Press.
DuPont, Q. (2017). Experiments in algorithmic governance: A history and ethnography of "The DAO," a failed decentralized autonomous organization. In M. Campbell-Verduyn (Ed.), *Bitcoin and beyond: Cryptocurrencies, blockchains, and global governance* (pp. 157–177). Routledge.
Ennis, P. J. (2017). *The gentrification of ICOs is underway*. CoinDesk. Retrieved November 15, 2022, from https://www.coindesk.com/markets/2017/11/19/the-gentrification-of-icos-is-underway/
Entertainment Software Association. (2021). *2021 Essential facts about the video game industry*. Entertainment Software Association. https://www.theesa.com/wp-content/uploads/2021/08/2021-Essential-Facts-About-the-Video-Game-Industry-1.pdf
Faustino, S., Faria, I., & Marques, R. (2021). The myths and legends of King Satoshi and the knights of blockchain. *Journal of Cultural Economy*, 15(1), 1–14. https://doi.org/10.1080/17530350.2021.1921830
Ford, B. (2020, November). *Identity and personhood in digital democracy: Evaluating inclusion, equality, security, and privacy in pseudonym parties and other proofs of personhood*. Bryan Ford's Home Page. https://bford.info/pub/soc/personhood/
Grauer, K., Kueshner, W., & Updegrave, H. (2022). *The Chainalysis 2022 crypto crime report*. Chainalysis. https://go.chainalysis.com/2022-Crypto-Crime-Report.html
Hoffman, D. (2020, September 17). *Ethereum: Slayer of Moloch* ⚔. Bankless. https://newsletter.banklesshq.com/p/ethereum-slayer-of-moloch-
Huizinga, J. (1949). *Homo Ludens: A study of the play element in culture*. Routledge & Kegan Paul.
Kavanagh, D., & Miscione, G. (2019). Carnival in the global village: Re-imagining information infrastructures. *The Information Society*, 35(5), 299–313. https://doi.org/10.1080/01972243.2019.1647321

Lopp, J. (2016). *Bitcoin and the rise of the cypherpunks*. CoinDesk. http://www.coindesk.com/the-rise-of-the-cypherpunk
Mackenzie, S. (2022). Criminology towards the metaverse: Cryptocurrency scams, grey economy and the technosocial. *The British Journal of Criminology*, 62(6), 1537–1552. https://doi.org/10.1093/bjc/azab118
Nakamoto, S. (2008). Bitcoin: A peer-to-peer electronic cash system. *Consulted*, 1(2012), 1–28.
Sales, R. (1983). *English literature in history 1780–1830: Pastoral and politics*. Hutchinson.
Soleimani, A., Bhuptani, A., Young, J., Haber, L., & Sethuram, R. (2019). *The Moloch DAO: Beating the tragedy of the commons using decentralized autonomous organizations* [White paper]. https://github.com/MolochVentures/Whitepaper/blob/aaf5afb64b7cbb8bfee1a70690cc10cda8758086/Whitepaper.pdf
Strange, S. (1986). *Casino capitalism*. Blackwell.
Suits, B. (1978). *The grasshopper: Games, life and Utopia* (B7918978). Scottish Academic Press.
US Bureau of Labor Statistics. (2022). *Union members summary*. https://www.bls.gov/news.release/union2.nr0.htm
Wacquant, L. (2015). For a sociology of flesh and blood. *Qualitative Sociology*, 38(1), 1–11. https://doi.org/10.1007/s11133-014-9291-y
Weyl, E. G., Ohlhaver, P., & Buterin, V. (2022). *Decentralized society: Finding Web3's soul* [SSRN Scholarly Paper No. 4105763]. Social Science Research Network. https://papers.ssrn.com/abstract=4105763
Wood, L. (2022, March 10). *$350+ billion worldwide sports industry to 2031*. GlobeNewswire News Room. https://www.globenewswire.com/news-release/2022/03/10/2400658/28124/en/350-Billion-Worldwide-Sports-Industry-to-2031-Identify-Growth-Segments-for-Investment.html

PART 3
DARE DEVILS

THE GAMBLER

Sandra Faustino

University of Lisbon, Portugal

ABSTRACT

This paper explores the influence of financialization in the post-2008 credit crisis, which led to a general mistrust in financial institutions and states. Simultaneously, Web3 and digital finance emerged as a way to navigate this problematic state of affairs, and many individuals were drawn to the agency of machines, code, and algorithms in making a deviation from austerity toward some form of liberation. Taking the form of an oracle reading, this paper uses the "Gambler" archetype to explore the subjective movement of those who engage with digital finance as a strategy to face the generalized climate of austerity and to claim their share of the economy, now that work has ceased to be a lifetime calling.

Keywords: Financialization; debt; risk; cryptocurrencies; oracle; parasite

Welcome to the cryptocarnival. You are probably a precarious worker, indebted, uncertain about the future, playing your odds on the crypto dice, exhausted by social networking, and working multiple jobs. In your pocket, one remaining token needs to be spent, before you exit the precinct and head home. As you arrive to this text, you may want to imagine you have used that token to buy your way into an oracle reading. You set out an intention: to gain insight into the mysteries that have taken hold of your financial life. Your card is "The Gambler."

I. LOSS

Let us raise the curtain in 2008, when the credit crisis initiated the period referred to as "The Great Recession" or "The Great Hangover" (Fair & Carter, 2010). This historical event has exerted a great influence on you. Before the crisis, financialization had already imprinted its logic onto markets as well as onto every other social sphere (Erturk et al., 2008), meaning that financial instruments and institutions had achieved a significant influence over your life, and the lives of many others, so heavily mediated by the massification of consumer credit (Ossandón, 2017). Surely, financialization can be traced back to the Atlantic slave trade (Baucom, 2005), but the 1980s marked a leap in its expansion under the promise of generating wealth that could then be injected into the "real economy" a promise equally flaunted by your liberal state. Around the turn of the millennium, during the peak of the dot.com bubble, it became obvious that "the future of finance was bound to become electronic" (Petry, 2020), and perhaps, in that case, held against higher scrutiny. Several crashes after, however, that generally optimistic atmosphere shifted to one of uncertainty (Beckert & Bronk, 2018). It became clear to you that finance intersects with gambling cultures far more than had previously been conceded (Nicoll, 2013), and what remained was a generalized mistrust in states and financial institutions. You were left with the urge of punishing the "greedy bankers" who were "set loose in an unregulated 'shadow' banking system, motivated increasingly by reckless speculation" (LiPuma & Lee, 2012, p. 291). But you were left hungover. States stepped in to bail out the bankrupt financial institutions and did so by reducing their social expenditure, offering you in return a life of either unemployment or precarious jobs, without proper access to education, housing, or health support. The post-crisis scenario left you broke, picking up the pieces of high-finance's "culture of risk." But in that period, you sensed something comic arising from the tragedy. The facticity of finance had been fully uncovered. The level of abstraction attained in financial markets, so well illustrated by the "exotic derivatives" created by "financial wizards" (Samman et al., 2015, p. 1), evaded the explanatory attempts of mathematics or economics. A clear disjunction between the human scale of reasoning and the "planetary" scope of computational infrastructures, including the speed at which financial markets are set to function, was laid out in the open (Benjamin, 2021). By 2015, a high-frequency trading system could complete a trade in just 740 nanoseconds, which equates to over 330,000 trades in the literal blink of an eye (Srnicek & Williams, 2014). This "technomorphing" of finance (Benjamin, 2021) seemed to produce a life form of its own that left everyone puzzled – including one of its architects, Alan Greenspan, head of the US Federal Reserve from 1987 to 2005, who said in a public hearing (Pro Publica, 2008): "I still don't fully understand why it happened." Tragic as it may be, there was a strange beauty in this foul human creation, before which "no one knew what was truth and what was fiction" (Stiglitz, 2009).

II. CONFRONTATION

This mutant financial realm now exerts an enchanting effect over subjects. Around you, a sense of opportunism lurks: "never let a good crisis go to waste," they say (Fuller, 2013). Online, financial gurus have become popular in helping people cope with the new indebted, securitized condition, steering them toward self-entrepreneurship: "stop working for someone else, work from home and get rich quick" (Martin, 2002, p. 46). The reprehensible culture of risk that led to the crisis has now found its way into everyday life, and something about this problematic state of affairs begs for resolution (Propp, 1968/1928). In this conjuncture, you feel drawn to Web3 and its ability to mediate the financialization process in a historically specific and novel way. Bored to death with the roulette of social security checks, job interviews, and credit-based entrepreneurialism, you allow yourself to become romantically playful with decentralized autonomous organizations (DAOs), cryptocurrencies, and non-fungible tokens (NFTs). You feel a reinvigorated faith in the Internet's beehive, still pregnant with the dreams of cryptographers and of the open-software movement, and you place your bet: if you cannot escape the casino, you might as well try to improve your odds. You are fascinated by the agency of things – machines, code, and algorithms – in making a deviation from austerity toward some form of liberation. The plasticity and playfulness of software feed your romanticism toward "the digital." You know that you cannot de-scale the speculative and abstract tendencies of global capital, but you can now create and access "moneyness," speculate, subvert, detour. In this sense, "The Gambler" is as romantic as it is ironic. It is not the disciplined and calculative dimensions of the casino that you wish to embrace but rather the unforeseeable, untamable nature of risk.

III. DEVIATION

Calculation means very little, and has by no means the importance attributed to it by some players: they sit with papers before them scrawled over in pencil, note the strokes, reckon, deduce the chances, calculate, finally stake and – lose exactly as we simple mortals who play without calculations. ("The Gambler," Dostoyevsky, 1966)

For this reason, you are not interested in Bitcoin's stardom in the investment portfolios of Goldman Sachs or in the adventures of stablecoins. Your path leads you closer to lay investors, hacktivists, self-taught coders, and digital artists. Your preferred terrain is the "noise" (Preda, 2017) that forms around big players, big headlines, and big plot-twists. This might be because you are an academic or theorist, artist, philosopher, or activist. You have a high level of formal education and an above-average financial literacy, as you have been socialized in an era of entrepreneurialism, risk, and calculation (Hall, 2011; Langley, 2008; Miller & Rose, 2008; Santos, 2020). But you are not a "professional" financier, and your engagement with finance is better understood from the point of view of the (romantic) amateur. You are often engaged with volunteerism, notwithstanding your regular situation of debt or unemployment. You might frame your actions as part of some collective militancy, foregrounding the affects, temporalities, dissidences, emotions, and contingencies that influence your financial practices, indifferent to the disciplining character of financial markets, banks, and trading rooms (Konings, 2020; Maurer et al., 2018). Under "The Gambler" archetype, your subjective move into digital finance is above all a strategy to face the generalized climate of austerity and to claim your share of the economy, now that work has ceased to be a lifetime calling (Kim, 2017). And magically enough, it is the machine itself which, once set up, is able to become a source of income (Srnicek & Williams, 2014), realizing "the right to make money" (Bjerg, 2014). Web3 presents you with the possibility of a post-work world, through new and unexplored territories – it enables a new set of moves in the game. The gambler, then, also acts as somewhat of a parasite. Not in a moral sense, but as a social metaphor (Serres, 1982): its actions are intended to upset an equilibrium and to make a deviation; intended to interrupt one set of moves and to make a new set of moves possible. It is not bound to the interests and conventions adopted by your institutions but rather navigates them as is deemed fit for its own survival. In other words, the gambler is like a joker. Be aware that the gambler can never dismantle the game; it can only add information and complexity to it; it can expand the repertoire of possible moves, creating both disturbance and continuity. You are bound to explore the emotional and affective logic of finance in everyday life, as the enchanting affordances of digital capital are coming your way.

REFERENCES

Baucom, I. (2005). *Specters of the Atlantic: Finance capital, slavery, and the philosophy of history*. Duke University Press.

Beckert, J., & Bronk, R. (Eds.). (2018). *Uncertain futures: Imaginaries, narratives, and calculation in the economy*. Oxford University Press.

Benjamin, J. J. (2021, March 8). *Horizonal machinery & the sites of non-anthropocentric worlding*. https://tripleampersand.org/horizonal-machinery-sites-non-anthropocentric-worlding/

Bjerg, O. (2014). *Making money: The philosophy of crisis capitalism*. Verso Trade.

Dostoyevsky, F. (1966). *The gambler, Bobok, a nasty story*. Penguin.

Erturk, I., Froud, J., Johal, S., Leaver, A., & Williams, K. (2008). *Financialization at work: Key texts and commentary*. Routledge.

Fair, V., & Carter, G. (2010). *The great hangover: 21 tales of the new recession from the pages of Vanity Fair*. Harper Collins.

Fuller, S. (2013). 'Never let a good crisis go to waste': Moral entrepreneurship, or the fine art of recycling evil into good. *Business Ethics: A European Review*, 22(1), 118–129. https://doi.org/10.1111/beer.12012

Hall, S. (2011). Geographies of money and finance I: Cultural economy, politics and place. *Progress in Human Geography*, 35(2), 234–245. https://doi.org/10.1177/0309132510370277

Kim, B. (2017). Think rich, feel hurt: The critique of capitalism and the production of affect in the making of financial subjects in South Korea. *Cultural studies*, 31(5), 611–633. https://doi.org/10.1080/09502386.2016.1264005

Konings, M. (2020). *The emotional logic of capitalism*. Stanford University Press.

Langley, P. (2008). *The everyday life of global finance: Saving and borrowing in Anglo-America*. OUP Oxford.

LiPuma, E., & Lee, B. (2012). A social approach to the financial derivatives markets. *South Atlantic Quarterly*, 111(2), 289–316. https://doi.org/10.1215/00382876-1548221

Martin, R. (2002). *Financialization of daily life*. Temple University Press.

Maurer, B., Musaraj, S., & Small, I. V. (Eds.). (2018). *Money at the margins: Global perspectives on technology, financial inclusion, and design* (Vol. 6). Berghahn Books.

Miller, P., & Rose, N. (2008). *Governing the present: Administering economic, social and personal life*. Polity.

Nicoll, F. (2013). Finopower: Governing intersections between gambling and finance. *Communication and Critical/Cultural Studies*, 10(4), 385–405.

Ossandón, J. (2017). 'My story has no strings attached': Credit cards, market devices and a stone guest. In F. Cochoy, J. Deville & L. McFall (Eds.), *Markets and the arts of attachment* (pp. 132–146). Routledge.

Petry, J. (2020). Securities exchanges: Subjects and agents of financialization. In P. Mader, D. Mertens, & N. Van der Zwan (Eds.), *The Routledge international handbook of financialization* (pp. 253–264). Routledge.
Preda, A. (2017). *Noise: Living and trading in electronic finance*. University of Chicago Press.
Pro Publica. (2008, October 23). *Greenspan says I still don't fully understand what happened* [Video]. YouTube. https://www.youtube.com/watch?v=R5lZPWNFizQ&t=287s
Propp, V., (1968 [1928]). *The morphology of the folktale*. University of Texas Press.
Santos, A. C. (2020). Cultivating the self-reliant and responsible individual: the material culture of financial literacy. In *Material cultures of financialisation* (pp. 56–68). Routledge.
Samman, A., Coombs, N., & Cameron, A. (2015). For a post-disciplinary study of finance and society. *Finance and Society*, *1*(1), 1–5.
Serres, M. (1982). *The parasite* (Trans. L. R. Schehr). Johns Hopkins University Press.
Srnicek, N., & Williams, A. (2014). On cunning automata: Financial acceleration at the limits of the dromological. *Collapse: Journal of Philosophical Research and Development*, *8*, 463–506.
Stiglitz, J. E. (2009, January). Capitalist fools. *Vanity Fair*.

WEB3 AND THE AMAZING COMPUTABLE ECONOMY

Jason Potts

RMIT University, Australia

ABSTRACT

This paper introduces the concept of a "computable economy" and discusses how it relates to the emergence of Web3 or the new type of economy that has arisen from the integration of digital technologies such as blockchain, smart contracts, and digital identity. A "computable economy" is one where those computational rule systems are integrated into a connected graph, allowing for decentralized cooperation and distributed coordination. This paper traces the trajectory of innovation in the economy from the development of industrial production technologies to the rise of information and communication technology (ICT) and the digital economy. It argues that the shift to a "computable economy" is a consequence of the transformation of analog economic institutions into natively digital institutions. This results in a "full stack" digital economy where all economic actions can be digitally constructed and implemented. This paper concludes by discussing the potential of Web3 to create a new type of economy, that is, "techno-utopian" and characterized by human flourishing, as the incursion of machines and computation leads to a new era of economic growth and transformation.

Keywords: Blockchain; institutions; innovation; economic dynamics; organizations

Web3 continues the innovation trajectory of the internet from Web2 (social media) and Web1 (email). And Web1-2-3 builds on the macro-techno-historical innovation trajectory of satellites and computers and telephone networks and transistors and silicon and glass and wire and electricity and logic and math.

Look what we've built with sand and lightning!

The 3 in Web3 is the supercluster of new digital technologies (crypto, blockchain, smart contracts, decentralised identity (DiD), non-fungible tokens (NFTs), decentralized autonomous organizations (DAOs), etc.) that make the internet a new type of economy. Web1 made the internet (which was built for the US military!) an open communication tool that became natively navigable. Think HTTP, search, and email. It was a new type of information processor. Web2 made the internet social. You could go there with friends and do things like shop, play games, and tell stories. But you had to bring much of the old world with you, such as banks and governments. It was a new place to visit. But you couldn't live there. It was still not yet self-sovereign.

Everything changes with Web3. The internet – these computers all strung together with machine language – becomes *a new type of economy* with digitally native money (crypto), digitally native agreements and law (smart contracts), digitally native property (tokens, NFTs), digitally native identity (DiDs), digitally native markets (DEXs), digitally native organizations (DAOs), and digitally native security, truth, and expectations (consensus protocols). Web3 is a further surge along the evolutionary innovation trajectory of the internet and computing and communication technologies.

Web3 is a world of human flourishing because of, not in spite of, the incursion of machines and computation. Over the past few hundred years, the discovery and application of new knowledge and technology, working with economic institutions that facilitated investment and trade, has lifted humanity from the normal miserable state of mass poverty. Industrial capitalism has given the world wealth and freedom. Now of course this induced second-order effects (externalities), including inequality and environmental pollution. But these are not my focus here. Rather, I want to follow the first-order effects through into their next generation. That will make this paper techno-utopian; so be it. You have been warned, and I leave critical reflections as an exercise for the reader. In any case, the world changing industrial innovation and economic growth and transformation occurred, in large part, by substituting machines for people, capital for labor, on every margin possible. Web3 continues this process but extends from *work* to *computation*.

Web3 is in this way the beginning of a new type of economy, something that grew out of a powerful trajectory in the industrial economy – the development of information and communication technology (ICT) – but is new because it is rebuilding economic institutions: money, contracts, markets, registries, organizations, and law and courts, that is, economic infrastructure. That is what is radically fundamentally new with Web3.

WEB3 = COMPUTABLE ECONOMY

Before I go further, let me elucidate what is meant by "computable," for it is an important concept in my argument here, yet one easily misunderstood. Computable does not mean "made of or reduced to number," which could imply soullessness and reductivism. I do not mean a computable economy as one stripped of humanity and empathy and the sublime and the soaring inexplicable imaginative leaps of faith and belief that have carried us up the mountain and through the valleys of our collective history. Rather, computable, which is an adjective, meaning capable of being computed, is meant as a verb: "to compute." To compute does not mean to reduce to a number but to follow a system of rules to an output, which then becomes a new part of the world, which can then be an input to new things. A computable economy is one where we find more and more ways to do that. And every time we do, the space of humanity gets bigger, just as with investment in capital goods.

So web3 can be defined as a new type of economy, as a transition from an industrial economy to a digital economy. It's a new institutional thing (digital economy, see Goldfarb & Tucker, 2019), caused by new technology (Web3). Yet we still need to unpack what is specifically "industrial" about an "industrial economy" and what is newly digital about a "digital economy." What's under the tent?

The concept of an industrial economy includes *industrial production* technologies:

- Iron, steel, minerals, engines, trucks, rockets, etc.
- Oil, synthetic materials, petrochemicals, pharmaceuticals, etc.
- Electrification, railways, satellites, etc.
- Transistors, lasers, computers, microelectronics, ICT, etc.

An industrial economy also refers to *industrial institutions*:

- The factory system and private corporations.
- Industrial sectors, industry policy, venture finance.
- Public economic institutions to support markets, for example, money, banks, property registries (including intellectual property rights (IPR)), courts, regulation, roads, ports, universities, etc.

Industrial economies have profoundly changed the global history of humanity. As Fig. 15.1 shows, they are the singular cause of modern human flourishing.

You will observe among the industrial production technologies a particular innovation trajectory, usually called ICT. Those digital technologies are the consequence of industrial innovation and industrial production. And so, computers, iPhones, and so on are produced in factories, protected by intellectual property, financed with capital markets, and sold in consumer markets. Industrial economies grow by producing digital things ever more cheaply and at ever greater scale (see Fig. 15.2).

But that industrial growth in the new digital or ICT sector is not what we mean by a digital economy. The digital economy is nowhere on those diagrams. It's not just the inevitable cumulative result of more or faster or cheaper computers, or more digital jobs or technology firms. Rather, the digital economy revolution specifically refers to the disruption and regrowth of *analog economic institutions in digital format*.

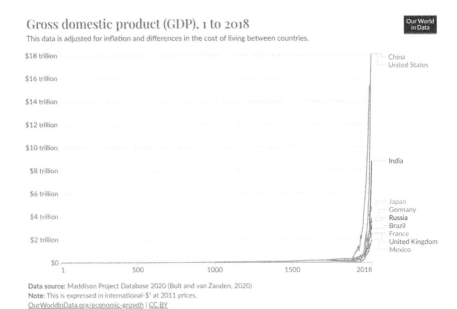

Fig. 15.1. Long-run Economic Growth. *Source*: From John C. McCallum (2022) – processed by Our World in Data.

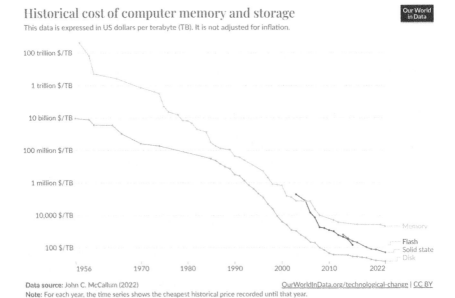

Fig. 15.2. Falling Cost of ICT. *Source*: John C. McCallum (2022) – Processed by Our World in Data.

The industrial economy is the proximate cause of the digital economy revolution, by advancing innovation and indeed industrial mass production of digital technology. But the epochal transition from an *industrial economy* to a *digital economy*, which is the specific significance of Web3, is a consequence of the transformation of industrial economic institutions (money, identity, contracts, registries, and economic organization, coordination, and governance in general) into natively digital institutions. The result is a "full stack" digital economy.

This is a statement to clarify *where* the digital disruption is occurring. It is not just the surface-industrial production layers that are being digitized. It is also occurring in the deeper institutional layers too, that is, "full stack." The distinction is captured by the idea of a fully "computable economy." So, what is meant by "computable"?

COMPUTABLE

"Computer" is a word from the 17th century, referring to a person who performs mathematical calculations by following rules. A computer, in other words, was an occupation not a thing. The picture in Fig. 15.3 from Wikipedia is titled "1954, NACA computer working with microscope and calculator." Note that the "computer" in this picture is the one sitting in the chair holding the pen.

Compare this with Fig. 15.4, which is of an "electronic computer," in which the operations of the computer have been replaced with a network of vacuum tubes, diodes, relays, and resistors. This is our modern definition of a computer as an "electronic machine for performing calculations" that processes data using rules.

But the deeper abstraction behind "computer" as occupation or tool is the idea of *computability*.

Fig. 15.3. A "Computer."

Fig. 15.4. An "Electronic Computer."

Consider the concept of a *computable number* (a.k.a. *recursive numbers* or *computable reals*), introduced by Alan Turing (1936) in a paper that gave rise to the concept of a *Turing machine*, so named by the logician Alonzo Church, in review of Turing's paper. That abstract machine implied by the mathematical model of computation is today simply known as a "computer."

Marvin Minsky (1967) defines a *computable number* as "one for which there is a Turing machine which, given n on its initial tape, terminates with the nth digit of that number [encoded on its tape]."

An *un*computable number is one that cannot be computed by a finite procedure (i.e., a universal machine, or "Turing machine"), that is, for which no such algorithm exists. Most numbers, it turns out, are uncomputable. And so, the concepts of computable numbers, a *universal state machine* and the formulation of the "halting condition" as a solution concept (decidability) are the foundations of modern computer science. Interestingly, another great genius of the early/mid-20th century, and who immediately built the next floor on those foundations, was John von Neumann with his concepts of the stored program architecture and automata theory.

COMPUTABLE ECONOMY

The concept of a computable number (or Turing machine, or state machine, or automata) is also a useful way to think about the meaning and definition of a "digital economy." Indeed, what is referred to as the information economy or digital economy can be elucidated with the idea of a "computable economy."

Just as computable and non-computable numbers exist, the corollary is that so do both computable and non-computable economies (and complexes of both).

An economy is computable in the same way, namely there exists a set of rules (i.e., institutions, technologies) that generates the economic output as a finite set of operations. Analogously, a fully computable economy is a "Turing complete economy."

A computable economy implies a field called *computable economics* (Tesfatsion, 2006), which Velupillai (1999) defines as follows (p. 2):

> Computable economics is about basing economic formalisms on recursion theoretic fundamentals. This means we will have to view economic entities, economic actions and economic institutions as computable objects or algorithms.

What do we gain from seeking such a quasi-formal definition (computable economy) rather than an empirically descriptive label (digital economy)?

The empirical observation is about the class and cluster of technologies. They are digital. They are generally and correctly described as ICT: that is, as information and communications technologies. But they also *compute*. And my claim is that it is the computing that is the core *economic* function in creating economic value.

The industrial concept of a digital economy usually means number of computers or jobs that use them, or investment in digital technology or some such input or output measure or spending, investment, or production (Carlsson, 2004; Mesenbourg, 2001). These are coherent and often useful empirical concepts but not what I mean here.

A computable economy is one where an economic action (i.e., transactions) can be digitally connected as part of an algorithmic process. A "Turing complete economy" is one where all economic actions can be digitally constructed and implemented.

The formal concept of a computable economy is not new. Even by the late 1950s and 1960s, Vernon Smith was developing algorithmic models of the market process, and Herbert Simon was developing algorithmic models of human (and machine!) decision-making using the logic of bounded rationality or satisficing, which is an operationalization of the halting condition. The theory of a computable economy has been subsequently anticipated or developed by Scarf (1989), Gode and Sunder (1993, 1997), Leijonhufvud (1993), Velupillai (1996, 1999), Richter and Wong (1999), and Mount and Reiter (2002), among others.

Nor is the general model of computation as the *lingua franca* of science a new idea (see, e.g., Hidalgo, 2015; von Neumann, 1966; Wolfram, 2004).

The concept of the economy as a *process of computation* is also not at all new. Philip Mirowski (2002) furnishes an exhaustive scholarly account of the computer metaphor in economic theory in his magisterial *Machine Dreams*, where he characterizes the trend of orthodox economic theory in the second half of the 20th century as that of "recasting the economic agent as an information processor." He writes:

> It goes without saying that the wartime development of the computer and its subsequent diffusion into nearly every sphere of intellectual discourse had quite a bit to do with what has been the most significant reorientation of the economics discipline in the last century. (Mirowski, 2007)

The "computer" is a compelling scientific metaphor for the operations of the economy. But the issue is not whether it is a useful metaphor – that is, how is an economy "like" a computer. The issue is more fundamental, or ontological, to what extent *is an economy actually a computer*, that is, performs computation?

The computable economy thesis implies that computers are not tools we use but an environment we live in. We don't use computers; computers use us!

HOW ECONOMIES COMPUTE

The issue of how economies compute goes to the heart of perhaps the most important debate in economics during the 20th century, the so-called "socialist calculation debate" (Boettke, 1998). This debate was nominally about the efficacy of economic planning, but it was really about whether markets were properly to be understood as computers. What makes this debate even more esoteric is that it began *before* (!) the invention of the modern electronic computer.

The debate took place between two factions of economic theorists: the neoclassicals (the orthodox view, along with the Marxists) and the "Austrians" (the heterodox view).

The neoclassicals argued that given the raw economic data relating to the technical conditions of economic production, the supplies of resources and preferences over goods, then, as Hayek (1945) explained, "the [economic] problem which remains is purely one of logic." As such, then the rational and optimal solution can be calculated by a sufficiently intelligent planner, ideally supported by sufficiently powerful calculating machinery.

Ludwig von Mises (an "Austrian") argued that Socialism was impossible because it was fundamentally unable to calculate. His point was that the data the neoclassical economists assumed to exist (viz. preferences, prices, uses of resources, etc.) did not actually exist in an ex ante state of nature. Rather, these data were themselves a product of the economic system.

Moreover, these data were produced through a stack of institutions and mechanisms: including property rights, exchange mechanisms to transfer property rights through bidding processes (markets), the broader social processes to legitimate those exchanges, as well as mechanisms for calculating value including accounting systems.

The outcome was a system of publicly observable prices, which could serve as common information to guide individual economic action, variously bringing more supply to market when prices were high, or economizing on consumption, or vice versa when prices fell. Prices were information for distributed coordination of economic actions. Indeed, Mises (1949, p. 679) argued that:

> Human cooperation under the system of the social division of labor is possible only in the market economy. Socialism is not a realizable system of society's economic organization because it lacks any method of economic calculation.

In a striking paragraph, Peter Boettke (2001, p. 33) outlines the depth and range of Mises argument:

To the economically illiterate, Mises had to explain how private property engenders incentives which motivate individuals to husband resources efficiently. To the more informed, but still economically uninformed, he had to explain how the exchange ratios established in a market allow individuals to compare alternatives by summarizing in a common denominator the subjective assessment of trade-offs that individuals make in the exchange and production process. To the trained economist, Mises had to explain how the static conditions of equilibrium only solved the problem of economic calculation by hypothesis, and that the real problem was one of calculation within the dynamic world of change, in which the lure of pure profit and the penalty of loss would serve a vital error detection and correction role in the economic process. And, finally, to scholars, activists, and political leaders, Mises warned that the suppression of private property leads to political control over individual decisions and thus the eventual suppression of political liberties to the concerns of the collective.

Hayek then built on Mises' calculation arguments by emphasizing the problem of knowledge. Hayek argued that the market mechanism was an ingenious device – a complex social technology not invented by anyone but rather that had evolved – that acted to gather and process distributed "local information" and compute them into "prices." These computed price signals – as outputs of the market computation – then worked to efficiently and effectively guide economic activity at scale.

The price system – itself built on institutions of private property, market mechanisms, profit and loss accounting – is a process of computation. The inputs into economic calculation, that is, the economic information for rational planning, does not exist outside of the market process but is created by it. Market mechanisms are distributed mechanisms that perform complex economic computation on knowledge, information, and resources.

In this view, an economy is clearly a type of computer.

A common error is to mistake the inputs or outputs of an economy for an economy itself, which is a computational process. The goods and services produced by an economy – the factors of production: land, labor, capital, resources, and so forth – are the inputs and outputs of an economy (including sets of things such as goods produced or measures such as decentralised exchange (DEX)). They are no more the economy than a set of input prompts or output files is a computer. An economy, like a computer, is a complex system of rules (algorithms, procedures, decision heuristics, institutions, administrative procedures, etc.) that performs a "state" processing function (see Fig. 15.5).

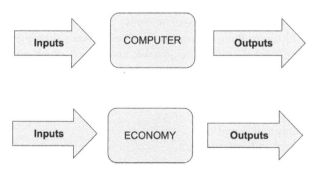

Fig. 15.5. Diagram of Computable Economy.

Economics comes from the Greek root οἶκος or house. But an economy is not a thing; it is not a pile of valuable objects. Rather, an economy is a process that is produced by a complex system of rules.

An economy is a *process-structure of rules* that *compute an output* that is a system of instructions that organize the coordination of resources to enable plans to mesh together. An economy is a rule system for economic computation.

These *generic rules* are separable and composable (Dopfer & Potts, 2008). Within each economic agent are *cognitive rules* for thinking and *behavioral rules* for action. There are *social rules* for coordinating people (e.g., firms, markets, institutions). Social rules can be tacit and informal, such as norms, or formal and legal, such as regulations and legislation. And there are *technical rules* that organize matter-energy (i.e., technologies). An economy is a complex system of rules, embedded and embodied in different types of substrates, operating by different mechanisms at different scales, and with different architectures and different properties. Together, these rules perform economic computation. An economy is a massively parallel and open dynamical system of rules – for decentralized cooperation and distributed coordination – for social computation.

A *computable economy* is one in which those computational rule systems are integrated (i.e., joined up) into a connected graph (Potts, 2000) and thus have a form of completeness (i.e., all parts are "computable"). The evolutionary process by which all parts become computable is the basic logic of the digital economy revolution.

A COMPUTER MADE OF COMPUTERS

Von Mises and Hayek's notion of the market or price mechanism as a form of economic computation, and therefore of a market economy as a computer, was an idea that the Austrian economists developed in the 1930s. This was broadly contemporary with Turing's and von Neumann's theoretical development of the mathematical model of computation and then the electronic instantiation of that – as the electronic computer.

By the 1970s, actual marketplaces had become actual (electronic) computers, as many major financial exchanges began a process of digital automation (e.g., NASDAQ launched in 1971, although futures only traded fully electronically in 1992 on CME Globex, see McCabe et al., 1991).

Economic historian Philip Mirowski (2007) proposes a theory of markets as evolving computational entities, or "market automata," which characterizes a marketplace as an algorithm that performs the following functions:

- Data dissemination and communications, plus rules of exclusion.
- Order routing through time and space.
- Order queuing and execution.
- Price discovery and assignment.

- Custody and delivery arrangement.
- Clearing and settlement, including property rights assignment.
- Record-keeping.

The evolution of a computable economy occurs as more parts of the economy become computable, that is, able to process and execute information algorithmically.

Computable economic agents evolve with the adoption of machine-assisted or automated decision-making in which software algorithms can be analytically conceptualized as both substitutes (on some margins) and complements for human decision-making. This ranges across the domain of bots and apps, smart wallets, and DAOs.

Computable money and finance arrives with cryptocurrencies and tokens that enable smart contracts to be wrapped around existing financial assets. Indeed, token-wrapped assets and non-fungible tokenized assets (NFTs) facilitate the development of *computable capital* (Banon et al., 2022). This digital wrapping (or "skin" or "twin") then interacts with other computable objects.

Computable capital is searchable, programmable, integrates with any economic agent (including internet of things (IoT) devices, algorithms, oracles, that is, tools that sense or emit information), and works at a global scale. Computable capital creates the ability to bring resources, as inputs into production (i.e., the definition of capital), into computable decision-making that can be executed in market contexts. These include searching for opportunities, verification of rights, assurance of the safety and efficacy of the exchange of property rights, or other mutually agreed-upon exchange and agreements in the space of possible contracts. Moreover, as agents and capital become computable then so too does entrepreneurship and innovation become potentially computable as embedded information and knowledge in databases and toolkits becomes machine accessible, for example, for discoverable trading opportunities for arbitrage or even the creation of new products and services (Potts, 2019).

ECONOMIES OF THE FUTURE

Web3 is the beginning of the future for new types of economies that can be built with natively digital institutions and infrastructure. Computable economies massively lower the cost of operating economies – that is, lower transaction, coordination, monitoring, and governance costs (Catalini & Gans, 2020) – but they also lower the cost of starting new economies and of experimentally designing them. If economies are much cheaper to build, we will build many more of them.

This opens a new world of "start-up" or "pop-up" economies that are easily instantiated and spun up for particular purposes at different scales as needed. They will have configurable institutional and governance parameters, that is, their own administrative and contract systems, money, identity, etc., that can be selected and designed as easily as it would be to say build a website. These "no-code economies" are the economies of the future.

On the whole, this is likely to be a very good thing for all of humanity. It creates a clear path to a truly native global economy by adding computability to everything. But it also creates safety and security by allowing any group to exit to their own economies by building their own infrastructure. The great disasters of the 20th century that trapped millions and billions of people inside broken and corrupt economic systems, causing untold human misery, suffering, and poverty, will hopefully be consigned to history.

There are major challenges. Many will resist due to investments in skills and capital or privileges that will be eroded by these new technologies. They will fight through political attempts to block the future, and if that fails then perhaps through violence. This is a sad but common theme of economic history (Juma, 2016).

There are also considerable education and access barriers to overcome. A digital economy requires high levels of digital literacy and access to digital technologies and infrastructure. There is a clear and urgent role for governments to provide these public goods.

But computable economies are not science fiction. They are the future that is already here in the guise of Web3. What we need to do is to deepen our understanding and appreciation of them and to accelerate our use of them.

REFERENCES

Banon, J., Berg, C., Davidson, S., & Potts, J. (2022). *How web3's 'programmable commerce layer' will transform the global economy*. World Economic Forum.

Boettke, P. (1998). Economic calculation: The Austrian contribution to political economy. *Advances in Austrian Economics*, 5, 131–158.

Boettke, P. (2001). *Calculation and coordination*. Routledge.

Carlsson, B. (2004). The digital economy: What is new and what is not? *Structural Change and Economic Dynamics*, 15(3), 245–264.

Catalini, C., & Gans, J. (2020). Some simple economics of the blockchain. *Communications of the ACM*, 63(7), 80–90.

Dopfer, K., & Potts, J. (2008). *The general theory of economic evolution*. Routledge.

Gode, D., & Sunder, S. (1993). Allocative efficiency of markets with zero-intelligence traders. *Journal of Political Economy*, 101, 119–137.

Gode, D., & Sunder, S. (1997). What makes markets allocatively efficient? *Quarterly Journal of Economics*, 105, 603–630.

Goldfarb, A., & Tucker, C. (2019). Digital economics. *Journal Economic Literature*, 57(1), 3–43.

Hayek, F. A. (1945). Use of knowledge in society. *American Economic Review*, 35(4), 519–530.

Hidalgo, C. (2015). *Why information grows: The evolution of order, from atoms to economies*. Basic Books.

Juma, C. (2016). *Innovation and its enemies: Why people resist new technologies*. Oxford University Press.

Leijonhufvud, A. (1993). Toward a not too rational macroeconomics. *Southern Economic Journal*, 60(1), 1–12.

McCabe, K., Rassenti, S., & Smith, V. (1991). Smart computer-assisted markets. *Science*, 254(5031), 534–538.

Mesenbourg, T. (2001). *Measuring the digital economy*. U.S. Bureau of the Census.

Minsky, M. (1967). The computable real numbers. In *Computation: Finite and infinite machines* (p. 159). Prentice-Hall. https://dl.acm.org/doi/10.5555/1095587.C1084696

Mirowski, P. (2002). *Machine dreams: Economics becomes a cyborg science*. Cambridge University Press.

Mirowski, P. (2007). Markets come to bits: Evolution, computation and markomata in economic science. *Journal of Economic Behavior and Organization, 63*(2), 209–242.
Mises, L. V. (1949). *Human action: A Treatise on Economics*. Yale University Press.
Mount, K., & Reiter, S. (2002). *Computation and complexity in economic behavior and organization*. Cambridge University Press.
Potts, J. (2000). *The new evolutionary microeconomics*. Edward Elgar.
Potts, J. (2019). *Innovation commons: The origin of economic growth*. Oxford University Press.
Richter, M., & Wong, K. C. (1999). Computable preference and utility. *Journal of Mathematical Economics, 32*(3), 339–354.
Scarf, H. E. (1989). Computation of general equilibria. In J. Eatwell, M. Milgate & P. Newman (Eds.), *General equilibrium* (pp. 84–97).
Tesfatsion, L. (2006). Agent-based computational economics: A constructive approach to economic theory. In H. Amman, D. Kendrick & J. Rust (Eds.), *Handbook of computational economics* (Vol. 2, pp. 831–880). Palgrave Macmillan UK.
Turing, A. M. (1936). On computable numbers, with an application to the Entscheidungs problem. *Proceedings of the London Mathematical Society, 42*(1), 230–265.
Velupillai, K. V. (1996). The computable alternative in the formalization of economics. *Kyklos, 49*(3), 251–272.
Velupillai, K. V. (1999). *Computable economics*. Oxford University Press.
Von Neumann, J. (1966). Theory of self-reproducing automata. *Mathematics of Computation, 21*(98), 745.
Wolfram, S. (2004). *A new kind of science*. Wolfram Media.

TRYING TO SELL THE CROW QUEEN IN WEB3: ON THE RESISTANCE OF VIDEO GAMERS TO CRYPTOCURRENCIES, NFTs AND THEIR FINANCIAL LOGIC

Diane-Laure Arjaliès[a] and Samuel Compain-Eglin[b]

[a]*Western University, Canada*
[b]*Video game artist, Canada*

ABSTRACT

This paper is an encounter between an artist creating characters for video games and an academic studying how people and things are being financialized. Exchanging about the appearance of non-fungible tokens (NFTs) and cryptocurrencies – technologies associated with Web3 in the video game industry, the academic, and the artist reflect on the place of playfulness, creation, and finance in our society. They observe that most North American and European players resisted NFTs and cryptocurrencies, while more Asian-Pacific ones embraced the latter. They conclude that those reactions were explained by the fact that gamers perceived cryptocurrencies and NFTs as institutional objects associated with a financial logic, whose presence threatened the gaming logic. As pragmatic friends, they nevertheless issued an NFT with this paper, a "Crow Queen." Time will tell if the Web3 society will praise this new form of digital joint academic/art production.

Keywords: Arts; cryptocurrencies; financial logic; NFTs; video games

ENCOUNTERING THE VIDEO GAME WORLD

It is estimated that 39% of the population actively plays video games, meaning more than 3 billion people (Howarth, 2023). I do not. My relationships with the virtual world have always been limited to a few exchanges over WhatsApp and Facebook. I gave up on Twitter only two days after signing up: too fast, too complicated, not enough time. I never played a game on my phone, never enrolled in Netflix, and belong to those species at risk of parents with a no-screen policy. I am not against technological progress; I do not understand it. The metaverse, non-fungible tokens (NFTs), and other cryptocurrencies are things that I have difficulty grasping, both cognitively and phenomenologically. I was probably the latest person on earth who could find any interest in the world of avatars, warcraft, and other crow queens and god-fall warriors. But I did. Now that I understand why 95% of our youth play video games, I will try to show you what you should care about them, too. Gaming has always been fundamental to forming communities (Mutch, 2021), and video games are increasingly central in our cultural, psychological, and social lives (Daniel & Garry, 2018; Vesa et al., 2017). Gamers' reactions vis-à-vis new technologies such as Web3 matter to our society and should be studied more. This paper is an invitation to do so.

But let's not go there yet. A little return in history is needed. London, Ontario, 2018: a college town in the great lakes' region, a historical fief of the loyalists to the British Empire, a classic of the classics known for well-tended gardens rather than its underground scene. I am shopping with my kids in an ugly mall on a Sunday morning when I hear a French Parisian accent, sounding just like mine. I am excited. I introduce myself. The mother and I agree to meet over a barbecue over the following weeks. I would learn it later, but the dad, Sam, felt I was weird: inviting people you meet once at a mall did not feel socially fit. Sam and I did not belong to the same worlds: he was a self-taught artist and lived in the virtual gaming realm; I was an academic evolving in the colonial legacy of a university campus. We should not have met, just as you should probably not read an essay on video games, NFTs, and weird social behaviors. But as you will discover, this encounter changed my perspective on a fascinating world I was missing, where many people belong, at least in their avatar forms, and where the future society is being shaped. I had a lot to learn from gamers.

While drinking in a sunny backyard, I asked Sam, "Why did you tattoo from your skull to your hand?" Sam explained, "It is to show that my creativity comes from my brain and travels toward my hand when I draw." Sam was a lead character artist: he created characters that would populate video games. He never attended an art school or a university; he self-taught using anatomy, anthropology, and other science fiction books.

> Teachers always told me that I would do nothing with my life. When I turned eighteen, I started working at McDonald's during the day and drawing the night. You can find software for creating characters that is free. So, I drew seven-eight hours per night, again and again. I posted my creations on my art station portfolio. Over the years, I became known in the video game world, and a company recruited me to create the characters for their game. It is not like in your world. Where you graduate from does not matter. What matters is your portfolio: showing what you can do.

THE CROW QUEEN: THE ARTISTIC LOGIC

After settling our initial differences, Sam and I discussed our creative practices further. Amused by our commonalities and differences, we agreed to work on a joint paper for a blockchain project on Web3 I was writing. Sam was drawing. But we were both studying, coding, and decoding the same information repeatedly to get better and better at accounting for what we saw. As we exchanged on our respective work and passion, we could relate in a way that surprised me. I could feel his creative process echoing mine, and he showed much interest in the research I conducted. It had been years since we had started speaking about a Crow Queen that he would draw, print, and hang in my living room. We decided this would be the art piece issued as an NFT – a non-fungible token or a digital art piece recognized through unique digital ownership, as an accompanying piece of this paper (see Fig. 16.1). I asked Sam to explain why he drew the Crow Queen as he did.

Fig. 16.1. The Crow Queen: Digital Art Piece Issued as a Free NFT as an Accompanying Piece to This Paper.

The low likelihood of earning money through the issuance encouraged us not to issue it on platforms like Opensea, where the NFT could be sold, as minting it would have cost us more than the selling price.

Sam answered,

The story of this character follows ... I love the different cultures and the divine representations when humans try to communicate with spirits, gods, and overall peoples' beliefs. So, I like all the imagery that comes off that. And in fact, we notice throughout the ages that this has always been necessary, whether in Christianity, Buddhism, Africa, or any other culture; there's always religious imagery that has been very strong. We can think of the Sistine Chapel, all the great artists of the Renaissance, and all the patrons who funded artists and allowed the development of new painting techniques. It was a real engine from an artistic perspective, spurring much creation. We were talking about the different types of games before and how they became fashionable; at one time, religion was fashionable, which led artists to create works to the glory of a God, to the glory of a hero, to the recognition of anything! So, I wonder a lot about religious symbolism. And how can we mix the codes from one religion to another? How can we bring principles, get other things, and so on? And I love everything voodoo and shamanic, so a couple of ideas came from it.

There is the priestess side. It is the priestess who can communicate with the dead, with the spirits, and with the other world. So, some codes are apparent: the skull and the bones have a strong symbolism for the world of the dead. You can also see the raven feathers: crows are in many religions. That's quite astonishing because even in some countries that didn't necessarily communicate at the time, the crow remains a messenger between the world of the living and the world of the dead. And it is an iconography that comes back and is relatively constant through several civilizations. So, it helps to reinforce the image. And likewise, these are things we put in place which are rarely known by the people who will look at them. They will understand instinctively, but they may be unable to explain it. And it's all the pleasure of the artist's work behind. It's how you code in what you do to talk to people, even if they can't put their finger on it. They feel it; they live it. You see, you have a base of general civilization. It's part of the culture. And, if you manage to type in it, you'll be able to make people feel what you want, and you'll be able to give emotion, an image, and so on.

And then you come back with the divine side. It is the same if you look at the representations of Christ and the angels in the European Christian culture. Well, you always have this kind of halo that gives the divine side, the angels, etc. And then, you use the same code. Except that it's extrapolated, it's with bones, with crow feathers. Raven feathers. But you have this kind of halo that is always present and radiates from the character's face. So that's also a code that you'll catch. You won't be able to put your finger on it because it's not a yellow halo that will shine. But on the other hand, visually, it will go around the head, take, and surround it. In addition, all the lines will go toward the center of the face, directing the gaze toward the front of the priestess. And it will encircle the face. So, the front will be covered, and everything will put the emphasis really on the priestess's face, on her expression a little bit lost, eyes in the void, or a little bit between the two worlds. And then, you'll continue with another curve that will make the transition to the image with the crow's skull. In the image's composition, on the first third line, I have the woman's face and the skull on the second third. It creates communication and a balance between the two, like tarot cards.

If you print it to make the skull at an actual size and hang it on a wall with your eyes facing the empty orbits, you'll lose sight of its open holes. Ultimately, you are not the priestess; you are only the mortal worshiping the gods and saints. And it's also this idea of having the human above the humans, and hell has always been represented below, and then the dead under the ground. So, it's all that too. When you think about composition, some codes are known, and you must use them to convey the right feelings and emotions and to direct the look. And above all, in the end, what is essential is that the player ... that you manage to win enough elements that are part of this kind of broad culture base. For that, people understand your image and the meaning that you want to convey.

I was stunned. To draw one character – a priestess, Sam relied on thousands of years of religious symbolism, studied dozens of representations of skull anatomy, and related to a lineage of artists returning to the Chapelle Sistine and Greek mythology. All these efforts were geared toward conveying the right emotion to the gamers, to make them feel that the virtual world in which they evolved was as real as it could be, the "affective component" that encouraged continuous experimentation (Jagoda, 2020, p. XV). Most European and North American gamers played to escape the mundane world to which they belonged and make this virtual world theirs. Games blur domain boundaries between life and work, private and public, virtual and physical, imaginary and real (Hulsey, 2019). Sam's job was to empower gamers to make their craziest dreams come true. The artistic production was beyond representation; it enabled gamers to identify with the virtual hero they incarnated. Gaming was a symbolic support to process individual and collective traumas, dreams, and societal past and future endeavors. This included re-living the crusades by playing assassin's creed, psychoanalytic and cathartic deaths exercise, or supporting the QAnon conspiracy fantasy (Haiven et al., 2022).[i] Sam explained:

> A video game is a universe you can move in, that is not material and where just your mind can escape. It's not something physical. It's something completely immaterial and in which you have all the powers. You are the hero in this world. And not just one human among millions. You are the hero of the story. That is the main idea. After that, it drifts because there are all kinds of video games. There are video games where you're going to collaborate with friends. You have some video games with social constructs all around them, where people get together on the Internet, and they can exchange. So, a game can be personal, but it can also be a community built around it. You cannot define it or pick up a controller and play. There are many, many possibilities. The video game has become something very vast.

FROM CREATING TO FINANCING GAMES

The more I learned about video games, the more interested I became. Sam and I started crossing each other's worlds. I invited him as a guest speaker to a conference to reflect on the artistic and scientific production of knowledge. He invited me to his company – a cool open space with free food and games everywhere, and an online webinar of the art developer team for a game he was conceiving: Dead Space, a science fiction survival horror classic.

Fig. 16.2 shows how 2,848 people worldwide joined to listen and enthusiastically comment on Sam's explanations of his color selection for the skin of his last zombie. This page alone was seen 135,000 times, and adding other platforms and the press, it probably crossed a million views. I would feel lucky if 10 people attended one of my Zoom seminars. Few cared about my research, but many were passionate about video games. I felt I had missed a big part of the world as it unfolded.

Playing is essential to human beings (Huizinga, 2014). Children learn and form their social practices through playing "as if" (Vygotsky, 1978). Psychoanalysis and psychological research have shown the critical role of play in our society,

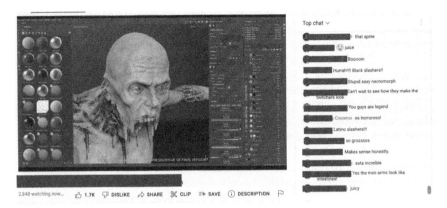

Fig. 16.2. Online Community Sharing Around Artistic Production in a Video Game. *Source*: A screenshot of Sam presenting his work during an online interactive presentation – May 12, 2022.

particularly video games (Cabeza-Ramírez et al., 2021; Granic et al., 2014). Beyond this crypto carnival project, research in social sciences on and involving playfulness is scarce. Except for media and cultural studies, very few disciplines have investigated the social practices associated with gaming and their impact on the industry and society more broadly (Corliss, 2011; Johnson & Woodcock, 2019). The video game industry is envisioned as a business (Shankar & Bayus, 2003; Zackariasson & Wilson, 2012). This is particularly the case in management, although gaming as a strategy arises in the marketing and communication/information technology (Marchand & Hennig-Thurau, 2013; Williams et al., 2007; Xi & Hamari, 2020).

We still need to learn about gamers and their world and how game-making is world-making; 95% of North American Gen Z and Millennials play video games in some capacity, the most frequent gamers spending an average of five to seven hours a week (YPulse, 2022). Not studying this field is a mistake, particularly given the rise of new technologies linked to Web3 or the "full digital experience." Soon, millions of avatars will move into a shared and persistent, three-dimensional (3D) virtual realm – or the metaverse.[ii] Will this world be like the one offered by video games? What will the impacts of Web3 be on gaming practices? What will it tell us about the other industries? We do not know. Understanding how today's gamers react to technologies such as NFTs and cryptocurrencies could help us understand what society would look like tomorrow.

The video game industry has become a giant economic actor. The global gaming industry will be worth US$321 billion by 2026. Social/casual gaming is expected to generate the highest revenue of US$242.7 billion, followed by PC games with US$42.2 billion, console games (US$31.5 billion), and integrated video game advertising (US$4.7 billion) (Read, 2022). Morgan Stanley's (2022) recent survey found that more than a quarter of those under 35 gamers believe gaming is a better social connection platform than social media platforms. The industry became bigger than movies and sports combined. Sam was an artist, but financial requirements also constrained him. When he designed his characters, he had to ensure the game would be successful.

> We have the initial idea. But quickly, we ask how much it will cost and how many people it will take to design it. It is about feasibility. We're going to have the profitability questions. Because the purpose of making a game is to raise enough money to make another game after. So, the questions we ask are: What player are you targeting? And as a result, how much money can you make? Likewise, when?
>
> When you create a game, you can have a great idea and everything, but you can only do what money allows. The day you present it to people who have money, can invest, come back with money to hire people, and pay for the software and office and marketing, they'll see it in terms of return on investment. And really, how do you build an idea that is solid enough and where people with different viewpoints, needs, and opportunities want to fund it? When you think about a game, it's not just about the art or gameplay, how you'll play, or what you'll do. There's a vast layer next to it that's less creative but necessary to have something viable in the end.

Since nobody attended my seminars, I wondered whether launching a video game was a good alternative: was there a business interest in sustainability games? I asked Sam whether he believed we could use video games to explain that the planet was dying and that people should care about it, as other scholars suggested (McGonigal, 2011). He explained,

> Video games are very dystopian. It is often a dark world where the planet has already been destroyed. But I wanted to create a game for my daughter where she would save the planet. But I don't have the money for it.

I did not understand:

> You do not have to work with these big companies. I thought creating video games was very cheap, thanks to those free software and those online communities. I heard about NFTs, where you can ask people to pay for your digital art pieces. I mean, gamers are virtual people; this should speak to them, no?

Sam commented,

> From my experience, it does not work. I know companies that tried to launch NFTs and cryptocurrencies, but they received backlash. I mean, as an artist, I would love to be able to fund my art through NFTs, but I have never done it. Most people who used NFTs were not artists.

WEB3 AND ITS RESISTANCE IN NORTH AMERICA AND EUROPE

I was puzzled. If there was one community I envisioned supporting Web3 and its accompanying technologies – NFTs, cryptocurrencies; it was the gamers. After all, I assumed those individuals to be young, digital natives and likely to question established practices to support their crowd. I decided to investigate. I formed a small research team and reviewed the gray literature on the topic – mainly reports published on the gaming industry and online platforms where gamers exchange. Below is a summary of our findings (see Anand et al., 2023).

Web3 games are characterized by the financialization of in-game items, where players can buy, sell, and trade digital assets using blockchain technology. Ubisoft, a major game developer, introduced limited edition NFTs within Ghost Recon Breakpoint, aiming to capitalize on the growing popularity of NFTs in gaming. However, implementing NFTs in the game was met with criticism and disappointment from players. Players expressed frustration over the extensive playing time required to earn a free in-game item – 600 hours of playing time to earn one free item – a cosmetic helmet for in-game avatars, complaining about the lack of value for the invested effort. Ubisoft's attempt to monetize through NFTs in Ghost Recon Breakpoint resulted in a commercial disaster, as only 15 NFTs were purchased for US$400 (Birnbaum, 2022). The discrepancy between player expectations and the perceived value of in-game items illustrates the challenges and risks of integrating NFTs into traditional gaming environments.

Web3 gaming allows for the decentralized ownership of in-game assets, meaning players own these assets beyond the confines of a single game, as Axie Infinity exemplifies. In Axie Infinity, players must own three Axie Infinity NFTs ("Axies") to play the game, requiring a substantial initial investment (of over US$1,000), especially during the game's peak popularity in August 2021 (Keller, 2022). The requirement to own Axies created sub-economies where lenders provided Axies to prospective players in exchange for a share of their earnings. Players could also trade Axie's native currency, $AXS, directly for fiat currency, enabling them to earn money by playing the game. Axie Infinity recorded significant revenue of US$1.3 billion in 2021, indicating the potential for players to earn substantial amounts through gameplay. Despite initial success, the popularity of Axie Infinity has decreased significantly, raising doubts about the sustainability of its earning potential. The decrease in popularity suggests challenges in maintaining the profitability of Web3 gaming ventures over the long term. Many players expressed dissatisfaction with the trend of monetization through NFTs and cryptocurrencies in gaming. Players perceived these trends as nickel-and-diming tactics aimed at maximizing profits rather than enhancing gameplay or benefiting gamers.

There has been a significant shift and resistance within the gaming community, particularly in North America and Europe, against integrating NFTs and cryptocurrencies into gaming, often associated with Web3 technologies. In 2022, North American gamers who hold cryptocurrencies only represented 15% of the global crypto gamers, with only 6% of regular gamers owning an NFT globally (Doll, 2022). Traditional gaming models, often called Web2, have involved monetization through microtransactions and "play to earn" models. One infamous example is electronic arts (EA) "Star Wars Battlefront II" release in 2017, which featured controversial loot box systems allowing players to purchase in-game advantages with real money. Including loot boxes sparked outrage among players who felt it gave an unfair advantage to those willing to spend more money (Davies, 2020; Jagoda, 2020). This controversy led to significant backlash against EA, including boycotts and calls for government regulation on gaming microtransactions. Despite the backlash against Web2 practices, resistance toward Web3 technologies, including NFTs and cryptocurrencies in gaming, appears to be even stronger. Unlike the tangible benefits of in-game advantages like powerful weapons or skills, NFTs and cryptocurrencies primarily increase financial gains for game owners. Many North American and European gamers perceive the integration of NFTs and cryptocurrencies as a departure from the traditional "gaming logic" and a betrayal of the gaming community's spirit. They resist being viewed solely as additional sources of revenue for game developers and owners.

WEB3 AS A SOURCE OF REVENUE FOR ASIAN-PACIFIC GAMERS

Gamers in Asia-Pacific view crypto gaming as a stable source of income despite the potentially low-profit margins. The high difference in exchange rates between local currencies and cryptocurrencies like Bitcoin and Ethereum contributes to the stability of earnings from crypto/NFT games. As a result, even modest earnings from playing crypto/NFT games can translate into significant income when converted into local currencies.

Crypto gamers, motivated by job loss or low wages, turn to P2E games to financially support themselves and their families. Players play games such as poker in the metaverse on behalf of others, earning up to US$1,500 monthly, rivaling, or exceeding earnings from traditional employment. In P2E games, players often share a portion of their earnings with the owner of the NFT or game assets they use, as seen in one player's case, where 40% of the proceeds go to the NFT owner. This model raises questions about the distribution of income and ownership rights within virtual economies and gaming platforms. Some individuals see P2E gaming as a viable alternative to traditional employment, questioning the value of hard work when they can earn more through gaming (Doll, 2022). This shift challenges conventional notions of productivity and meaningful work, particularly in the context of digital and virtual economies. For the first time, this resulted in the Asian-Pacific region overtaking North America in terms of revenue in the video gaming industry, standing at US$157.3 million compared to US$80.3 million as of 2020 (Kameke, 2022). This trend underscores the economic significance and potential of crypto gaming and P2E models in reshaping the global gaming landscape.

THE PROBLEM AT PLAY: CRYPTOCURRENCIES AND NFTS AS INSTITUTIONAL OBJECTS

North American, European, and Asian-Pacific gamers all associated cryptocurrencies and NFTs with a financial logic. The main difference between the two groups was that the first one did not need an additional source of revenue as severely as the second one. Sam summarized,

> The main advantage of those new technologies is adding money flows. They do not add anything from a development perspective or improve the gaming experience. If I use an NFT, it

is only to raise more funding. From a player's point of view, what's complicated is that I play because I want some entertainment. I work all day to earn some money to live. I play to escape this life. If I can make a little money playing, why not? But the primary impression today is that if I want to make $0,10 by playing, the company will get $1. There is this impression of being used as a cash cow, that you will work for them for free, and that everything you do will increase the company's wealth.

As developers, we are between a rock and a hard place. You must make money to live, pay people, and make the next game. So, having other threads of money is attractive. But on the other hand, we don't want to look like a bunch of scrooges to the players. Because if a company has a bad image in the community, people will be less willing to buy these games. You must satisfy the financiers because you must make money. But it would be best if you also satisfied the players because they're the ones who will buy the products. As a developer, you must try to please everyone and act as a buffer between the two to ensure everyone is happy. That's the feeling I have; again, it's personal. It's not a value; it's not a universal truth. It's my feeling today about the world of video games, the way it works.

Cryptocurrencies and NFTs appear to be institutional objects – objects constitutive of an institutional logic – in this case, the financial logic. Most objects are not institutional, in the sense that their meaning and social significance vary according to the situation (Friedland & Arjaliès, 2021). One can look at some glasses, pens, or computers without considering particular social practices. In sharp contrast, institutional objects immediately evoke an "institutional logic," like a crucifix is associated with religion or ballot papers with democracy. As we can see in this paper, there are three main institutional logics in the gaming industry: artistic, gaming, and financial. Players associate cryptocurrencies and NFTs with the financial logic and interpret those technologies as endangering the gaming logic by penetrating gaming practices (e.g., through selling NFTs inside the game). This rejection was particularly strong when gamers played to escape the capitalistic world where they had to work to earn a living. In this context, anything that made them think they were being used to generate wealth for a company spurred massive reactions. Asian-Pacific gamers who welcomed those technologies were searching for additional revenues: they were not playing for play but to earn money.

As a developer, Sam felt squeezed between the financial and gaming logics – struggling to meet both. As an artist, he also questioned the benefits of those technologies to support his artistic creation. NFTs were envisioned as an additional source of revenue for artists through the issuance of digital art pieces. Graphic designer Mike Winkelmann, known in the digital art world as "Beeple," was perhaps the most famous NFT digital artist. *Everyday: The first 5,000 Days* – a collection of all his digital works in one big piece – was auctioned off in early 2021 at Christie's for almost US$70 million. However, in 2021, most NFT sales were US$200 or less (Kinsella, 2021). Additionally, most NFTs were used to sell "collectibles" whose artistic added value was questionable. For instance, Crypto Kitties, launched in 2017, enabled buying, selling, and creating NFTs in the form of virtual cats. The game went viral; it made up 10% of transaction traffic and congested the entire Ethereum network but eventually lost its interest among players (Serada et al., 2021). The artistic qualities of crypto kitties in Fig. 16.3, compared to those of the Crow Queen in Fig. 16.1, can be easily

Trying to Sell the Crow Queen in Web3 187

Fig. 16.3. Cryptokitties. Generated by BingAI on January 30, 2024.

assessed. The multiplication of collectibles negatively impacts the unique digital artworks artists propose through NFTs, thus endangering the industry's artistic logic, in addition to the gaming one.

CONCLUSION: FINANCIALIZATION IN DISGUISE?

What are the implications of our work for the study of gaming, Web3, and institutional logics more broadly? First, our findings show the essential role of playfulness in our society. The video game industry has become a capitalistic empire, with multi-millions investors, professional players whose compensation exceeds regular jobs, and intense competition with fads, many losers, and a few (temporary) iconic winners. Still, most gamers refused the inclusion of NFTs and cryptocurrencies in their games. As institutional objects associated with a financial logic, they threatened the gaming logic that needed to be preserved – at least on the surface – to gather gamers' support. The association of NFTs and cryptocurrencies with a financial logic is ironic, given that the first cryptocurrencies were launched as an alternative to financial institutions (Arjaliès, 2021). The love and need of gamers to play in a world outside of the capitalistic realm might push NFTs and cryptocurrencies away from the industry, which is now at a crossroads. Faced with the backlash but seeing the growing Asian-Pacific market, the major North American and European companies hesitate. Although problematic from a business perspective for those companies, the fact that human beings are still fighting to keep playfulness in their life might appear reassuring. Financialization might not have corrupted (yet) all the layers of our societal and personal lives.

Second, gamers' reactions could help us envision the future of Web3. A subset of gamers – mainly from Southeast Asia – turned the gaming logic into a financial one. Using NFTs and cryptocurrencies as a source of revenue, they created a new constellation of practices within the industry. Whether those practices constitute a separate realm or have penetrated existing gaming communities remains unclear. Some games seem geared toward those financial practices openly, while others include possibilities to make money, although the latter remains marginal or even hidden. There might be gamers with different purposes (gaming or financial) within the same game. However, the penetration of Web3 objects might disturb the social and cultural practices of the gaming communities in the long term. It is unlikely that all objects associated with Web3 will be institutional. For instance, objects like artificial intelligence processing or virtual reality devices might be considered technical objects. But the subtle presence of financial institutional objects, like NFTs and cryptocurrencies, might be enough to spur the financialization process against which gamers fought above. From this perspective, Web3 bears the risk of becoming an incarnation of a form of capitalism 3.0.

Lastly, our study offers novel insights into institutional theory. As explained above, the concept of institutional objects (Friedland & Arjaliès, 2021) provides a theoretical and methodological apparatus to study practices grounded in objects. Web3 like other digital forms of organizing, such as the decentralized autonomous organizations (DAOs) (Hsieh & Vergne, 2023), do not exhibit the same features as previous forms of organizing, including those of Web2 and Web1. They are distributed and constantly evolving, combining human and non-human actors and multiple institutional logics and goals. Their objects (e.g., codes) seem to be the most reliable source of information in their governance and institutional systems. Identifying the institutional objects in Web3 and their associated logics offers a way to understand the mechanisms at play in this digital new world. Institutionalizing those objects will likely shape the constellation of practices in place. Likewise, actors' resistance to those objects could prevent Web3 from catalyzing around specific logics. Our study shows that financialization in the form of cryptocurrencies and NFTs might not be part of all the layers of our future Web3 society. Some actors will probably keep resisting those new institutional (financial) objects (e.g., actors pursuing gaming and artistic logics) until, maybe, their virtual practices – which they do not fabricate – are being infused with those objects. This could be especially true if capital owners (e.g., investors) impose NFTs and cryptocurrencies into economic and cultural practices (e.g., gaming) for financial reasons. If this happens, artists like Sam might become the ultimate barrier between capitalism and what seems to remain one of the latest realms outside of the latter: playfulness.

NOTES

i. We thank Matteo Ronzani for those important insights.

ii. In 2021, two of my former students launched Flirtual, an open-source and open-algorithm virtual reality social platform or in other words a digital world where 50,000 avatars are already flirting. https://flirtu.al/

REFERENCES

Anand, H., Kumar, L., & Arjaliès, D.-L. (2023). *Blockchain, cryptos and NFTs in the gaming industry: A tale of two worlds*. Western University. https://ir.lib.uwo.ca/iveypub/64

Arjaliès, D.-L. (2021). "At the very beginning, there's this dream." The role of utopia in the workings of local and cryptocurrencies. In R. Raghavendra, R. Wardrop, & L. Zingales (Eds.), *Handbook of technological finance* (pp. 95–137). Palgrave.

Birnbaum, J. (2022). *Why video game makers see huge potential in blockchain – And why problems loom for their new NFTs*. https://www.forbes.com/sites/justinbirnbaum/2022/01/06/why-video-game-makers-see-huge-potential-in-blockchain-and-why-problems-loom-for-their-new-nfts/?sh=3e673d3e43d7

Cabeza-Ramírez, L. J., Fuentes-García, F. J., & Muñoz-Fernandez, G. A. (2021). Exploring the emerging domain of research on video game live streaming in web of science: State of the art, changes and trends. *International Journal of Environmental Research and Public Health, 18*(6), 2917.

Corliss, J. (2011). Introduction: The social science study of video games. *Games and Culture, 6*(1), 3–16.

Daniel, M., & Garry, C. (2018). *Video games as culture: Considering the role and importance of video games in contemporary society*. Routledge.

Davies, W. (2020). Post-liberal competitions? Pragmatics of gamification and weaponization. In D. Stark (Ed.), *The performance complex: Competition and competitions in social life* (Vol. 187, pp. 197–198). Oxford University Press.

Doll, I. (2022). *Argentines flock to crypto games as economy eats up salaries*. Bloomberg. https://www.bloomberg.com/news/articles/2022-03-22/argentines-flock-to-crypto-games-as-economy-eats-up-salaries

Friedland, R., & Arjaliès, D.-L. (2021). Putting things in place: Institutional objects and institutional logics. *Research in the Sociology of Organizations, 71*, 45–86.

Granic, I., Lobel, A., & Engels, R. C. (2014). The benefits of playing video games. *American Psychologist, 69*(1), 66.

Haiven, M., Kingsmith, A., & Komporozos-Athanasiou, A. (2022). Dangerous play in an age of technofinance: From the GameStop hunger games to the Capitol Hill Jamboree. *TOPIA: Canadian Journal of Cultural Studies, 45*, 102–132.

Howarth, J. (2023). *How many gamers are there?* [New 2023 statistics]. https://explodingtopics.com/blog/number-of-gamers

Hsieh, Y., & Vergne, J. (2023). The future of the web? The coordination and early-stage growth of decentralized platforms. *Strategic Management Journal, 44*(3), 829–857.

Huizinga, J. (2014). *Homo Ludens: A study of the play-element in culture*. Mansfield Centre.

Hulsey, N. (2019). *Games in everyday life: For play*. Emerald Insight.

Jagoda, P. (2020). *Experimental games: Critique, play, and design in the age of gamification*. University of Chicago Press.

Johnson, M. R., & Woodcock, J. (2019). The impacts of live streaming and twitch. Tv on the video game industry. *Media, Culture & Society, 41*(5), 670–688.

Kameke, L. (2022). *Gaming market in the Asia-Pacific region – Statistics and facts*. Statista. https://www.statista.com/topics/2196/video-game-industry-in-asia/

Keller, L. (2022). *Top NFT game Axie Infinity generated $1.3B in revenue last year*. Yahoo! Finance. https://finance.yahoo.com/news/top-nft-game-axie-infinity-140000481.html

Kinsella, E. (2021). *Think everyone is getting rich off NFTs? Most sales are actually $200 or less, according to one report*. Artnet News. https://news.artnet.com/market/think-artists-are-getting-rich-off-nfts-think-again-1962752

Marchand, A., & Hennig-Thurau, T. (2013). Value creation in the video game industry: Industry economics, consumer benefits, and research opportunities. *Journal of Interactive Marketing, 27*(3), 141–157.

McGonigal, J. (2011). *Reality is broken: Why games make us better and how they can change the world*. Penguin.

Morgan Stanley. (2022). *Into the metaverse: Why gaming could level up in 2022*. https://www.morganstanley.com/ideas/video-gaming-industry-2022

Mutch, A. (2021). Challenging community: Logic or context? *Organization Theory, 2*(2), 1–18. https://doi.org/10.1177/26317877211004602

Read, S. (2022). *Gaming is booming and is expected to keep growing. This chart tells you all you need to know*. World Economic Forum. https://www.weforum.org/agenda/2022/07/gaming-pandemic-lockdowns-pwc-growth/

Serada, A., Sihvonen, T., & Harviainen, J. T. (2021). CryptoKitties and the new ludic economy: How blockchain introduces value, ownership, and scarcity in digital gaming. *Games and Culture, 16*(4), 457–480.

Shankar, V., & Bayus, B. L. (2003). Network effects and competition: An empirical analysis of the home video game industry. *Strategic Management Journal, 24*(4), 375–384.

Vesa, M., Hamari, J., Harviainen, J. T., & Warmelink, H. (2017). Computer games and organization studies. *Organization Studies, 38*(2), 273–284.

Vygotsky, L. S. (1978). The role of play in development. *Early years education: Histories and traditions*, 199–211.

Williams, D., Caplan, S., & Xiong, L. (2007). Can you hear me now? The impact of voice in an online gaming community. *Human Communication Research, 33*(4), 427–449.

Xi, N., & Hamari, J. (2020). Does gamification affect brand engagement and equity? A study in online brand communities. *Journal of Business Research, 109*, 449–460.

YPulse. (2022). *Gen Z, millennials, and Gen alpha's favorite video games of 2022*. https://www.ypulse.com/article/2022/12/19/gen-z-millennials-and-gen-alphas-favorite-video-games-of-2022

Zackariasson, P., & Wilson, T. L. (2012). *The video game industry: Formation, present state, and future*. Routledge.

BLOCKCHAIN AND WEB3: MIRRORS, "JOUISSANCE" AND SOCIAL AND PERSONAL IDENTITY FORMATION

Victoria Lemieux

The University of British Columbia, Canada

ABSTRACT

This paper argues that the concept of "jouissance" can help us understand the popularity of blockchain protocols, meme-coins, and non-fungible tokens (NFTs) in the world of Web3. These technologies act as mirrors to project reflections that allow people to imagine social and personal selves differently. Meme-coins use dark humor to oppose mainstream society, and the popularity of NFTs cannot be fully explained by artistic merit or return on investment. Instead, each collectible NFT allows the collector to explore various possible representations of the self. It is argued that blockchains must be seen as socio-informational-technical systems that participate in the formation of the symbolic social structures giving rise to social and personal identity. By recognizing the personal and social significance of jouissance, we can appreciate the darker, more primal aspects of these phenomena that other theories and approaches cannot fully explain.

Keywords: Web3; non-fungible tokens; blockchain; identity; jouissance

When I was growing up in Southern Ontario, Canada, traveling carnivals would visit small towns across the province throughout the summer. This included the town in which my grandmother lived and with whom I would customarily stay for a time during the summer months. The carnivals were a great source of delight for me during these visits. There were rollercoasters with blaring music that whizzed me around in circles until I was dizzy and, truth be told, a bit queasy. There were Ferris wheels manned by mysterious (at least to me) and possibly dangerous (at least to my grandmother) "carnies," who traveled with the fun fair to assemble and dismantle the rides and collect tickets from those making their circumnavigational journey around the wheel. There were shooting games with large, dusty teddy bear prizes (never won). But most intriguing of all of the carnival offerings was the "fun house" where I could wander through a maze of mirrors, each one designed to present me with a slightly different, distorted, image of myself. In the hall of mirrors, I would gaze in fascination first at a reflection of myself as a two-foot by two-foot (or half-meter by half-meter, if you prefer) dwarf, then another where I had been transformed into a tall, skinny giant, and another where I morphed into a Picasso-esque squiggly line. Due to the careful positioning of the mirrors, these simultaneously familiar, yet strange, reformulations of the physical "me" seemingly went on to infinity.

While the fun house was "fun," there was always something inexplicably unsettling about it as well. Why should a hall of mirrors be so horrifyingly thrilling? After all, I knew that the mirrors did not project back the "real" me or that I would not be permanently transfigured into a dwarf, a giant, or a squiggly line. Nor was I likely to be trapped in the infinity of the mirrors forever. It was only years later, on reading about Julia Kristeva's Lacanian-inspired concept of "jouissance," that I began to understand what I might have been feeling and experiencing (Kristeva, 1982). Jouissance is a French term meaning "enjoyment" with sensual overtones, but in Kristeva's Lacanian-inspired interpretation of the term, it also takes on the mantle of a perverse and picante delight experienced through the process of abjection or casting down and being separated from the norms of the self and society.[i] It is in this carnival memory of my youth that I find a path to deeper understanding of today's explosion of blockchain protocols, especially the "meme coins" and endless non-fungible tokens (NFTs) in the world of Web3. I argue that these can be seen as mirrors designed to project reflections that allow us to imagine social and personal "selves" differently.

To access this deeper appreciation of blockchains and Web3, it is necessary to abandon any notion of them as mere technical artifacts. Instead, the path to understanding must be followed by reformulating blockchains and Web3 as socio-informational-technical systems that participate in the formation of the symbolic social structures that give rise to social and personal identity (i.e., identity in the Lacanian sense[ii]) shaping human social relations and consciousness. A simple technical view of blockchains fails to fully account for what early innovators of the technology sought to achieve with them (i.e., Nakamoto wrote about generating greater social trust through disintermediating the banks) and the popularity of the technology as a social phenomenon. Instead, it is more fruitful to view blockchains as expressions of the complex network of relations (in the Latourian sense) that gives rise to our social "life world" and our personal place in this world (Husserl, 1970/1954). John Searle's "speech act" theory

(1985) introduces the notion that speech, including speech that is captured in the form of text, is capable of performing declarative acts that summon a society into existence. Through successive speech acts, a culture intersubjectively constructs and reproduces its life-world (Berger & Luckmann, 1966). The work of library scientist and document theorist Jesse Shera – who, with his colleague Margaret Egan, first introduced the field of "social epistemology" – argued that text forms "the basic bonds through which individuals achieve unity in a culture" and that "[a] culture, almost by definition produces a 'transcript,' a record in more or less permanent form that can be transmitted from generation to generation" (cited in Martinez-Ávila & Zandonade, 2020). So, it is by means of what can, in some cases, materialize as a shared ledger, if we accept Searle's and Shera's ideas, that a society takes shape and expresses its unique cultural identity and that we find our personal place within the broader culture. From this perspective, all societies are socio-informational-technical ecosystems constituted of, and by, social actors, communications, and technologies – such as blockchains – of cognition and communication that enable the creation and continuation of the identity of individual and social groups over time and space.

Kristeva (1982) argues that the connection between the anthropological, or the social, and the psychological, or the subjective, follow the same logic. Taking this line, I suggest that we can draw upon Kristeva's Lacanian-inspired theories of identity formation to gaze into the mirror of processes of personal and social identity formation as these are configured through blockchains in the same playful spirit as the fun-house carnival game. This line of thought connects blockchain-based social and personal identity formation to Kristeva's notion of jouissance.

I have written about blockchains as reflections of our social selves drawing upon Taylor's notion of utopian imaginaries (Lemieux, 2022; Taylor 2020; see also Dylan-Ennis, this volume). For example, the original blockchain – Bitcoin – sought to redress the broken trust perpetrated by financial institutions through rendering the banks obsolete. Subsequent protocols have sought to make improvements to the originary Bitcoin model not only to provide additional technical capabilities, as in Ethereum's smart contracts, but to create a better social future. In Taylor's writings, imaginaries help us reach a desirable future state, to explore different standards to steer by through experimentation with new sorts of imagined communities (Taylor, 2020, pp. 23–24). In this sense, blockchain protocols take on the form of a social wish (Lemieux, 2022, p. 201). The intention of the utopian social imaginary, then, is to break away from, or cast down, the usual social norms and rules in order to create a prefigurative image of a preferable or desirable society, an image that is able to transform society as it exists now in order to exchange it for a better future. It may or may not achieve this positive social transformation, as many critics of utopianism observe; nevertheless, that is its intention.

This idea is well exemplified by the iconography of pink-haired unicorns and rainbows associated with Ethereum Classic, visual metaphors expressing a collective hope (Cuen, 2020). Dancing is also an expression of the utopian wish within the Ethereum community:

> The dance is a promise "until next year," the leaders say on stage. It's a celebration of what the community has achieved so far and what it will achieve. The dance is a way to communicate with Ethereans from all around the world .... (Cuen, 2020)

To some, the dancing expresses Ethereum's cultural values related to "freedom, creative expression, fun, unconventionality, and even the desire for collective unity" around a vision that is bigger than any one individual (Cuen, 2020).[iii]

Blockchain-based meme-coins and cartoonish NFTs are not meant as Tayloresque utopian imaginaries like Ethereum unicorns and rainbows, however. Though it would be oversimplifying to draw sharp distinctions, meme-coin and NFT imaginaries occupy a social place more along the lines of the hall of mirrors of my youth or, even more so, the "Dutty Mas" of Jamaican and other Caribbean carnivals. In the Jamaican Carnival tradition, Dutty Mas takes place the night before "Pretty Mas," the daylit, brighter and "cleaner" version of carnival. Pretty Mas embraces the desirable allure of glitter, color, and light embodied in the elaborate feathered costumes worn by "band" members (Sheriff, 2014). Dutty Mas, on the other hand, sometimes called J'Ouvert (jour ouvert) or Bacchanal, hints at a darker, more sensual, kind of carnival. In both forms of mas, the usual social norms and rules are dispensed with, but in Dutty Mas, celebrants cover themselves with mud, oil, and brightly colored splashes of powder or paint (literally getting dirty, or in Jamaican patois, "dutty") and dance in the streets from darkness until dawn. Dutty Mas is the epitome of Kristeva's notion of the spirit of jouissance.

To elaborate, according to Lacan (2014), the psyche, or human consciousness formation, can be divided into three major perspectives, which correlate roughly to the three main moments in the individual's development. The first of these is the Imagery perspective/moment, which is the start of ego formation wherein subjects became distinct from objects (the process of objectification). It is at this moment that an infant is able to recognize itself in a mirror, or other symbolically reflective device, and perceives itself as an object outside of itself – it becomes objectified.[iv] Once a child begins to recognize that its body is separate from the world and its mother, it begins to feel anxiety, which is caused by a sense of lost unity (Felluga, n.d.). Kristeva (1982, p. 13) gives a social example of the process in describing the way that some "primitive" societies use ritual to demarcate the boundary between the society and the threatening world of animals and animalism. In both the cases of the human and society, this moment is crucial for entry into the Symbolic order or moment, which requires that the individual understands itself as separate from others.

Now, once the separation of subject and object has taken place, and the sense of loss and anxiety and the Symbolic (i.e., the world of language, rules, norms, and institutions) becomes known, desire for reunification with the self and the mother begins. This moment opens up the space of abjectification. Kristeva (1982) describes this space as follows:

> [...] there is nothing either objective or objectal to the abject. It is simply a frontier, a repulsive gift that the Other, having become alter ego, drops so that "I" does not disappear in it but finds, in that sublime alienation, a forfeited existence. Hence a *jouissance* [emphasis added] in which the subject is swallowed up but in which the Other, in return, keeps the subject from foundering by making it repugnant. (p. 9)

and

> The sense of abjection that I experience is anchored in the superego. The abject is perverse because it neither gives up nor assumes a prohibition, a rule, or a law; but turns them aside, misleads, corrupts; uses them, takes advantage of them, the better to deny them. (Kristeva, 1982, p. 15)

In this way, abjectification, and the experience of jouissance that it engenders, is a way of dealing with the pain of separation from ourselves (i.e., the ideal state of pre-linguistic nature from which we have been separated at birth and to which we can never return). In the debasement of ourselves and casting aside the normal rules of self and society, what is reflected back to us in the mirror (symbolic or otherwise) is not something we desire (even as we still desire a return to our ideal state). As a result, we can take perverse and cathartic pleasure in both perceiving ourselves as separate in this distorted form and using the revulsion it creates in us to sublimate our eternal and unquenchable desire to merge with the Other in order to re-unify ourselves.

Unlike Pretty Mas or Taylor's utopian imaginary, then, Dutty Mas (and the carnival fun house as well) does not invoke imagery of attraction or aspiration but rather imagery of abjection (to use Kristeva's term). Moreover, the goal of celebrants of Dutty Mas and those entering the fun-house carnival hall of mirrors is not adoption of the image but to experience a perverse enjoyment in participating in the effects of the image and, through simultaneous revulsion with, and attraction to, the image, coupled with knowledge of the transience of the experience, to achieve catharsis. Kristeva accounts for the experience in this way:

> A big fire at night always produces an exciting and exhilarating effect; this explains the attraction of fireworks; but in the case of fireworks, the graceful and regular shape of the flames and the complete immunity from danger produce a light and playful effect comparable to the effect of a glass of champagne. A real fire is quite another matter: there the horror and a certain sense of personal danger, combined with the well-known exhilarating effect of a fire at night, produce in the spectator (not, of course, in one whose house has burnt down) a certain shock to the brain and, as it were, a challenge to his own destructive instincts, which, alas, lie buried in the soul of even the meekest and most domesticated official of the lowest grade. This grim sensation is almost always delightful. I really don't know if it is possible to watch a fire without some enjoyment. (Kristeva, 1982, p. 16)

This acknowledgment of a darker, more primal, form of social imaginary associated with blockchain meme-coins and NFTs does not reject the brighter, lighter notion of utopian imaginaries. As Caribbean carnival traditions teach us, both co-exist. However, they serve different purposes.

Through the use of dark humor, meme-coins, for example, exist in opposition to more mainstream coins, and more mainstream society, just as the Dutty Mas exists within Caribbean carnival culture as a Bacchanalian parody of Pretty Mas, which in turn arose in opposition to the post-Lent balls and masquerades of colonial occupiers as a way of drawing attention to hypocrisy, greed, or the mean-spiritedness of these celebrations. Similarly, in the form of abject and perversely comic depictions of crypto culture, meme-coins use parody as a fun-hall mirror reflection of what is to be rejected the better to highlight the ideal. In doing so, such parody brings about a cathartic jouissance.

Dogecoin is the standard bearer for such meme-coin jouissance. Founded by Jackson Palmer[v] and Billy Markus in 2013, it is represented by the ridiculous image of a Shiba Inu dog, and "has combined a serious devotion to the decentralized idea of cryptocurrencies with utter refusal to take themselves seriously" (Floyd, 2018). Dogecon 2018, an "un-conference" held in Vancouver, Canada, that I attended, bore all the trappings of jouissance characteristic of a Dutty Mas: weird costumes, games, drops of free coins, and partying through the night (Kertonegoro, 2018).

In a similar vein to Dogecoin, Pied Piper Coin (PPL) began as parody based upon the home box office (HBO) sitcom *Silicon Valley* in order to use

> humor [symbolic abjection] to help remind the cryptosphere of all the shady things that have occurred and to help the broader community avoid these mistakes. [...] People need to learn their history before they can progress into the future. Our way of teaching is through humor. (Floyd, 2018)

PPL holds up a mirror that both repulses through highlighting the lost ideal and attracts, through the use of parody, in such a way as to render the repulsive safe.

Jouissance also helps explain the popularity of NFTs, the demand for which cannot be fully accounted for by either artistic merit or return on investment. In Lacanian theory, the power of the image is not due to any intrinsic quality but to the place which it occupies in a symbolic structure ("Fantasy," n.d.). In relation to jouissance and identity formation, the succession of artificial intelligence (AI)-generated NFT artworks is personal. Each collectible NFT is a slight variation on a theme like the mirrors in the carnival fun hall – a variant Krypto Kitty, Bored Ape, Peace Punk, Woman Warrior, or what have you. The collector is able to ask, "does this image reflect me?" to explore various possible representations of the self and acquire the image that best expresses a playful fantasy version. This phenomenon is exemplified by the use of NFTs as profile pictures for X (Twitter) users. "Introducing NFT profile pictures," an X (Twitter) marketing campaign announces, "ownership is stored on a blockchain ... NFT profile pictures are displayed in a special hexagonal shape ...." The collector knows that the image is impossible or improbable. It is not an image to be aspired to or achieved; rather, it is one that frees the collector to mentally experiment with versions of their identity that are outside of the embeddedness of their usual existence in a personal or social sense – somewhat like a sexual fantasy would be. And because there is something abject in the image – who would want to look like a Bored Ape? – the image provides cathartic access to the comfort of knowing "this is not really me." This instantiates the collector's particular mode of jouissance in that it enables the collector to project onto the NFT (the Other) an impossible desire that they cannot experience (i.e., a fantasy), while at the same time using the possession and ownership of the NFT to compensate for a sense of lack. As such, the fantasy image of the NFT represents an escape from the dissatisfaction created by a disunity of self and the demands of social reality (i.e., the Symbolic order). NFTs therefore can be considered the natural foil to the utopian imaginaries of more mainstream blockchain protocols or the comic darkness of meme-coins in that they provide personal jouissant comfort as a salve for the sense of lack or anxiety-producing loss experienced as part of human consciousness and social existence.

Consideration of blockchain and Web3 phenomena through the lens of jouissance provides a distinct image, like those of the fun-house carnival hall of mirrors, through which to gaze and playfully consider the personal and social meaning and identity of these phenomena. There are, of course, many other mirrors to be discovered in the blockchain and Web3 fun house – as the other contributions to this unique publishing experiment will attest to – but jouissance is a concept that helps account for the fascination and popularity of certain aspects of blockchains, Web3, and crypto culture that other theories and approaches cannot fully. In uncovering and exploring blockchain and Web3 through the lens of jouissance, it is possible to appreciate the need for a Dutty Mas version of the crypto carnival, offering a darker, more primal, explanation of this world than the Pretty Mas of Taylorian or technical utopianism.

NOTES

i. The Collins-Robert French Dictionary Complete and Unabridged defines jouissance as follows: "pleasure, enjoyment, delight (sensuelle), sensual pleasure, orgasm, climax." "Jouissance," *Harper-Collins French Dictionary Complete and Unabridged,* 7th ed. (New York: Harper-Collins, 2005).

ii. The other two perspectives or moments are: the Symbolic perspective/moment, which is the world of language, rules, norms, and institutions – symbolically, the Father and the Real perspective/moment, which is the ideal state of pre-linguistic nature from which we have been separated from birth. These are not necessarily conceived of by Lacan as temporally distinct or linear perspectives or moments; an individual can oscillate among, and wrestles with, them throughout life. See, Ellie Ragland-Sullivan, *Jacques Lacan and the philosophy of psychoanalysis* (Urbana: University of Illinois Press, 1986).

iii. Anthropologist Ann Brody cited in Leigh Cuen. The following video encapsulates the circa 2018 philosophy of the protocol, a mix of dedication to practical work (i.e., "BUIDL") and utopian ideals: https://youtu.be/xC8DrG5KSLU. For an example of the dancing, see https://youtu.be/kUheuFDHSvI.

iv. Jacque Lacan writes in "The Mirror Stage as Formative of the Function of the I as Revealed in Psychoanalytic Experience," delivered at the 16th International Congress of Psychoanalysis, Zurich, July 17, 1949, that "We have only to understand the mirror stage as an identification, in the full sense that analysis gives to the term: namely, the transformation that takes place in the subject when he assumes an image – whose predestination to this phase-effect is sufficiently indicated by the use, in analytic theory, of the ancient term imago" (Lacan, 2014).

v. Recently, Palmer, who left Dogecoin in 2015, abandoned the parody of the memecoin to express his revulsion with the current "mirror image" of crypto more directly: "After years of studying it, I believe that cryptocurrency is an inherently right-wing, hypercapitalistic technology built primarily to amplify the wealth of its proponents through a combination of tax avoidance, diminished regulatory oversight and artificially enforced scarcity" (Jackson Palmer Tweet, July 14, 2021, https://twitter.com/ummjackson/status/1415353985406406658?s=46&t=h2XsfTibFT5xPgFY5cENTg).

REFERENCES

Berger, P. L., & Luckmann, T. (1966). *The social construction of reality: A treatise in the sociology of knowledge.* Anchor Books.

Cuen, L. (2020, July 27). *Ethereum as lifestyle brand: What unicorns and rainbows are really about.* CoinDesk. https://www.coindesk.com/markets/2020/07/27/ethereum-as-lifestyle-brand-what-unicorns-and-rainbows-are-really-about/

"Fantasy." (n.d.). No *subject:* An *encyclopedia of Lacanian psychoanalysis*. Wiki. https://nosubject.com/Fantasy

Felluga, D. (n.d.). *Modules on Lacan: On the structure of the psyche. Introductory guide to critical theory*. http://www.purdue.edu/guidetotheory/psychoanalysis/lacanstructure.html

Floyd, D. (2018, July 17). *Is pied piper serious? How HBO inspired crypto's most confounding coin*. CoinDesk. https://www.coindesk.com/markets/2018/07/17/is-pied-piper-serious-how-hbo-inspired-cryptos-most-confounding-coin/

Husserl, E. (1970/1954). *The crisis of European sciences and transcendental phenomenology: An introduction to phenomenological philosophy* (Trans. D. Carr). Northwestern University Press.

Kertonegoro, S. (2018, June 21). *Dogecon: 'A celebration of radical decentralism and absurdist cryptoeconomics'*. Enjin [blog]. https://blog.enjincoin.io/dogecon-a-celebration-of-radical-decentralism-and-absurdist-cryptoeconomics-f512fbdce2b3

Kristeva, J. (1982). *Powers of horror* (Vol. 98). University Presses of California.

Lacan, J. (2014). The mirror stage as formative of the function of the i as revealed in psychoanalytic experience. In D. Birksted-Breen, S. Flanders, & C. D. Stivale (Eds.), *Reading French psychoanalysis* (pp. 97–104). Routledge.

Lemieux, V. L. (2022). *Searching for trust: Blockchain in an age of disinformation*. Cambridge University Press.

Martinez-Ávila, D., & Zandonade, T. (2020). Social epistemology in information studies: A consolidation. *Brazilian Journal of Information Science*, *14*(1), 7–36. https://doi.org/10.36311/1981-1640.2020.v14n1.02.p7

Searle, J. (1985). *Expression and meaning: Studies in the theory of speech acts*. Cambridge University Press.

Sheriff, N.-W. (2014). J'ouvert speaks to the present. *Journal of Emerging Dance Scholarship*, *1*, 1–26. http://www.jedsonline.net/wp-content/uploads/2014/06/Sheriff-.pdf

Taylor, C. (2020). What is a 'social imaginary?' In C. Taylor (Ed.), *Modern social imaginaries* (pp. 23–30). Duke University Press.

BLOW THAT MAUSOLEUM DOWN

Bill Maurer

University of California, Irvine, USA

ABSTRACT

Drawing on anthropological perspectives, this paper argues that the fungibility of objects and the ability to exchange them for money is a defining characteristic of capitalist markets. In contrast, other systems of reckoning value emphasize the unique relationships within which objects are embedded and their inability to stand for just any other thing. This paper further highlights the role of slavery in the origins and continued dominance of capitalism and the existence of alternative systems such as cooperativism and sharing that are often overlooked. This paper then examines the Saussurean and Peircean semiotics underlying the concept of money as an abstract sign and argues that non-fungible tokens (NFTs) in blockchain technology contradict these theories by emphasizing pure uniqueness and rendering objects non-transformable or inconvertible. This paper concludes by warning against the dangers of a future where fungibility is absent, as it is necessary for life and the generation of new and different possibilities.

Keywords: Fungibility; slavery; capitalism; regeneration; cooperativism; semiotics

Insofar as Web 3.0 imaginaries are propelled by the promise of decentralization and inspired by blockchain, they stand to make some very old mistakes. Granted, they might lead to inventions that "work," that is, function or do whatever it is they seek to do. But just because something works in practice does not mean it is on any kind of solid epistemological, ontological, or moral footing. One huff, puff, and you blow the house down.

Kind of like capitalism.

In capitalism, the story goes, anything can stand for any other thing. Money is the great leveler and equalizer, whose magic allows things as eternal as the land and ephemeral as a promise to enter into a great marketplace where anything can be exchanged for money. The very fact of this ability – of anything to be transacted – is what makes capitalist markets so unique, so vibrant, so violent.

In anthropology, we have long contrasted capitalism with other systems of reckoning value by spotlighting the instances, in those systems, where anything cannot stand for just any other thing. In some systems, we say, it is the relationships within which a thing is embedded that make it unique; it can only be substituted for a thing that can insert itself into those same relations, taking its place or taking its part or playing its role. When a marriage takes place, and there is an exchange of pigs and yams and other items, it is not just any pig that can stand in relation to the parties to the marriage transaction but this particular pig, which is held to take the same position in a system of relations as a human person (Strathern, 1991). We therefore often say that other economies are "human" economies (Hart, 2000) or "peopled" economies (Lofving, 2005) – which is ironic, of course, since most of the things involved are not humans or are humans and pigs substituting for one another, for example. But we say they are "human" because of our own deeply held assumption that humans themselves are unique and non-fungible. When we do see actual, whole humans as the object of interchangeable exchange, any human for any other human, any human for money, we call it slavery, and we say that our system abhors it. Even though our system was founded upon it (Cooke, 2003) and even though our system still uses slaves and does not honor human bodily autonomy. This is what I mean when I reference the huffing and puffing and blowing the house down: most of our stories of capitalism are made of sticks and straw.

Capitalism was supposedly born of free labor, depending on the valuation of the unique skills or attributes of unique human beings and a marketplace to sort them out. Consider John Stewart Mill (1869):

> Nobody thinks it necessary to make a law that only a strong-armed man shall be a blacksmith. Freedom and competition suffice to make blacksmiths strong-armed men, because the weak armed can earn more by engaging in occupations for which they are more fit. (p. 32)

Never mind that in his day, smithing was a hereditary occupation (think surnames like Smith or Miller). Yet capitalism was built on a solid foundation of the objectification and violent abstraction of the human such that it (not him/her/they) could enter into a calculus of money and exchange. No chattel slavery and transatlantic slave trade and no rise of capitalism on the industrial plantation model with its own modes of accounting, money, and insurance (see Baucom, 2005; Ralph, 2018; Rosenthal, 2018). This is why we so politely say that it is the labor, not the actual human being, that is being exchanged. Which, of course, is silly. Marx's insight was to insist that, as with the pigs, there are always human social relations underpinning those abstractions and exchanges: the ability of anything to be transacted is our fiction masking those real relations underneath.

The recognition that slavery is at the origins and remains at the heart of capitalism (Robinson, 2000) also belies capitalism's uniformity and dominance. Its hegemony may be due to the ideological, theoretical, legal, or political props or struts holding it up (liberal theory, property law), but it is never "one" system, or even that systematic, since it is shot through with other "systems" (slavery, indenture, cooperativism, sharing; Gibson-Graham, 2006) or harnesses those systems to its own ends (see Meillassoux, 2008; Tsing, 2021). I have long argued that "alternatives" are mischaracterized as such, as alter or other, insofar as they lie right alongside the relations and rules we attribute to and hold as defining capitalist orders. They are not separate systems, bounded off or far away, but right here, albeit in different spatiotemporal phases from the stuff that we tell ourselves that we see all around us, even if we think of ourselves as having been disabused of the fetishism of the commodity: money, markets, labor, and property.

THE STRUCTURE OF ABSTRACTION AND FUNGIBILITY

To stick with the fiction, however, capitalism rests on the ability of anything to be abstracted from its own context and placed in the context of the market, where its valuation is determined by supply and demand, or the expropriation of labor, which adds a differential of value to raw materials by the capitalist. Money is its universal and universalizing sign. Money itself is also an abstract sign. It is not the physical dollars or coins or lumps of gold that matter; it is the idea that those pieces of paper and metal signify abstract value according to which all things are measured. Money, like all things in capitalism, is therefore fungible: any bit of money can stand in for any other bit because they all name just one relation, the market's relation of valuation by price. I do not need to use "this" dollar or "that" euro to buy a particular thing; I can use any dollar or any euro; indeed, digital abstractions of the abstractions of money (i.e., cryptos) will do just fine.

This notion of money as a particular kind of sign that can stand for anything, and of money and all things as interchangeable and fungible insofar as they can all be measured according to one yardstick of value, rests on a special understanding of signs and symbols. In this rendering, the sign is arbitrary. It could be pennies, or euros, or digital messages, or tallies on a piece of wood, all signifying the abstract value of money. Ferdinand de Saussure (1916/1983, p. 115) made this point in his *Course on General Linguistics*:

> To determine what a five-franc piece is worth one must therefore know: (1) that it can be exchanged for a fixed quantity of a different thing, e.g. bread; and (2) that it can be compared with a similar value of the same system, e.g. a one-franc piece, or with coins of another system (a dollar, etc.).

It's worth remembering that Ferdinand Saussure's theory of the sign as arbitrarily standing for a signified was developed in conversation with the economics of Vilfredo Pareto (Ponzio, 1990). For Saussure, the system of signs, each in arbitrary relation to their signifieds yet, importantly, organized in relation to each other, revealed an underlying structure, which should be the *proper object of linguistics*.

For Pareto, similarly, the relations among competitive agents in a marketplace revealed value through price and thereby an underlying structure despite the diversity of forms, forces, and fungible items in the world. That structure would be the *proper object of economics*.

If Saussure was influenced by economists thinking about markets, another semiotician, Charles Peirce was influenced by ... rocks, coastlines, gravity, and geography (Baker, 2009). Developing his semiotics against the backdrop of seemingly unalterable (by humans) yet dynamic physical systems, Peirce famously emphasized the determinate qualities of things (with concepts like firstness and qualisign), their ontological interconnectedness or intertwining or, really, in his words, their partaking all of the same primordial protoplasmic substance, the appearance of order or structure being the result of habit (Peirce, 1892). Things and signs are what they are, not because of some underlying structure, but because they have moved and flowed and been inflected in such and such a way for some time – their previous flows creating channels that constrain but do not determine their future movements. For rivers can overflow their banks; oceans can erode coastlines. And if everything is changeable, nothing is strictly speaking fungible with anything else because it already *is* everything else.

But nothing is unique, singular, or transcendent, either. Again, since everything itself partakes of the same protoplasm and congeals into the manifold and manifest world through habit, everything is simultaneously (part of, composed of) everything else. This is a profoundly monist position. And, again, I'd argue that because his philosophy was developed in tandem with a deep appreciation of the physical world, this makes sense: the "I" that is me and my physical stuff sparking life to that "I" is carbon, nitrogen, oxygen, hydrogen, calcium, phosphorus, and a handful of other elements, common to just about every other thing in the physical universe. I am but a momentary congealing. I am held together by habit (Nöth, 2010).

How odd, then, that we persist in believing in our own uniqueness, our own individuality. What is but an eddy in the cosmic flow we take to be something super-duper special and singular. Doing so helps us deal with the void. And helps us stomach the abstractions of capitalism: I am me, and me is mine; and I am selling my labor, not myself or my soul. Really, honestly, truly! Just my labor! Not my life!

SEEKING ALPHA AND JUDGING SINGULARITIES

Now let's look at what's going on with some imaginaries propelling Web3. Take decentralized identities. They're belying both the Saussurean and the Peircean semiotics. No arbitrary sign but a nailed down "self-sovereign" identity, and self-sovereign identity for all! For people, and things, and objects of property whose relations are utterly obscured by code and ideological underpinnings that make every digital transaction unique. Everything will be tokenized, every physical and digital world thing, indeed, infinitely partible pieces of every such thing, rendered unique and unalterable and resolutely, purely, Itself. It is thus utterly non-arbitrary and utterly removed from the flow and flux of space–time–matter. No oneness, but infinite, separate, unique atoms.

Now exactly how are you going to make meaning and money with that? The investors who are professionally committed to profiteering trade an elusive substance called "alpha," which gives them the edge over the market. In traditional capital markets, alpha is a measurement of your ability to beat the all-knowing, perfectly efficient market. Usually, you can only get alpha from sociological events, information asymmetries, superior analysis, or market inefficiencies. For example, insider trading is very alpha. But in crypto markets, especially decentralized finance (DeFi), alpha is more elusive (Rodriguez, 2021). First, there is no known way to meaningfully measure the crypto market. The closest parallels to the S&P 500 are indexes based on each crypto's "total market cap," a number that has a mimetic resemblance to the sum price of traditional stock certificates but does not stand for value in the same way. Rodriguez recognizes this dilemma and suggests that the price of governance tokens might be a better measure of a crypto's market value but acknowledges that this too is a poor metric. So, they continue to hunt for alpha, maybe investing in mining to get their edge or join a shady "alpha group" that coordinates pump and dump schemes and supposedly trades advance and inside information.

The alpha that professional investors seek is intangible and not just a measure of their financial success. Rather, alpha is the process of conferring judgment, and moreover, the passing of information about where alpha is, how to get it, and how to exploit it is how price gets set. Lucian Karpik's (2010) economic theory offers an account of how the price of singularities (like artworks or non-fungible tokens (NFTs)) and other kinds of provenancial goods can be understood.

Singular goods cannot be explained with the neoclassical model, Karpik explains, because each item is incommensurable: utterly unique, impossible to compare, and therefore no basis for a rational market. Rather, the market for singular goods requires supporting "judgment devices" (e.g., networks of friends, quality labels, rankings, expert opinions, etc.). Karpik outlines eight "regimes of coordination," each operating through particular kinds of devices, which fall into two broad categories: *personal devices* (which operate through *personal networks, shared convictions,* and *professional reputation*) and *impersonal devices* that are either substantial and formal devices for small and large markets. That is, small markets are coordinated through *authenticity* and *expert opinion*, while large markets are coordinated through *branding* and *common opinion*.

Perhaps, a research project could inquire into how these devices operate in the context of Web3 and NFTs? Indeed, Dallyn (2017) used Karpik's ideas to think about how Bitcoin is valued, making the point that value cannot be reduced to price because that leaves open the question of how value is judged. This is aligned with research on how market devices work to produce prices and make markets work (Çalışkan & Callon, 2009, 2010; Muniesa et al., 2007; Neyland et al., 2019). As always, crypto offers a test case for understanding the limits of heterodox economies.

But when I see investment strategies that return great alpha on market singularities, I think of St Catherine of Siena, Oliver Plunkett, Jeremy Bentham, Lenin,

Kim Il Sung ... all those preserved heads and body parts of the saints, authoritarian rulers, and the occasional philosopher, whose gods and ideologies strive to hold back the inevitability of death and decay. But rot is transformation, that which such acts of eternal preservation seek to forestall. Rot is new life, the shifting of that protoplasmic substance into new congealings, alternative formations, and pure possibility. This is what goldbugs and crypto alike would seek to deny by freezing singularities in a house of bricks. The wolf didn't try hard enough: it's time to blow that house down. Indeed, the political ascendance of "forever" rulers and ideas and denial of alternatives makes it ever more urgent to nurture alternative space–time–matters, now, right now! For no transformation, no life. No life, no future. Just all the work and energy required to maintain stasis in the mausoleum of Web3.

ACKNOWLEDGMENTS

I would like to thank Quinn DuPont, Donncha Kavanagh, and Tom Boellstorff for comments on earlier versions of this paper, and Quinn DuPont especially for a final round of editing. This paper is based on research supported by the US National Science Foundation under grant number 1455859. Any opinions, findings, and conclusions or recommendations expressed in this material are those of the author and do not necessarily reflect the views of the National Science Foundation.

REFERENCES

Baker, V. R. (2009). Charles S. Peirce and the "light of nature." In G. D. Rosenberg (Ed.), *The revolution in geology from the Renaissance to the enlightenment. Geological society of America memoirs* (Vol. 203), 259–266. https://doi.org/10.1130/2009.1203(18)

Baucom, I. (2005). *Specters of the Atlantic: Finance capital, slavery, and the philosophy of history*. Duke University Press.

Çalışkan, K., & Callon, M. (2009). Economization, part 1: Shifting attention from the economy towards processes of economization. *Economy and Society*, *38*(3), 369–398.

Çalışkan, K., & Callon, M. (2010). Economization, part 2: A research programme for the study of markets. *Economy and Society*, *39*(1), 1–32.

Cooke, B. (2003). The denial of slavery in management studies. *Journal of Management Studies*, *40*(8), 1895–1918. https://doi.org/10.1046/j.1467-6486.2003.00405.x

Dallyn, S. (2017). Cryptocurrencies as market singularities: The strange case of Bitcoin. *Journal of Cultural Economy*, *10*(5), 462–473. https://doi.org/10.1080/17530350.2017.1315541

Gibson-Graham, J. K. (2006). *A postcapitalist politics*. University of Minnesota Press.

Hart, K. (2000). *Money in an unequal world: Keith Hart and his memory bank*. Texere.

Karpik, L. (2010). *Valuing the unique: The economics of singularities*. Princeton University Press.

Lofving, S. (2005). *Peopled economies: Conversations with Stephan Gudeman*. Interface.

Meillassoux, Q. (2008). *After finitude: An essay on the necessity of contingency*. Continuum.

Mill, J. S. (1869). *The subjection of women*. Longmans, Green, Reader, and Dyer.

Muniesa, F., Millo, Y., & Callon, M. (2007). An introduction to market devices. *The Sociological Review*, *55*(2_suppl), 1–12. https://doi.org/10.1111/j.1467-954X.2007.00727.x

Neyland, D., Ehrenstein, V., & Milyaeva, S. (2019). On the difficulties of addressing collective concerns through markets: From market devices to accountability devices. *Economy and Society*, *48*(2), 243–267. https://doi.org/10.1080/03085147.2019.1576432

Nöth, W. (2010). The criterion of habit in Peirce's definitions of the symbol. *Transactions of the Charles S. Peirce Society, 46*(1), 1–20.

Peirce, C. S. (1892). Man's glassy essence. *The Monist, 3*(1), 1–22.

Ponzio, A. (1990). *Man as a sign: Essays on the philosophy of language*. De Gruyter Mouton.

Ralph, M. (2018). Value of life: Insurance, slavery, and expertise. In S. Beckert & C. Desan (Eds.), *American capitalism: New histories*. Columbia University Press. https://doi.org/10.7312/beck18524

Robinson, C. J. (2000). *Black Marxism: The making of the black radical tradition*. University of North Carolina Press.

Rosenthal, C. (2018). *Accounting for slavery: Masters and management*. Harvard University Press.

Strathern, M. (1991). *Partial connections*. Rowman & Little.

Tsing, A. L. (2021). *The mushroom at the end of the world: On the possibility of life in capitalist ruins*. Princeton University Press.

IMMEDIATE GRATUITOUSNESS

Finn Brunton

University of California, Davis, USA

ABSTRACT

"Immediate Gratuitousness" puts cryptocurrency and its sister industries into a history of performances of extravagance, daring, and waste. My assertion is that the people to read at this point in the development of crypto are not Mazzucato or Galbraith, Minsky or Perez (or Hayek and Mises), but Antonin Artaud, playwright of the theater of self-destruction and gratuitous gestures. This account of crypto situates it in a context of value produced through performance and ruinous waste, from burning a million British pounds on the Isle of Jura in 1994 to the production of proof-of-burn minting mechanisms, and explains how to make sense of our carnivalesque moment through the logic of the extravagantly destructive.

Keywords: Gold; YOLO; speculation; finance; Artaud; cryptocurrency

They kept fighting among themselves, picking up anything that could be used as a weapon, snatching each other's spoils, taking possession of all they could lay hands on, even the most useless objects, then dropping them and running after some other plunder. What they could not take away they destroyed. (Anna Kavan, *Ice*)

ARTAUD'S CARNIVAL

Antonin Artaud – playwright, director, actor, writer, founder of the Theater of Cruelty, magus and sorcerer, semi-pro madman – had a profound insight into the *gratuitous*.

The term has a double meaning, positive and negative, that's shared in French and English alike. It is *free,* or given freely: gratuitous assistance, for which no money changes hands. This is the basis of calling a tip a *gratuity* because the tip is not part of the payment. You give it freely. This positive meaning of "gratuitous" has fallen into disuse outside of a few specialist communities like free and open-source software, who make precise distinctions between *libre* and *gratis*. (Libre is free in a more substantive sense, the sense of rights; gratis is merely free of charge [Suber, 2008].)

Gratuitous is now more commonly a pejorative, reflecting its second meaning: unwarranted, done without good reason, *sans raison,* as one says of a movie having gratuitous violence or gratuitous nudity. We can describe a friend's overreacting freakout as "so gratuitous." In this way, the meaning has begun to colloquially shift from something unjustified to something excessive.

Searching for theater and performance in their purest forms, Artaud looked to the gratuitous in both meanings. He studied actions that escaped the conventional systems of utility and value, without any purpose beyond themselves, devoid of useful function, because they were the places where pure theatrical presentation could begin. Therefore, he studied people and events in which the civilizational order was overturned or pulled inside-out and became unwarranted and excessive.

This may sound like the carnivalesque. Indeed, Artaud's areas of theatrical interest share the key dynamics of the carnival: the profaning of the sacred, the collapse or inversion of hierarchies, the melding of traditionally distinct things, the expression of latent impulses. Artaud's carnival, though, went much further in the work of collapse and inversion.

Not the language of the carnival, in Mikhail Bakhtin's (1984, pp. 122–132) terms, earthy and joyfully rude; but the failure of language into glossolalia, screaming, muttering, vacuous statements, silence. Not the celebration of the body, food, sexuality; Artaud was interested in deliberate self-starvation, in castration and needless cruelty, incest, the body as a vector for viruses and black magic. Not the inversion of values, making the low high and the high low; instead, the collapse of all existing values in frenzy, squandering, waste, and ruin. Finally, not sacrifice but destruction, and with the destruction, Artaud's perennial curtain-whisking big reveal: that there was nothing behind the gratuitous action – the *acte gratuit* – at all. It had been stupid and meaningless.

On April 6, 1933, Artaud (1958) delivered a public lecture called "Theater and the Plague." Famously, this lecture was his kind of trainwreck, gradually shifting from informational content into acting out his onstage death from *la peste* (Nin, 1966, pp. 191–192). He began sweating and cramping as he talked, shaking, struggling to breathe and hold on to his papers. Amid excessively – gratuitously – detailed body-horror bubonic plague effects, he described the social process of an outbreak in Marseilles in the 18th century. He sketched the breakdown of civic order, the funeral pyres, the costumes of the doctors, and the aristocratic retreat to fortified positions (where the Masque of the Red Death awaits the courtiers). The most important moment of all, for Artaud and for us in this paper, happened amid this tumult.

"The dregs of the population," he said, "apparently immunized by their frenzied greed, enter the open houses and pillage riches they know will serve no purpose or profit. And at that moment the theater is born. The theater, an immediate gratuitousness provoking acts without use or profit." (p. 24)

Draping yourself in the robes of a defunct extravagance, and seizing fistfuls of coins with no future and no one with whom to exchange, which you will not likely live to spend: this is, for Artaud, the purest theatrical gesture of all. At the intersection of plague, frenzy, and money, performance is born.

YOLO IDEOLOGY

People live for the morrow, because the day-after-tomorrow is doubtful. All our road is slippery and dangerous, while the ice which still bears us has grown unconsciously thin: we all feel the mild and gruesome breath of the thaw-wind. (Nietzsche, 1967, p. 40)

During the plague years of COVID-19, quarantined and isolated, the normies got crypto.

Celebrity spokesmen pointed out what an emasculated loser you were for not putting your cash into cryptocurrency and its adjacent financial instruments. Credulous news content implied that this eccentric alpha-rollout technology was home to the real investment action and belonged in the savvy portfolio. Civic buildings were renamed. Stunts proliferated. The mayor of New York City took paychecks in Bitcoin. The president of El Salvador commissioned architectural models of a gleaming, golden, Bitcoin-themed city.

Artists found themselves in the non-fungible token (NFT) business, a party-scene gold rush that worked like any one of a thousand Conceptual Art pieces from the 1970s. It could have been typed on an index card and pinned to the gallery wall: you own the exclusive rights to a claim of ownership over an image of which countless perfect copies exist – but this one is *yours,* in a complex, esoteric, *de jure* fashion. "Web3" became a terminological fundraising tool, slapped on Twitter bios and slide decks, with the science fictional properties of the monster in *The Blob* or the "grey goo" scenario in nanotechnology. Anything Web3 touched dissolved and became a part of it, absorbed into its scenario – video games, virtual reality, the vaporous Metaverse, social networks, email, and gig labor.

The enumeration of capital lost all meaning, in tandem with another explosively inflated bubble in tech stocks. Values of many millions, billions, tens of billions, and hundreds of billions were announced for tokens which were virtually never exchanged, for platforms on which almost no transactions took place, for systems which had no use case or killer app. These tokens, platforms, and systems in turn became the basis of millions, hundreds of millions, and billions "under management" by various funds and firms. Their operations had a recursive, self-referential meta-fraudulence. They would issue financial instruments backed by the assets of other firms – firms which, themselves, were in turn backed by the assets of the very firms they were backing, like Baron Munchausen pulling himself up out of the ocean by his own topknot. Everyone had improbably leveraged loans out to everyone else, a chain of dependencies in which each link had its own unique weaknesses.

CEOs' hustling investment cash traveled the world under "the flag of technology," as venture capital culture-warrior Balaji Srinivasan identified the Bitcoin logo in a social media bio (Srinivasan, 2019). Some of these travelers were bitter Bitcoin maximalist holdouts, fuming about all the gatecrashers for whom this was a party rather than the righteous financial apocalypse: a revelation in which all the books would be opened, all insolvencies revealed, and all debts settled forever in a deflationary Big Crunch. As grimly carnivorous prepper survivalists – "Bitcoin carnivores" are a thing, eating only beef and holding only BTC (Pearson, 2017) – this crew was not amused by new products of their milieu: the NFT hipsters, the comically insecure trading platforms, the hundreds of pumped-and-dumped tokens, and the decentralized autonomous organizations (DAOs).

This cohort and their predecessors were the primary subjects of my book *Digital Cash* (2019). They were ideologically committed, with their roots in American libertarian political philosophy, Austrian economics, and a science fictional sensibility and philosophy of history. They had shared interests in signature libertarian projects like precious metal currencies, micronational, offshore, seasteading schemes, private spaceflight companies, drug legalization, anti-surveillance technology, and access to firearms and weapons platforms. They had every right to feel perturbed by the lack of conviction on the part of the wave of late adopters taking up their technology – and the subsequent tsunami of rubes, suckers, and personal investors that the new crew onboarded.

Bitcoin, and some of the major cryptos that spun off in its wake, is the most popular culturally libertarian (as opposed to neoliberal) project in history. Yet, as it grew, it shed its original agenda and model of history, those ideological structures early Bitcoin wore like a mech suit for surviving the collapse of statist civilization. The original technology was not meant to be a fun, tech-hobbyist speculation, part of a high-risk portfolio. Nor was it to be a mere payment system, like a debit card but worse – painfully slow, requiring considerable technical expertise to set up and use, unlikely to be available in any normie context, monstrously energy-hungry, and productive of an eternal, public transactional record.

Instead, it was supposed to be the global reserve currency for a new emergent order. It was supposed to witness the default and demolition of the Federal Reserve Bank of the United States, of the European Central Bank, and of the People's Bank of China; the fall of Wall Street, of the City of London, and of the International Monetary Fund; and the abolition of every taxation and financial regulatory body. This was a technology investment in which the technology and the investment were one and the same and made the same bet. The bet was not on business cycles, disruptive innovation, or the tendency of the rate of profit to fall but on a model of history. It was a bet on the inevitability of debasement, inflation, and failure of territorial currencies, the end of state intervention in markets, and the reordering of the global neoliberal consensus. In the titles of two prescient and influential libertarian investment books sharing this theory of history, it was the anticipation of *Blood in the Streets* (Davidson & Rees-Mogg, 1987) and the coming of *The Sovereign Individual* (Davidson & Rees-Mogg, 1997).

The precedent for this monetary project was not some quant savant running a hedge fund with a new portfolio optimization algorithm, but something much older: the small and hardened crew of ideologically driven gold and silver commodity investors. Long before crypto, they had been sitting on their hoard, buying the dip, holding on, and waiting for "fiat currency" (their term) to crack. Not only before crypto, but before PayPal, they had launched successful digital gold currency (DGC) payment platforms – so successful that they were shut down for their abuse by money laundering operations (Mullan, 2016). This position is still present deep in parts of cryptocurrency and blockchain technology and culture, and it can explain some puzzling things about how they work, but it has been elided and in some cases wholly replaced in the technology's popular reception and adoption.

I call what has replaced it *YOLO ideology*. What distinguishes YOLO ideology is that its model of history is vacant, and its future is opaque. The past does not have any meaningful data for us. What happens now makes no sense in terms of prior history; we are in uncharted waters. The future is too volatile to be predicted – or even hedged against. YOLO operates in a perpetual and absolute present.

It offers not the joyous upset of the carnival, where the commoner can be crowned king of the day, but something more: an expectation of permanent upset. YOLO ideology therefore emphasizes action, the deed, as pure performance between a past emptied of significance and a future horizon that's only a few weeks out at best. Fittingly, it's a term for performance itself: a credo that's also a verb. You Only Live Once is something you can do, by "YOLOing" your next month's rent into some random crypto. "It's either a Lambo or food stamps," as the Wall Street Bets meme had it – "and I guess it's food stamps," followed up by one YOLOer as their rent money evaporated (Deeps, 2021).

YOLO ideology is about the big swing, the ruinous bet, the sweeping financial gesture that is as productive of *media* and theater – of memes, clout, astounded "lol"s – as it is of any return on investment. It's an image macro of a screenshot of a banking or investment browser interface, documenting the buy, hashtagged YOLO, which will perhaps make you "stupid rich," or dead broke and defaulting on a string of short-term loans taken out to buy the crypto dip. It embraces the frenzy, the bubble, the disbelief of the tedious index-funders, and the willful and hilarious stupidity of many of its vehicles: the crude, ugly NFTs, the asinine in-joke crypto drops and DAO schemes. Its epitome is the "diamond hander" imperturbably holding on to his coins as they crater into worthlessness, "to no purpose or profit," YOLOing to the end.

YOLO is finance without the future, as the very name would suggest. You Only Live Once is a perfect inverse of the famous (and widely misunderstood) remark of John Maynard Keynes: "*In the long run* we are all dead" (Keynes, 1929, p. 80). This lone sentence is often taken out of context as a kind of laissez-faire argument for present joys regardless of the future consequences. In 1923's *Tract on Monetary Reform,* Keynes was in fact arguing for deliberate, aggressive state intervention in the economy in the present precisely to manage current uncertainty and secure the future. He was arguing against the hands-off economists whose premise was that the economy would return to equilibrium in "the long run," if we were only sufficiently patient. "Economists set themselves too easy, too useless a task," he continues from that famous sentence, "if in tempestuous seasons they can only tell us that when the storm is past the ocean is flat again." In other words, the future demands planning and intervention from us. YOLO ideology is Keynes' misunderstood position realized: you only live once, in the long run we are all dead, so *go for it*, bro.

In a financial environment where one has no meaningful stake in the future, the language of the Securities and Exchange Commission (SEC)'s rule 156 – "a statement that past performance does not guarantee future results" – takes on a new significance, particularly the idea of *performance* (SEC, 2019, b/2/ii/B). If one's experience is of wild volatility and disconnection from the fundamentals, punctuated by national and global financial crises, bubbles, and busts, then the pretense of financial probity based on the lessons of the past seems like nothing so much as performance: play-acting, theater. From the perspective of the Bitcoin classicists and the hard-metal goldbugs who preceded them, the whole of state-issue currency is a performative act. It realizes the aphorism of Lichtenberg's: to imagine that a monarch announces, "on pain of death," that everyone must agree that an ordinary stone is a diamond (Lichtenberg, 2012, p. 97). The *fiat* of fiat currency – let it be thus – should evoke for us not just the command that something pass as "legal tender," but the whole class what J.L. Austin called "speech acts," those *performative utterances* that make something happen by our shared understanding of the rules (Austin, 1962).

Libertarians and YOLO actors agree on this fundamental theatricality, but their sense of what it means is distinct. For libertarians, this performance enacted a vast and secret transfer of power, granting statists, bureaucrats, and various Ayn Rand villains the ability to control the rules of reality itself: to set prices, manage markets, empower one group over another, and extract value through taxes and currency debasement. To defeat these foes would restore objective fact to a position of power. Behind the theater, there is reality; the end of the carnival brings with it a restoration of the "real order," the proper hierarchy. For the YOLO theory, by contrast, there is nothing behind the performance. Their adversaries are not people with a different but coherent theory of power that must be overcome, but rather those who do not concede that all is theater and have allowed their performance to become excessively serious, self-important, pompous, and staid. YOLO is looking for the purest expression of financial performance, to find out what is revealed by the most gratuitous action. The brokerage firms, hedge funds, and investment bankers are bourgeois repertory, doing Shakespeare or Molière for the thousandth time. YOLO is Artaud, seeking a new kind of reality inside the consensual illusion of the market. YOLO is the financial Theater of Cruelty.

"IT JUST WANTS TO BE A FIRE"

On August 22, 1994, Bill Drummond, Jimmy Cauty, Alan Goodrick, and Jim Reid, a reporter, arrived on the Isle of Jura in Scotland's Inner Hebrides carrying one million British pounds in fresh 50-pound notes (Reid, 1994).

It was Drummond and Cauty's money. Hybrid artist-musician-producer-impresarios, they had a string of dance-music hits as the KLF (among other names) in the late 1980s and early 1990s. They outlined their pragmatic and genially cynical approach to pop music production in their 1988 how-to book *The Manual (How to Have a Number One the Easy Way)* (Drummond & Cauty, 1999). The fortune from this success was given over to the K Foundation – also Drummond and Cauty – which began disbursing the money in a string of provocative and bizarre art projects conducted with impeccable seriousness. They gave anti-awards, identified bundles of cash as artworks and priced them under cost, and planned a world tour of a shipping container full of pound notes that would travel by train, ship, and truck to celebrate the end of cash.

Getting the Foundation's million pounds in cash was difficult. A private security firm had to be hired to collect it and supervise the transit from a NatWest facility. Once it was in Drummond and Cauty's hands, they stowed it in two big suitcases. Drummond, Cauty, Goodrick, and Reid took a chartered flight to Islay, and the ferry from there to Jura, with almost the entirety of the Foundation's remaining money literally in hand.

That night they made a fire in a disused boathouse and, bundle by bundle, burned all of it.

Reid's account squares with the footage shot by Goodrick: burning a million quid is a tedious process, peeling off handfuls of crisp 50-pound notes and feeding them into the fire over the course of two hours or so. The bundles of 50 grand, substantial plastic-wrapped bricks were too tightly packed to burn well. They came out "singed, charred, but perfectly legal" and had to be broken up and poked back into the fire. Some unknown tens of thousands of pounds blew away up the chimney before they could ignite. (Days later, the Isle's police began investigating numerous discoveries of charred money washing up on the beaches.)

They passed a bottle of whisky. "I don't think people should find out about it," Cauty said. "[I]t doesn't want to be a shocking thing; it just wants to be a fire." After it was done being a fire, Reid wrote, "all that was left was the cold and the rain and the ashes." On that August night, Drummond and Cauty inaugurated the YOLO ideology.

They went on tour with their film of the destruction, asking viewers: what do you think about this? What does this mean? Why did we do it?

The reactions were understandably by and large extremely strong: horrified, furious, vituperative. Seen from a macroeconomic perspective, all they had done was to make everyone else's UK currency worth imperceptibly more, by pulling their small chunk of it from circulation. No one disputed that the money was theirs to do with what they wished; rather than spending it on a small mansion, a smaller Basquiat, or a big recording studio, they had incinerated it. Yet there was something obscene in the pure squandering, the waste, of a sum that few people would ever possess. The comments were collected in a document from the tour, *K Foundation Burn a Million Quid* (Brook, 1997), and taken together, they express the fundamentally liquid character of money: what had been destroyed here was a mass of pure potential. It could have been housing for the indigent, assistance for the community, any given philanthropic possibility; it could have fed, grown, taught, aided; it could have got many of artistic projects off the ground; anything would have been better than this. Drummond and Cauty had opened a void in the future, a black hole into which possibilities kept falling.

It was arguably the most genuinely shocking act in the history of popular music, so extreme it has been blocked out of broader memory. The most deliberately transgressive provocateurs and offenders of public taste understand that you never mess with the money. The KLF performed the Joker's move from Christopher Nolan's *Dark Knight* film: having amassed his villainous fortune into an enormous pyramid of money filling a warehouse, he burns it – a demonstration, more significant than many murders, of his utterly alien value system. (The Joker is a favorite YOLO meme-and-media figure, along with characters like Leonardo DiCaprio's version of Jordan Belfort, from *The Wolf of Wall Street*, throwing cash at a federal agent from the deck of a yacht.) It was not sacrifice, which translates things from one order of value into another, but waste: gratuitous, the state in which the possibility of theater can be realized.

It was performance, but also real – a real loss of real possibilities, real as cash in hand. YOLO, likewise, gets its theatrical charge from the realities of the situation: taking the performance to the end of the line. Like the carnival, drawing transgressive power from the hierarchies and customs it overturns, YOLO's stoic, low-affect "lol" about the outcome of a major bet gets its power, its sting, from the reality of losing one's savings, wrecking relationships, moving back in with friends or parents, facing massive debt or tax burdens without hope of repayment, being the *bagholder* who ended up with little but "unrealized losses" in crypto and NFTs for which the market has gone. When the avant-garde director Peter Brook embarked on staging Artaud's work and reviving the Theater of Cruelty, he had an actor with a pistol turn suddenly and fire at the audience; part of YOLO media is the promise of disaster as well as the possibility of wild success. The many disasters, the rug-pulls and rip-offs and financial destruction, are part of the show itself: lambos or food stamps.

Artaud's ultimate point in "Theater and the Plague" was a theory of theater as a kind of contagion – a "contagious delirium" (p. 26), pulling you into its shared world, awakening fearsome drives, energies, and fantasies. It reveals new and different, and rather awful, appetites that are latent within the existing order: "the action of theater, like that of plague, is beneficial, for, impelling men to see themselves as they are, it causes the mask to fall, reveals the lie, the slackness, baseness, and hypocrisy of our world" (p. 31). None of it ever added up. The lies of the current situation are disclosed by the mortality of the plague, the fantasies of the theater, and the contagions of finance. You only live once, and what matters is the gratuitous nature of the act, reckless, gestural, and impulsive, costumed in the finery of the plague-abandoned house, carrying coins and jewels no one needs – the password to a wallet of worthless crypto: not carnival, but pure theater at last.

REFERENCES

Artaud, A. (1958). The theater and the plague. In *The theater and its double* (M. C. Richards, trans.) (pp. 15–32). Grove.
Austin, J. L. (1962). *How to do things with words*. Clarendon.
Bakhtin, M. (1984). *Problems of Dostoevsky's poetics*. University of Minnesota Press.
Brook, C. (1997). *K Foundation burn a million quid*. Ellipsis.

Brunton, F. (2019). *Digital cash: The unknown history of the anarchists, technologists, and utopians who created cryptocurrency*. Princeton.

Davidson, J. D., & Rees-Mogg, W. (1987). *Blood in the streets: Investment profits in a world gone mad*. Simon & Schuster.

Davidson, J. D., & Rees-Mogg, W. (1997). *The Sovereign individual: Mastering the transition to the information age*. Touchstone.

Deeps. [@JayCeeTrades]. (2021, May 19). *I bought the dip. Lambo or food stamps, there's no in between #dogecoins* [Tweet]. Twitter. https://twitter.com/JayCeeTrades/status/1395112209726935041

Drummond, B., & Cauty, J. (1999). *The manual (how to have a number one the easy way)*. Ellipsis.

Keynes, J. M. (1929). *A tract on monetary reform*. MacMillan & Co.

Lichtenberg, G. C. (2012). *Philosophical writings*. State University of New York.

Mullan, P. C. (2016). *A history of digital currency in the United States: New technology in an unregulated market*. Palgrave.

Nietzsche, F. (1967). *The will to power*. Random House.

Nin, A. (1966). *The diary of Anaïs Nin* (Vol. 1, pp. 1931–1934). Swallow Press.

Pearson, J. (2017, September 29). *Inside the world of the 'Bitcoin carnivores': Why a small community of Bitcoin users is eating meat exclusively*. Vice. https://www.vice.com/en/article/ne74nw/inside-the-world-of-the-bitcoin-carnivores

Reid, J. (1994, September 25). Money to burn. *The Observer* (pp. 127–129).

Securities and Exchange Commission. (2019). *17 CFR § 230.156 – Investment company sales literature*. https://www.law.cornell.edu/cfr/text/17/230.156

Srinivasan, B. [@balajis]. (2019, October 29). *Bitcoin will become the flag of technology* [Tweet]. Twitter. https://twitter.com/balajis/status/1189270395712626689

Suber, P. (2008). *Gratis and libre open access. SPARC Open Access Newsletter 124*. https://dash.harvard.edu/bitstream/handle/1/4322580/suber_oagratis.html

Printed and bound by CPI Group (UK) Ltd, Croydon, CR0 4YY
19/11/2024

14595309-0002